T0327653

The Analytics Lifecycle Toolkit

Wiley & SAS Business Series

The Wiley & SAS Business Series presents books that help senior-level managers with their critical management decisions.

Titles in the Wiley & SAS Business Series include:

The Analytic Hospitality Executive by Kelly A. McGuire

The Analytics Lifecycle Toolkit: A Practical Guide for an Effective Analytics Capability by Gregory S. Nelson

Analytics: The Agile Way by Phil Simon

Analytics in a Big Data World: The Essential Guide to Data Science and Its Applications by Bart Baesens

Bank Fraud: Using Technology to Combat Losses by Revathi Subramanian

Big Data Analytics: Turning Big Data into Big Money by Frank Ohlhorst

Big Data, Big Innovation: Enabling Competitive Differentiation through Business Analytics by Evan Stubbs

Business Analytics for Customer Intelligence by Gert Laursen

Business Intelligence Applied: Implementing an Effective Information and Communications Technology Infrastructure by Michael Gendron

Business Intelligence and the Cloud: Strategic Implementation Guide by Michael S. Gendron

Business Transformation: A Roadmap for Maximizing Organizational Insights by Aiman Zeid

Connecting Organizational Silos: Taking Knowledge Flow Management to the Next Level with Social Media by Frank Leistner

Data-Driven Healthcare: How Analytics and BI Are Transforming the Industry by Laura Madsen

Delivering Business Analytics: Practical Guidelines for Best Practice by Evan Stubbs

Demand-Driven Forecasting: A Structured Approach to Forecasting, Second Edition by Charles Chase

Demand-Driven Inventory Optimization and Replenishment: Creating a More Efficient Supply Chain by Robert A. Davis

Developing Human Capital: Using Analytics to Plan and Optimize Your Learning and Development Investments by Gene Pease, Barbara Beresford, and Lew Walker

The Executive's Guide to Enterprise Social Media Strategy: How Social Networks Are Radically Transforming Your Business by David Thomas and Mike Barlow

Economic and Business Forecasting: Analyzing and Interpreting Econometric Results by John Silvia, Azhar Iqbal, Kaylyn Swankoski, Sarah Watt, and Sam Bullard

Economic Modeling in the Post Great Recession Era: Incomplete Data, Imperfect Markets by John Silvia, Azhar Iqbal, and Sarah Watt House

Enhance Oil & Gas Exploration with Data Driven Geophysical and Petrophysical Models by Keith Holdaway and Duncan Irving

Foreign Currency Financial Reporting from Euros to Yen to Yuan: A Guide to Fundamental Concepts and Practical Applications by Robert Rowan

Harness Oil and Gas Big Data with Analytics: Optimize Exploration and Production with Data Driven Models by Keith Holdaway

Health Analytics: Gaining the Insights to Transform Health Care by Jason Burke

Heuristics in Analytics: A Practical Perspective of What Influences Our Analytical World by Carlos Andre Reis Pinheiro and Fiona McNeill

Human Capital Analytics: How to Harness the Potential of Your Organization's Greatest Asset by Gene Pease, Boyce Byerly, and Jac Fitz-enz

Implement, Improve, and Expand Your Statewide Longitudinal Data System: Creating a Culture of Data in Education by Jamie McQuiggan and Armistead Sapp

Intelligent Credit Scoring: Building and Implementing Better Credit Risk Scorecards, Second Edition by Naeem Siddiqi

JMP Connections by John Wubbel

The Analytics Lifecycle Toolkit

A Practical Guide for an Effective
Analytics Capability

Gregory S. Nelson

WILEY

Copyright © 2018 by John Wiley & Sons, Inc. All rights reserved.

Published by John Wiley & Sons, Inc., Hoboken, New Jersey.

Published simultaneously in Canada.

For general information on our other products and services or for technical support, please contact our Customer Care Department within the United States at (800) 762-2974, outside the United States at (317) 572-3993, or fax (317) 572-4002.

Wiley publishes in a variety of print and electronic formats and by print-on-demand. Some material included with standard print versions of this book may not be included in e-books or in print-on-demand. If this book refers to media such as a CD or DVD that is not included in the version you purchased, you may download this material at http://booksupport.wiley.com. For more information about Wiley products, visit www.wiley.com.

Library of Congress Cataloging-in-Publication Data is Available:

ISBN 978-1-119- 42506-9 (Hardcover)
ISBN 978-1-119-42509-0 (ePDF)
ISBN 978-1-119-42510-6 (ePub)

Cover Design: Wiley
Cover Image: © mattjeacock/Getty Images

Printed in the United States of America.

10 9 8 7 6 5 4 3 2 1

To Nick and MaryLu, for showing me what it means to be a part of something bigger than yourself.

Contents

Preface

The modern enterprise is often characterized as "data rich, but information poor." This challenge is exacerbated by the pure volume and variety of data generated at the point of interaction (e.g., customers, patients, suppliers) and careening outward. Whether you are preparing, analyzing, presenting, or consuming data, having a strong foundation in data and analytics is paramount for conveying ideas effectively.

In this book, I translate the world of big data, data science, and analytics into a practical, comprehensive guide where you can explore the art and science of analytics best practices through a proven framework for managing analytics teams and processes.

The focus of the book is on creating effective and efficient analytics organizations and processes in order to strengthen the role of data and analytics in producing organizational success.

When I started thinking about writing about this specific topic, it was primarily in response to the lack of information about "the people and process" side of analytics. That is, for over a decade, authors have written about the concept of analytics, its importance in business, and specific implementations of technologies such as Python, R, or SAS, among others. However, those resources generally do not address the tactics of analytics model development or business case development, nor do they address the impact of analytics on operational processes.

The issues that organizations have grappled with over the past 10 years since Tom Davenport and Jeanne Harris published their seminal work *Competing on Analytics* (Davenport & Harris, 2007) have shifted from "What problems can we solve with analytics?" to "How do we find, nurture, and retain analytics professionals?" This shift from the "what" to the "how" supports the basic premise of this book. I also think the timing is right for the book, as entire industries are transforming themselves with the use of data and analytics. While many organizations have solved the barriers of effectively using analytics in everyday operations as well as strategic decision making, other industries are just now getting on the "analytics bandwagon," and they see the promise of analytics without a clear roadmap for getting there. For the former, the challenge is one of effectiveness and improved efficiencies. For the latter, the real struggle can often be with creating an organizational culture—or mindset—for analytics, justifying the development of an analytics capability, and organizing for success.

My personal inspiration for this book came from the works of Ralph Kimball. I remember reading his first edition of the *Data Warehouse Toolkit* (Kimball, 1996) and thinking to myself, "This makes sense." It was so very different from the conceptual treatments often found in business and technology books, in that Kimball gave us the language, tools, and processes to actually do data warehousing. He provided a solid overview of the areas relevant to someone who was either familiar with or completely new to data warehousing, along with a framework for the data warehousing lifecycle and key process areas. I hope that you will find that *The Analytics Lifecycle Toolkit* lives up to this inspiration and that it provides a comprehensive and practical guide to the Analytics Lifecycle with focus on creating an effective analytics capability for your organization.

This book differs from other "how-to" books in that it is not designed as a cookbook of analytics models, but rather, is a primer on the best practices and processes used in analytics. It is intended for:

- *Organizational leaders and analytics executives* who need to understand what it means to build and maintain an analytics capability and culture, including those in newly minted chief analytics officer or chief data officer positions.

- *Analytics teams* on the front lines of designing, developing, and delivering analytics as a service or as a product. This group includes analytics product managers, team leads, analysts, project managers, statisticians, scientists, engineers, data scientists, and the "quants" who build analytics models.

- *Aspiring data champions*, those who use data or consume analytics products in their role as fact-based, problem solvers. The data champion is anyone who wishes to use data to improve performance, support a decision, or change the trajectory of some business process.

This book is organized in three sections:

1. **The Foundation of Analytics:** Starts by outlining what analytics is and how it can be applied to a number of problems in the organization. The focus shifts to analytics as an organizational capability, outlining a different perspective on how analytics can serve the organization's purpose, and how analytics (and data) strategy informs what we do and how we deliver those capabilities. Then this section will address how to deliver analytics capabilities through resources—that is, people, processes, technology, and data.

2. **Analytics Lifecycle Best Practices:** Introduces analytics products and how to support the design, development, and delivery of analytics products and/or services. The lifecycle is then broken down into five best practice areas with specific processes that support analytics product development.

3. **Sustaining Analytics Success:** Rounds out the discussion of how to ensure that analytics products have the greatest impact on the organization and sustain improvements. The discussion includes how to measure effectiveness and efficiency for analytics programs and apply lessons learned from other disciplines such as behavioral economics, social psychology, and change management.

In the first chapter, you will see that the language of analytics can be confusing and even down right daunting. Terms like *the science of, the discipline of,* and *the best practice of* generally refer to the usual manner in which analytics are conceptualized.

However, terms like *method, methodology,* or *approach* typically mean the processes used in common practice.

One of my goals in writing *The Analytics Lifecycle Toolkit* is to assume nothing and to clarify things along the way. To that end, I will do my best to make analytics accessible by providing explicit examples and using precise language wherever possible.

You've made it this far, so perhaps you agree that this topic is interesting and worth the price of admission. But if you need 10 more reasons, here they are:

This book:

1. Offers a practical guide to understanding the complete analytics lifecycle and how to translate that into organizational design and efficient processes.

2. Provides a framework for building an analytics team in the organization, including functions and team design.

3. Explores the people and process side of analytics with a focus on analytics team effectiveness and design thinking around the creation of analytics products.

4. Discusses the analytics job families and roles needed for a successful analytics program.

5. Includes case studies from real-world experiences.

6. Bridges concepts appropriate to an analytics culture such as data-centrism and numeracy with data and technology strategies.

7. Creates understanding and awareness for analytics leaders and a toolbox for practitioners.

8. Provides access to a library of tools and templates that include areas of best practice that support leadership, process improvement, and workforce enablement.

9. Begins with fundamentals of the analytics lifecycle, discusses the knowledge domains and best practice areas, and then details the analytics team processes.

10. Was written by someone who does analytics for a living and has seen hundreds of unique customer perspectives and applications across multiple industries.

Hopefully, this book will provide some useful guidance for those just starting their analytics journey and some tips for those more experienced. Happy trails!

Acknowledgments

This work would not have been possible without the support of my colleagues and clients who gave me the space to write. I am especially indebted to Monica Horvath, PhD, for picking up the pieces I dropped along the way. Not only did she provide scrutiny during technical review of this book, but was my sounding board and co-conspirator for the past several years at ThotWave as we helped clients improve the "people and process side of analytics." Much of the content around organizational design and our analytics competency model was rooted in these efforts.

I am grateful to all of those with whom I have had the pleasure to work during this project. I learn from each of my clients at Thot-Wave and my professional colleagues throughout the industry as they continue to teach me a great deal about the real-world implications of analytics and the real struggles that organizations have.

I am indebted to those who agreed to review drafts of this book. In particular, I want to thank Anne Milley from JMP Software; Marc Vaglio-Luarin, analytics product manager from Qlik Software; Linda Burtch, founder of Burtch Works; Mark Tabladillo, lead data scientist from Microsoft; Randy Betancourt from Accenture; Robert Gladden, chief analytics officer at Highmark Health; Mary Beth Ainsworth, product marketing at SAS for artificial intelligence and text analytics; and Teddy Benson from the Walt Disney Company. Your contributions to this work made it a better product.

I would especially like to thank my personal copyeditor, MaryLu Giver. Despite the massive amount of red ink, she was encouraging, thorough, and incredibly kind. In addition, thanks goes to the editorial team at Wiley and, in particular, Julie Kerr, who made the process of publishing a book easy and allowed me to focus on the writing.

Nobody has been more important to me in the pursuit of this project than the members of my family. I would like to thank my family, whose love and guidance are with me in whatever I pursue. They are the ultimate role models. Most importantly, I wish to thank my loving and supportive wife, Susan, who makes me a better person, and my daughter and grandson, who give me hope.

REFERENCES

Davenport, T. H., & Harris, J. G. (2007). *Competing on analytics: the new science of winning*. Boston: Harvard Business School Press.

Kimball, R. (1996). *The data warehouse toolkit: practical techniques for building dimensional data warehouses*. New York: John Wiley & Sons.

PART I

The Foundation of Analytics

CHAPTER 1

Analytics Overview

*... what enables the wise commander to strike and
conquer, and achieve things beyond the reach of ordinary
men, is foreknowledge. Now, this foreknowledge cannot
be elicited from spirits ...*

The Art of War, Sun Tzu (as seen in Giles, 1994)

FUNDAMENTAL CONCEPTS

Peter Drucker first spoke of the "knowledge economy" in his book *The Age of Discontinuity* (Drucker, 1969). The knowledge economy refers to the use of knowledge "to generate tangible and intangible value." Nearly 50 years later, organizations have virtually transformed themselves to meet this challenge, and data and analytics have become central to that transformation.

In this chapter, we highlight the "fundamentals" of analytics by hopefully creating a level playing field for those interested in the moving from the *concept* of analytics to the *practice* of analytics. The fundamentals include defining both *data* and *analytics* using terms that I hope resonate. In addition, I think it is important to consider analytics in the wider context of how it is used and the value derived from these efforts. Finally, in this chapter, I relate analytics to other widely used terms as a way to find both common ground and differentiation with often-confused terminologies.

Data

Data permeates just about every part of our lives, from the digital footprint we leave with our cell phones, to health records, purchase history, and utilization of resources such as energy. While not impossible, it would require dedication and uncanny persistence to live "off-the-grid" in this digital world. Beyond the pure generation of data, we are also voracious consumers of data, reviewing our online spending habits, monitoring our fitness regimes, and reviewing those frequent flyer points for that Caribbean vacation.

But what is data? At its most general form, data is simply information that has been stored for later use. Earliest forms of recording information might have been notches on bones (Sack, 2012). Fast forward to the 1950s, and people recorded digital information on Mylar strips (magnetic tape), then punch cards, and later disks. Modern data processing is relatively young but has set the foundation for how we think about the collection, storage, management, and use of information.

Until recently, we cataloged information that wasn't necessarily computable (e.g., videos, images); but through massive technological change, the class of "unstorable" data is quickly vanishing. Stored information, or data, is simply a model of the real world encoded in a manner that is usable, or for our purposes "computable" (Wolfram, 2010).

The fact that data is a persistent record or "model" of something that happened in the real world is an important distinction in analytics. George Box, a statistician considered by many as "one of the greatest statistical minds of the 20th century" (Champkin, 2013) was often quoted as saying: "All models are wrong, but some are useful." All too often, we find something in the data that doesn't make sense or is just plain wrong. Remember that data has been translated from the real, physical world into something that represents the real world—George's "model." Just as the mechanical speedometer is a standard for measuring speed (and a pretty good proxy for measuring velocity), the model is really measuring tire rotation, not speed. (For those interested in a late-night distraction, I refer you to Woodford's 2016 article "Speedometers" that explains how speedometers work.) In sum, data is stored information and serves as the foundation for all of analytics. In visual analytics, for example, we make sense out of the data using visualization techniques that enable us to perform analytical reasoning through interactive, visual interfaces.

Analytics

Analytics may be one of the most overused yet least understood terms used in business. For some, it relates to the technologies used to "beat data into submission," or it is simply an extension of business intelligence and data warehousing. And yet for others, it relates to the statistical, mathematical, or quantitative methods used in the development of models.

According to Merriam-Webster (Merriam-Webster, 2017), **analytics** is "the method of logical analysis." Dictionary.com (dictionary.com, 2017) defines analytics as "the science of logical analysis." Unfortunately, both definitions use the root word of *analysis* in the definition, which seems a bit like cheating.

The origin of the word *analysis* goes all the way back to the 1580s, where the term is rooted in Medieval Latin (analȳticus) and Greek (analȳtikós), and means to break up or to loosen. Throughout this book, I frame analytics as *a structured approach to data-driven problem solving*—one that helps us break up problems through careful consideration of the facts.

What Is Analytics?

There has been much debate over the definition of analytics (Rose, 2016). While the purpose of this book is not to redefine or challenge anyone's definition, for the current discussion I define analytics as:

a comprehensive, data-driven strategy for problem solving

I intentionally resist using a definition that views analytics as a "process," a "science," or a "discipline." Instead, I cast analytics as a comprehensive strategy, and as you will see in Part II of this book, it encompasses best practice areas that contain processes, along with roles and deliverables.

Analytics uses logic, **inductive and deductive reasoning**, critical thinking, and quantitative methods—along with data—to examine phenomena and determine its essential features. Analytics is rooted in the scientific method (Shuttleworth, 2009), including problem identification and understanding, theory generation, hypothesis testing, and the communication of results.

Inductive reasoning

Inductive reasoning refers to the idea that accumulated evidence is used to support a conclusion but with some level of uncertainty. That is, there is a chance (probability) that the final conclusions may differ from the underling premises. With inductive reasoning, we make broad generalizations from specific observations or data.

Deductive reasoning

Deductive reasoning on the other hand makes an assertion about some general case and then seeks to prove or disprove it with data (using **statistical inference** or **experimentation**). We propose a theory about the way the world works and then test our hypotheses.

We will explore this in more detail later in this chapter.

Analytics can be used to solve big hairy problems such as those faced by UPS that helped them "save more than 1.5 million gallons of fuel and reduced carbon dioxide emissions by 14,000 metric tons" (Schlangenstein, 2013) as well operational problems like optimizing the scheduling of operating rooms for Cleveland Clinic (Schouten, 2013). With success stories like those, it is no wonder that analytics is an attractive bedfellow with technology vendors (hardware and software) and other various proponents. Of course, the danger in the overuse of analytics can be seen in the pairing of the term with other words such as:

- Big data analytics
- Prescriptive analytics
- Business analytics
- Operational analytics
- Advanced analytics
- Real-time analytics
- Edge or ambient analytics

While these pairings offer distinctive qualifiers on the type and context to which analytics is applied, it often creates confusion, especially in C-suites, where technology vendors offer the latest analytics solutions to solve their every pain. My perspective (and one that is shared with lots of other like-minded, rational beings) is that analytics is not a technology but that technology serves as an enabler.

Analytics is also often referred to as "any solution that supports the identification of meaningful patterns and relationships among data." Analytics is used to parse large or small, simple or complex, structured and unstructured, quantitative or qualitative data for the express purposes of understanding, predicting, and optimizing. Advanced analytics is a subset of analytics that uses highly developed and computationally sophisticated techniques with the intent of supporting the fact-based decision process—usually in an automated or semi-automated manner.

Advanced analytics typically incorporates techniques such as data mining, econometrics, forecasting, optimization, predictive modeling, simulations, statistics, and text mining.

How Analytics Differs from Other Concepts

Vincent Granville, who operates Data Science Central, a social network for data scientists, compared 16 analytics disciplines to data science (Granville, 2014). Without repeating those here (but definitely worth the read!), it is useful to highlight the differences between analytics and similar concepts as a way to clarify the meaning of analytics. Here, analytics will be described as it relates to concepts and methods:

- **Concepts**
  - Business intelligence and reporting
  - Big data
  - Data science
  - Edge (and ambient) analytics
  - Informatics
  - Artificial intelligence and cognitive computing
- **Methods**
  - Applied statistics and mathematics
  - Forecasting and time series
  - NLP, text mining, and text analytics
  - Machine learning and data mining

To start with, it is important to distinguish between **concepts** and **methods**.

Concepts

Concepts are generalized constructs that help us understand what something is or how it works.

Methods

Methods, in this context, are the specific techniques or approaches that are used to implement an analytic solution.

Another way to think about this is that methods describe approaches to different types of problems. For example, we might consider something as an optimization problem or a forecasting problem, whereas big data is a mental model that helps us understand the complexity of modern data challenges. Similarly, as we will see later in this chapter, machine learning can be thought of as simply the current state of artificial intelligence—the latter being the concept and the former being the method.

ANALYTICS CONCEPTS

An analytics concept can be thought of as an abstract idea or a general notion. We differentiate concepts from implementation to highlight the fact that the idea necessarily can take on multiple forms when implemented. For example, the concept of artificial intelligence can be seen in self-driving cars, chatbots, or recommendation engines. The specific implementations are essentially the current state implementation of the concept.

In the following section, I outline my interpretation of what I see as the fundamental definition of **business intelligence**, **reporting**, **big data**, **data science**, **edge analytics**, **informatics**, and the world of **artificial intelligence** and **cognitive computing**.

Business Intelligence and Reporting

There is little consensus as to how analytics and business intelligence differ. Some categorize analytics as a subset of business intelligence, while others position analytics in an entirely different box. In a paper I wrote in 2010 (Nelson, 2010), I defined business intelligence (BI) as "a management strategy used to create a more structured and effective approach to decision making ... BI includes those common elements of reporting, querying, Online Analytical Processing (OLAP), dashboards, scorecards and even analytics. The umbrella term 'BI' also can refer to the processes of acquiring, cleansing, integrating, and storing data."

There are those who would classify the difference between analytics and business intelligence as differences between (1) the complexity of the quantitative methods used (i.e., algorithms, mathematics, statistics) and (2) whether the focus of the results is historical or future-oriented. That is to say, business intelligence is focused on the presentation of historical results using relatively simple math, while analytics is thought of as much more computationally sophisticated and capable of predicting outcomes of interest, determining causal relationships, identifying optimal solutions, and sometimes also used to prescribe actions to take.

The limit of most business intelligence applications lies not in the constraints of technology but, rather, in the depth of analysis and the true insights created that inform action. Telling me, for example, that something happened doesn't help me understand what to do to change the future—often, that is left for *offline analysis*. The promise of analytics is that it creates actionable insights about what happened (and where, why, and under what conditions), what is likely to occur in the future, and then what can be done to influence and optimize that future.

Note that the BI dashboard depicted in Figure 1.1 relays facts about the past such as sales, call volumes, products, and accounts, making it easy to get a quick snapshot of the current state of the organization's sales position or activities.

Business intelligence and its little sister, "reporting," are the techniques used to display information about a phenomenon, usually at the tail end of the data pipeline where visual access to data and results

Figure 1.1 BI dashboard

Source: © QlikTech International AB. Reprinted with permission.

11

are surfaced. Analytics, on the other hand, goes beyond description to actually understand the phenomenon to predict, optimize, and prescribe appropriate actions.

Business intelligence has traditionally suffered from two shortcomings. These shortcomings are related to the fact that BI typically (1) focuses on creating awareness of the facts of the past in that it measures and monitors rather predicting and optimizing; and (2) it is often not quantitatively sophisticated enough to build accurate insights that could be used to influence meaningful change (although the right report or visualization can influence change).

In cases where business intelligence is properly coupled with in-depth "analysis" rather than the mere awareness of facts, it gets closer to analytics. But it often lacks the advanced statistical and mathematical sophistication or "learning" seen in advanced analytics solutions.

To that end, I view analytics as a natural evolution of the concepts contained within the general framework of business intelligence. It places more emphasis on the full pipeline of activities necessary to create insights that fuel action. Analytics is more than just the predefined visual elements used in self-service dashboards or reporting interfaces.

Big Data

Big data is a way to describe the cacophony of information that organizations must deal with in their efforts to turn data into insights. The phrase *big data* was first used by Michael Cox and David Ellsworth in 1997 (Cox, 1997) who referred to the "problem" as follows:

> Visualization provides an interesting challenge for computer systems: data sets are generally quite large, taxing the capacities of main memory, local disk, and even remote disk. We call this the problem of big data. When data sets do not fit in main memory (in core), or when they do not fit even on local disk, the most common solution is to acquire more resources.

Think of big data as a concept that highlights the challenge of utilizing traditional methods of data analysis because of the size and complexity of that data. We contrast big data with traditional "small" data by its volume (how much data we have), velocity (how fast the data is coming at us), and variety (numbers, text, images, video).[1]

If big data is a concept used to describe the complexity of today's information, analytics is used to help us analyze that complexity in proactive (predictive and prescriptive) ways versus reactive ways (i.e., the realm of business intelligence).

Data Science

It would seem that defining big data was a cakewalk as compared with data science as such little consistency can be found in the term. There is a lot of debate about what it means and whether it is different at all from analytics. Even those who would attempt a definition might do so by discussing the people (data scientists), the skills they need to have, the roles they play, the tools and technologies used, where they work, and their educational backgrounds. But this doesn't give one a meaningful definition.

Rather than describing data science by the people or the types of problems they address, it might be more accurate to define it as follows:

> Data Science is the scientific discipline of using quantitative methods from fields like statistics and mathematics along with modern technologies to develop algorithms designed to discover patterns, predict outcomes, and find optimal solutions to complex problems.

The difference between data science and analytics is that data science can help support or even automate the analysis of data, but analytics is a human-centered strategy that takes advantage of a variety of tools, including those found in data science, to understand the true nature of the phenomenon.

Data science is perhaps the broadest of these concepts in that it relates to the entirety of the science and practice of dealing with "data." I think data science is analytics engineered by computer scientists. In practice, however, data science tends to focus on macro,

---

[1] Note: The three Vs of Big data have evolved into five Vs that also include veracity (trustworthiness) and value.

generalized problems, whereas analytics tends to address particular challenges within an industry or problem space. In Chapter 10, I extend this by defining the relationship between data science and analytics by referring to data science as an enabler of analytics.

Edge (and Ambient) Analytics

Analytics is a predominant activity for most modern organizations that see it as their directive to **democratize data** through data-driven, human-centered processes. Edge analytics refers to distributed analytics where the analytics are built into the machinery and systems where information is generated or collected as part of the "unconscious" activities of an organization.

Edge analytics is often associated with smart devices where the analytical computation is performed on data at the point of collection (e.g., equipment, sensor, network switch, or other device). Rather than relying on traditional data-pipeline methods where data is collected, transmitted, cleansed, integrated, and warehoused, analytics are embedded within the device or nearby.

 DEMOCRATIZE DATA

The democratization of data refers to "freeing" data so that everyone that can and should have access to data is given the tools and the rights to explore the data and these are not limited to the privileged few.

As an example, consider the fact that traditional credit card fraud detection relies on a machine (e.g., card reader) and a connection to an authorization "broker" to validate the transaction by sending a request and very quickly (hundredths of a millisecond) applying an algorithm to authorize or flag the operation and the device receives the authorization. In edge analytics, the algorithm would run on the instrument itself (think smart chip reader with embedded analytics).

Edge analytics is often linked with the Internet of Things (IoT), and a recent IDC FutureScape for IoT report found that "by 2018, 40% of IoT data will be stored, processed, analyzed and acted upon at the edge of the network where it is created" (Marr, 2016). As IoT evolves, we will likely see more attention paid to the Analytics of Things (AoT), which refers to the opportunity of analytics to bring unique value to IoT data.

Ambient analytics is a related term whose name implies that "analytics are everywhere." Just as the lighting or acoustics of a room often go unnoticed but set the stage for mood, ambient analytics will support and influence the context of how we work and play. We are seeing ambient intelligence play out in everyday scenarios, such as detecting glucose levels and administering insulin. Similarly, home automation devices can detect when you are nearing your home and adjust the temperature and turn on lighting. Ambient analytics goes beyond simple decision rules and utilizes algorithms to decide on the appropriate course of action.

There is little doubt that edge and ambient analytics will continue to challenge the traditional human-centered processes for operationalizing (e.g., understanding, deciding, and acting) analytics.

Informatics

Informatics is a discipline that lies at the intersection of information technology (IT) and information management. In practice, informatics relates to the technologies used to process data for storage and retrieval. In essence, informatics deals with the realm of how information is managed and refers to the ecosystem of data and systems that support process workflows rather than the analysis of the data found therein.

Often used in information sciences and used heavily in healthcare and research, health informatics is a specialization that sits between health IT and health information management and links information technology, communications, and health care to improve the quality and safety of patient care. It lies at the heart of where people, information, and technology intersect.

Health policy refers to decisions, plans, and actions that are undertaken to achieve specific health-care goals within a society. Because health policy makers want to see health care become more affordable, safer, and of higher quality, information technology and health informatics are often the means prescribed to do this. In fact, one of the

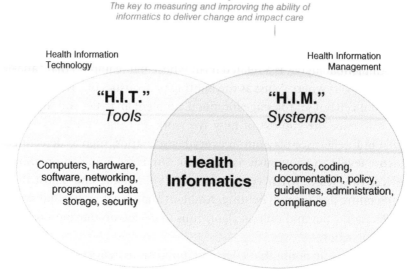

Figure 1.2 The difference between health information management, health IT, and informatics

biggest mandates is to position data resources as to enable a 360-degree view of every patient, and only data sharing can accomplish this (see Figure 1.2).

Analytics integrates with all of these concepts and relies on the underlying data, supporting technologies, and information management processes.

Artificial Intelligence and Cognitive Computing

Artificial intelligence (AI) is "the science of making computers do things that require intelligence when done by humans" (Copeland, 2000).

The difference between artificial intelligence (AI) and **machine learning** is that AI refers to the broad concept of using computers to perform the "intelligence" work of discovering patterns, whereas machine learning is a part of AI that relates to the notion that computers can learn from data.

Machine learning is a subset of artificial intelligence that can learn from and make predictions based on data. Rather than following a particular set of rules or instructions, an algorithm is trained to spot patterns in large amounts of data.

Artificial intelligence (and machine learning) can be used in the Analytics Lifecycle to support discovery (e.g., how data is structured, what patterns exist). The application of artificial intelligence found in analytics usually comes in the form of machine learning (as seen above) or cognitive computing.

Cognitive computing is a unique case that combines artificial intelligence and machine-learning algorithms in an approach that attempts to reproduce (or mimic) the behavior of the human brain (Feldman, 2017).

Cognitive computing systems are designed to solve problems the way people solve problems, by thinking, reasoning, and remembering. This approach gives cognitive computing systems an advantage that allows them to "learn and adapt as new data arrives" and to "explore and uncover things you would never know to ask about." (Saffron Technologies, 2017). The advantage of cognitive computing is that once it learns—unlike humans—it never forgets.

> *In the battle of man vs. algorithm, unfortunately, man often loses. The promise of Artificial Intelligence is just that. So if we're going to be smart humans, we must learn to be humble in situations where our intuitive judgment simply is not as good as a set of simple rules.*
>
> Farnham Street Blog (Parrish, 2017, Do Algorithms Beat Us at Complex Decision Making?)

In slightly pejorative terms, artificial intelligence acts on behalf of a human, whereas cognitive computing provides information to help people decide.

Learn More

To learn more about the difference between AI and cognitive computing, please review the referenced article by Steve Hoffenberg (Hoffenberg, 2016).

THE METHODS OF ANALYTICS

In the prior section, we discussed analytics and some of the related concepts such as big data and data science. We now turn our attention to the practical methods used in analytics, including the tools in the analytics toolbox.

Specifically, in this section, I will outline the methods found in statistics, time series analysis, natural language processing, machine learning, and operations research.

Applied Statistics and Mathematics

Like many of the concepts that have already been discussed, there is a wide disparity about how people define **statistics** and how it differs from mathematics in general. Some would argue that statistics is a branch of mathematics (Merriam-Webster, 2017b), and others (like John Tukey (Brillinger, 2002)) suggest that it is a science. Most would agree that like physics, statistics uses mathematics but is not math (Milley, 2012).

For present purpose, statistics deals with the collection, organization, analysis, interpretation, and presentation of data. Using that broad definition, it sounds an awful lot like analytics. However, analytics and data science both use the quantitative underpinnings of statistics but their focus is wider than that of traditional statistics. While there are dozens of perspectives about the conceptual relationship between statistics and other disciplines (Taylor, 2016), I have represented what I see as the relationships among those concepts discussed here in Figure 1.3.

Mathematics has a certain absolute and determinable quality about it, and the way that math is taught (at least in US schools) imbues a deterministic way of viewing the quantitative world around them. That is, we are taught to believe that all facts and events can be explained. Statistics, on the other hand, views quantitative data as probabilistic or stochastic. That is, facts may lead to conclusions that may be generally true (beyond simple randomness), but it must be acknowledged that there is some random probability distribution or pattern that cannot be predicted precisely.

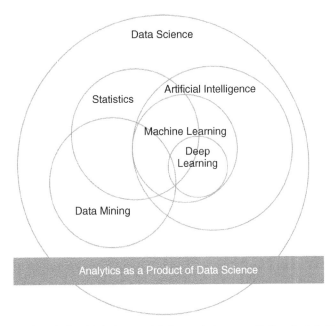

Figure 1.3   The relationship between statistics and other quantitative disciplines

---

Learn More

To learn more about the history of statistics and how it transformed science, please see David Salsburg's book *The Lady Tasting Tea* (Salsburg, 2002).

As shown in Figure 1.4, mathematical thinking is deductive (i.e., it infers a particular instance by applying a general law or principle) whereas statistical reasoning is inductive (i.e., it infers general laws from specific instances).

This difference is important in the context of analytics in that we apply both inductive and deductive reasoning to analytics problem solving. Thus, the application of both mathematics and statistics to analytics is appropriate and necessary. If analytics is a comprehensive strategy, then statistics and mathematics are tools in our proverbial analytics toolbox that help deliver on that strategy.

Linear programming, for example, can be used to support special types of problems in analytics that are loosely defined as an

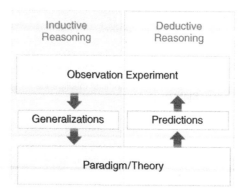

Figure 1.4 Inductive reasoning compared to deductive reasoning

optimization problem. For example, The Walt Disney Company uses linear, nonlinear, mixed integer, and dynamic programming in its data science work to support the optimization of restaurant seating, reduce wait times for park rides, and schedule staff (i.e., Cast Members). Note that I do not call out operations research, **mathematical optimization, decision sciences**, or **actuarial sciences** separately for the purposes of this discussion, as my perspective is that they serve as tools in our proverbial analytics toolkit—just as critical thinking and problem solving.

 LINEAR PROGRAMMING

Linear programming is a mathematical method for problem solving where the output is a function of a linear model. For example, we might want to optimize emergency department throughput by looking at several factors, including surgical complexity, number of staff required, and potential complications, for example.

Forecasting and Time Series

In discussing the methods that support analytics, forecasting and time series methods are grouped together, not because they are the same thing but, rather, because they both fall into the same class of problem—the process of characterizing and predicting time-ordered data based on historical information.

Forecasting and time series refer to methods for analyzing time-sequenced data to extract meaningful characteristics from the data. Most often, forecasts are seen as trends represented as a visual display of historical data values, with some providing future predictions. Time series analysis is different than forecasting. You need time series data to make forecasts, but not all time series analysis is done to make a forecast. For example, time series analysis can be used to find patterns or similar features in multiple time series, or to perform statistical process control. Similarly, seasonality can be used to identify patterns.

Time series analysis utilizes a variety of approaches, including both quantitative and qualitative methods. The objective of time series analysis is to discover a pattern in the historical data (or time series) and then extrapolate the trend into the future. In Figure 1.5, note that there are generally four types of time series approaches.

Quantitative methods are the most common type of forecasting, but both qualitative and decision analysis approaches are in widespread

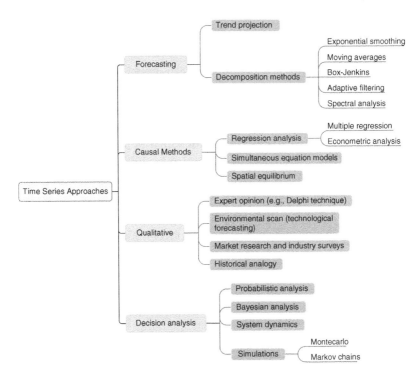

Figure 1.5 Approaches to forecasting and time series analysis

use, where historical, quantitative data may not be available or in cases where the "cone of uncertainty" is at its broadest (Saffo, 2007).

Natural Language Process

Natural language processing (NLP) refers to approaches used to understand and generate "natural language" through the use of computers.

NLP is a field of study that focuses on the interactions between human language and computers and sits at the intersection of computer science, artificial intelligence, and computational linguistics. Text mining and text analytics are often used interchangeably and refer to precursor activities to NLP as well as the application of NLP itself.

The goal of NLP is the understanding of natural language in computerized text. NLP is used for classification, extraction, and summarization, but the advances both in our understanding and in technology are quickly driving NLP to the forefront of a number of applications in analytics and beyond. For example, in analytics, we have historically taken information found in narratives (text, documents, tweets, speech) and processed them to categorize (taxonomy development) or to understand the sentiment. Sentiment analysis is particularly useful for understanding how people perceive products or services. In health care, sentiment analysis is used to measure "joy" in patients (Freed, 2017) as well as those at risk of heart failure (Eichstaedt, Schwartz, & Kern, 2015). These abstractions of text are then used as input to analytics processes such as predictive modeling, decision analysis, search, or question-answer applications.

Figure 1.6 highlights this as a generalized process.

A practical application of NLP can be seen in marketing; text is used to understand the overall "sentiment" of something (usually a brand or a product). Sentiment refers to the concept of understanding how emotions can be characterized in a body of work. Beyond sentiment analysis, NLP can be used in a variety of applications including:

- Grammar checking
- Entity extraction
- Translation
- Search
- Standardization
- Question answering

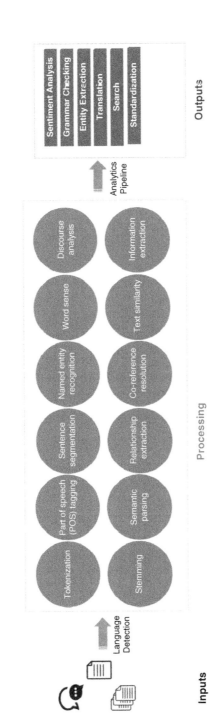

Inputs

Language Detection

Processing

Tokenization
Part of speech (POS) tagging
Sentence segmentation
Named entity recognition
Word sense
Discourse analysis

Stemming
Semantic parsing
Relationship extraction
Co-reference resolution
Text similarity
Information extraction

Analytics Pipeline

Outputs

Sentiment Analysis
Grammar Checking
Entity Extraction
Translation
Search
Standardization

Figure 1.6 Natural language processing conceptual workflow

23

Learn More

To learn more about the terminologies used in natural language processing, please see the article by Matthew Mayo at https://www.kdnuggets.com/2017/02/natural-language-process ing-key-terms-explained.html.

Natural language generation (NLG) is a subset of both artificial intelligence and NLP and is the process of automatically producing text from structured data in a readable format with meaningful phrases and sentences. Unlike NLP, the goal of NLG is to go the other way. That is, NLG takes data or some other form of information as input and produces text as output.

NLG has been popularized by chatbots which range in applications from customer service (Pathania & Guzma, Chatbots in Customer Service) to diagnosing symptoms (Facebook, 2017). Chatbots are only one application of NLG, and others include the automation of such things as:

- Summarizing business intelligence reports into complete narratives (Qlik, Tableau, TIBCO, Microstrategy, Sisense, Information Builders)
- Automatically creating financial reports complete with analysis (Nanalyze)
- Producing daily sports recaps (StatsMonkey)
- Providing automated performance reviews on customer service representatives (Quill by Narrative Science)
- Suggesting opportunities for customer relationship management systems by automatically creating CRM scripts (Yseop's Savvy)
- Helping a small business with a "financial analyst in a box" (Recount by Arria)

The field of natural language processing historically has involved the direct hand coding of rules—ontologies—that defined the structure, content, and context of words and how they are used in everyday language. Modern advances in statistical computing, computational linguistics, and machine learning are transforming the world of NLP at unprecedented rates.

Text Mining and Text Analytics

Perhaps one of the most confusing aspects of text analytics in general is the distinction between NLP and text mining. Think of this like **data mining**, where we are trying to extract useful information from data. The data, in this case, happens to be text and the extracted information includes the discovery of patterns and trends found in the textual data.

Text mining deals with the text data itself, where we attempt to answer questions such as the frequency of words, sentence length, and presence or absence of certain text strings. We can solve problems such as those outlined in Chapter 8 (e.g., classification using techniques found in NLP). In essence, text mining is often a precursor to NLP.

Text analytics often refers to advanced methods than span statistical analysis, machine learning, and other techniques but is generally recognized as equivalent to text mining. I think this is a gray area. Note the phrase *text analytics* is often used by the BI folks and represents more simple actions that can be done automatically and visualized via typical reporting means (e.g., word clouds, frequencies, etc.). Text mining would be the moniker used by the data scientists who have a wide swath of more advanced methods, but they would still do all of the counting of things as part of their effort. I think this fits my perspective that analytics is a natural evolution of BI and makes the important point of how different communities use different words, which can cause confusion. See, for example, www.linguamatics .com/blog/are-terms-text-mining-and-text-analytics-largely-inter changeable.

Machine Learning

SAS, the largest privately held US software firm and analytics giant, defines machine learning as (SAS, 2017):

> ... a method of data analysis that automates analytical model building. Using algorithms that iteratively learn from data, machine learning allows computers to find hidden insights without being explicitly programmed where to look.

At its core, machine learning is a class of quantitative methods that uses algorithms to build analytical models, helping computer models "learn" from data. It differs from human-centered processes in that the computer learns to find patterns in the data rather than the person building the model directly. The concept of model building and model management, in general, is that it brings repeatability to ongoing decision making rather than the high touch analysis that often accompanies statistical analysis.

With recent advances in computing power, machine learning can be used to automatically apply complex mathematical calculations to big data that heretofore would have been impossible.

Humans can typically create one or two good models a week; machine learning can create thousands of models a week.
Thomas H. Davenport, Analytics thought leader (Davenport, 2013)

Figure 1.7 highlights common methods used in machine learning.

Learn More

To learn more about these and other terms used in machine learning, please visit the Google Developers Machine Learning Glossary found here: developers.google.com/machine-learning/glossary/.

Machine learning algorithms are most often categorized by the "learning style" (remember, machine learning is all about having computers learn what matters by looking at patterns in the data). That is, there are different ways an algorithm can model the real world (problem) based on the data it sees.

There are four learning styles, or learning models, that an algorithm can use. Each differs in the roles the input variable can take on and how the data must be prepared for the model.

Table 1.1 highlights the differences in machine learning algorithms.

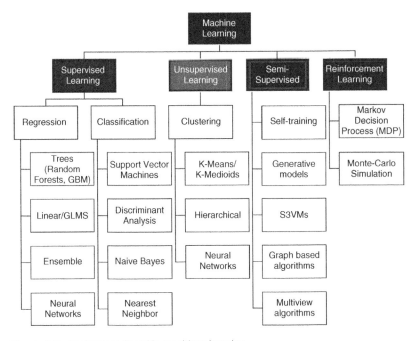

Figure 1.7 Techniques found in machines learning

Data Mining

 DATA MINING

Data mining is a process of discovering and interpreting patterns in (often large) data sets in order to solve business problems.

Data mining was popularized in the late 1990s and early 2000s as a way to analyze large databases in order to generate new or novel information. The holy grail of data mining is finding the "needle in the

Table 1.1 Styles of machine learning

Learning Style	Model Building	Example
Supervised	The model is trained through a human-centered process of identifying which outcomes are examples (labels) of true cases versus those that are not.	Patients with and without a given disease are labeled in a historical dataset. The supervised model is intended to use that historical information to predict patients with the disease in a new (unseen) database.
Unsupervised	The model attempts to self-describe or organize data in an attempt to discover novel interactions.	In an exploration of consumer behavior, we might want to understand what distinguishes people who visit our website. Without an a-priori hypothesis, unsupervised methods can help us classify types of visitors.
Semi-supervised	In cases where labeling is impractical, the model is built by labeling "some" of the cases and letting the algorithm learn.	Perhaps the most common example of semi-supervised models is image categorization. The model can identify "events" in a picture—say, of a child with a basket on a grassy lawn at an Easter Egg hunt.
Reinforcement	The algorithm "decides" on a course of action in response to seeing a new data point, and the model is "rewarded" based on how good that decision was.	NLG algorithms can be taught to improve how it structures content and syntax, uses punctuation, or expresses colloquialisms in spoken dialogue systems (SDS) based on reward systems. This essentially maximizes rewards through reinforcement mechanisms.

haystack" and differs from statistics in that there is not necessarily an **a-priori** theoretical-driven hypothesis before discovery can begin.

 A-PRIORI

A-priori is defined as "from the earlier," or simply, beforehand. An a-priori hypothesis is one that is stated prior to an experiment being conducted or the data collected.

Data mining uses traditional statistical methods as well as artificial intelligence and machine learning techniques. It is ultimately focused on identifying previously unknown patterns in our data and in making predictions.

Just like other techniques in analytics, data mining follows a lifecycle that usually begins with framing the problem, then making sense of the data, doing model construction, and acting on the results. In typical fashion, the data miner identifies the outcome variable of interest and then uses a variety of techniques to pre-process the data (such as clustering, principal components analysis, and association rule learning), then applies those outputs as inputs to data mining algorithms such as regression, neural networks, decision trees, or support vector machines. A critical part of the data mining process is in model evaluation and ensuring that we don't overfit the model. I will discuss this in greater detail in Chapter 8.

THE GOAL OF ANALYTICS

Things get done only if the data we gather can inform and inspire those in a position to make a difference.

Mike Schmoker, PhD, author, former administrator,
English teacher, and football coach

Analytics is a comprehensive strategy to support change. It informs interventions or change strategies. The goal of analytics is to support a data-driven, fact-based process of discovery. It is all about building confidence in our knowing and using that knowledge to understand, explain, predict, and optimize.

Analytics Is about Improving Outcomes

We analyze to understand, frame, and solve problems, make decisions, and create insights that can be used to drive change. We use what we know to make sense out of our worlds—that is, we "describe, discover, predict, and advise" (Blackburn & Sullivan, 2015). But advice falls short when analytics neither creates change nor produces outcomes. Results are interesting at best. The litmus test we should use is whether analytics has real-world impact. Fortunately, there are plentiful examples of how analytical thinking and its resultant products create change throughout organizations across various industries.

Analytics has the power to transform businesses and has proven its utility in hundreds if not thousands of examples. So why all the attention? To answer that, here are some of the outcomes that can be achieved with analytics.

Case Studies @
www.analyticslifecycletoolkit.com

See case studies organized by industry, method, and outcome.

In sum, the biggest opportunities for analytics may include those areas where the need involves:

1. An integrated, unified view of data

2. Going beyond description and discovery of the unknown to prediction, prescription, and optimization

3. A problem significant enough to be considered urgent and solvable

All three are required and not merely a "nice to have" to ensure that analytics has its permanent place in businesses.

Analytics Is about Creating Value

We are already overwhelmed with data; what we need is information, knowledge, and wisdom.

Dr. John Halamka, CIO Beth Israel Deaconess Medical Center

As indicated, outcomes are a critical component of analytics in that we must create something that is worthwhile. In discussing analytics, it's hard not to talk about value creation. After all, many view analytics in the same light as the countless information technology (IT) projects that they see fail. There are lots of reasons why projects fail (Bartels, 2017). As Jeremy Petranka, PhD notes, failed projects often relate to the fact that the linkage between the undertaking and organizational strategy is absent.

While the reasons may vary, I find in my advisory work that projects often fail when the fundamental value proposition was never fully realized. That is, the promise of the value to be "delivered, communicated, and acknowledged" was not accomplished (Value Proposition, n.d.).

Value has many definitions including the net result of [benefits − costs]. I prefer to look at value with a quality component, depicted as:

$$\text{Value} = \frac{(\text{Quality} + \text{Outcomes})}{\text{Cost}}$$

The quality component is critical in that analytics without quality presents risk, uncertainty, and unrealized potential. Quality comes in the form of robustness, repeatability, reliability, and validity. When the ratio is less than one—that is, when costs outweigh the quality plus outcomes—then we have failed to meet our fundamental value proposition (the reason for doing analytics in the first place). However, the full value isn't enough. Instead, we expect analytics to be a "force multiplier" (Kaufman, 2010) for organizations, and as such, it should be far greater. Of course, return on investment (ROI) for analytics isn't the only measure of value, as other things must be considered, such as mitigating risk, avoiding missed opportunities, or committing to improving the lives of customers, patients, or other stakeholders.

Rather, analytics is about creating value in that we achieve outcomes through the scientific approach we refer to as the **Analytics Lifecycle**. Analytics requires a multidisciplinary approach to achieving value.

 ## ANALYTICS LIFECYCLE

Analytics Lifecycle refers to the series of changes that occur during the life of an analytics product. Throughout this book, we consider the evolution of a business question to what changes must be affected in order to improve the organization and its processes.

We will discuss tools and best practices for measuring value in Chapter 10 when we outline the "Value Management" as a critical component of Analytics Product Management.

Analytics Is about Discovery

Even more than what you think, how you think matters.

Dr. Atul Gawande, author and surgeon

If business intelligence (BI) is about knowing the knowable, then analytics helps us with knowing the unknown. As the adage goes, "We can never know something until we discover it." The power of analytics is that it supports discovery. We use our skills of reasoning and sensemaking to unearth patterns in data and are, in fact, often pivoting between deductive and inductive reasoning when we "problem solve" with data.

Discovery runs throughout this book and is specifically described in a number of best practice areas as a way to frame problems (Chapter 6), unearth patterns and discover relationships (Chapter 7), and activate analytics results (Chapter 9).

Analytics Is about Change

Don't rely solely on data to drive decisions; use it to help drive better leadership behaviors.

John W. Boudreau, PhD, professor and research director, University of Southern California's Marshall School of Business and Center for Effective Organizations

I know of few people who like and embrace change. Yet change is inevitable and perhaps the only constant organizations should count on. The impetus for change can come in many forms but for some organization it can come in the form of a crisis such as disaster, deregulation, declining profits, government mandates, failed systems, or public health scares.

Change has afforded entire industries the opportunity to transform how they operate. Take, for example, the case of the Oakland A's as depicted in the book *Moneyball* (Morris, 2014) and their use of analytics to drive competition. Major League Baseball has been transformed by analytics, and its decisions around players will never be the same.

I began this section with words like value, outcome, and impact. For me, these are key to analytics—driving change to improve outcomes and creating value. If we look at some of the most celebrated cases of analytics we see evidence of organizational change (i.e., the impact of how decisions are made or work is performed) as a result of analytics:

- Disney uses analytics and linear programming to optimize party size at restaurants throughout their resorts to optimize capacity and resource utilization.
- Cleveland Clinic uses advanced forecasting models to schedule operating room staff.
- Boston Public Schools improves how they make bus stop assignments to support over 25,000 school bus riders.
- University of Utah predicts outbreaks of Respiratory Syncytial Virus (RSV) three weeks before it happens for high-risk patients.

In each of these cases, whether we use analytics to improve customer experience, spur innovation, or redesign and optimize service delivery processes, change is inevitable, as the impact to the organization necessarily involves altering how work gets done.

We will explore the impact of analytics change throughout this book but special attention will be paid to this topic in Part III where we explore making analytics actionable.

CHAPTER SUMMARY

Analytics is resilient, in large part, because of its ability to impact the way that we work, the decisions we make, and the outcomes we achieve. Analytics is often seen hanging in the same circles as big data, data science, informatics, and even business intelligence.

However, analytics should be considered as an organizational strategy, and the **Analytics Lifecycle** is a set of best practices, each having complementary processes. In fact, I operationally defined analytics for the purposes of this book as *a comprehensive, data-driven strategy for problem solving.* This definition does not diminish those who would tie it to statistics, computational algorithms, data visualization, or massively large databases. But in doing so, it does acknowledge that (1) they aren't the same thing and (2) while useful, many of these things are tools and not disciplines required to engage in a data-driven, fact-based discovery, and problem-solving process. That is, I know plenty of capable, analytical thinkers who do not have a PhD in statistics.

Analytics should be framed as a process, as supported by the following observations. Analytics:

- … is not a destination, but rather the process of gaining insights to effect change. Analytics is the art and science of turning data into actionable interventions.

- … allows us to discover meaningful patterns in data and supports the examination of data with the intent of drawing a conclusion (taking action).

- … is not a technology, although technology is used to support the process.

- … is more than simply counting things or using basic math, but takes advantage of what we know about the past to predict and optimize the future.

- … can include but does not require computationally intense algorithms that can only be driven by the "data scientists" of Silicon Valley but rather by the curious—anticipators we call Data Champions.

- … necessarily creates an artifact that is used as input to a "decisioning" process; that is, the process of analytics creates a data product—large or small, reusable or not—that feeds another process.

Like many organizational strategies that have preceded modern analytics, we continue to evolve our thinking and raise our proficiency in how we make sense of the world. We benefit from the accumulated knowledge of our prior work including the scientific process, statistics, exploratory data analysis, data mining, artificial intelligence, data visualization, computational sciences, psychology and behavioral economics, lean thinking, Six Sigma, and so on. The world of analytics has benefited from each of their unique contributions as applied to thinking, learning, problem solving, decision making, and behavior change.

EXPLORATORY DATA ANALYSIS

Exploratory data analysis (or EDA) is the process of understanding data and determining what questions to ask before undertaking analytics.

In Part III of this book, we offer a practical perspective on *actioning* analytics. While not officially a word, actioning is used because it implies movement; that is, actioning is an organized activity to accomplish an objective or outcome.

REFERENCES

Bartels, E. (2017). Jeremy Petranka on IT strategy. Retrieved from events .fuqua.duke.edu/facultyconversations/2017/06/20/jeremy-petranka-on -it-strategy/.

Blackburn, F., & Sullivan, J. (2015). Field guide to data science. Retrieved from www.boozallen.com/s/insight/publication/field-guide-to-data-science .html.

Brillinger, D. R. (2002). John Wilder Tukey (1915–2000). *Notices of the AMS, February 2002.* Retrieved from Notices of the AMS website: www.ams.org/ notices/200202/fea-tukey.pdf.

Champkin, J. (2013). George Box (1919–2013): a wit, a kind man and a statistician. *Significance.* Retrieved from www.statslife.org.uk/history-of-stats-science/448-george-box-1919-2013-a-wit-a-kind-man-and-a-statistician.

Copeland, J. (2000). What is artificial intelligence? Retrieved from www .alanturing.net/turing_archive/pages/Reference%20Articles/What%20is %20AI.html.

Cox, M., & David, E. (1997). *Application-Controlled Demand Paging for Out-of-Core Visualization.* Paper presented at the Proceedings of the 8th Conference on Visualization '97, Phoenix, Arizona, USA.

Davenport, T. H. (2013). Industrial strength analytics with machine learning. Retrieved from blogs.wsj.com/cio/2013/09/11/industrial-strength-analy tics-with-machine-learning/.

dictionary.com. (2017). Analytics. Retrieved from www.dictionary.com/ browse/analytics.

Drucker, P. (1969). *The age of discontinuity: guidelines to our changing society* (1st ed.). New York: Harper & Row.

Eichstaedt, J., Schwartz, H. A., & Kern, M. L. (2015). Psychological language on Twitter predicts county-level heart disease mortality. *Psychological Science.*

Facebook. (2017). Florence chat. Retrieved from www.messenger.com/t/florence.chatbot.

Feldman, S. E. (2017). Cognitive computing. Retrieved from en.wikipedia.org/wiki/Cognitive_computing.

Freed, D. (2017). Joy for Facebook Messenger. facebook.com/hellojoyai/.

Granville, V. (2014). 16 Analytic disciplines compared to data science. Retrieved from www.datasciencecentral.com/profiles/blogs/17-analytic-disciplines-compared.

Hoffenberg, S. (2016). IBM's Watson answers the question, "What's the Difference Between Artificial Intelligence and Cognitive Computing?" Retrieved from www.vdcresearch.com/News-events/iot-blog/IBM-Watson-Answers-Question-Artificial-Intelligence.html.

Kaufman, J. (2010). *The Personal MBA.*

Marr, B. (2016). Will 'analytics on the edge' be the future of big data? Retrieved from www.ibm.com/think/marketing/will-analytics-on-the-edge-be-the-future-of-big-data/.

Merriam-Webster. (Ed.) (2017a) Merriam-Webster.

Merriam-Webster. (Ed.) (2017b).

Nelson, G. S. (2010). BI 2.0: Are we there yet? Paper presented at the SAS Users Group International.

Pathania, A., & Guzma, I. (Chatbots in Customer Service). Retrieved from www.accenture.com/t00010101T000000__w__/br-pt/_acnmedia/PDF-45/Accenture-Chatbots-Customer-Service.pdf.

Rose, R. (2016, June). Defining analytics: a conceptual framework. *ORMS Today, 43.*

Sack, J. (2012). Early human counting tools. Retrieved from mathtimeline.weebly.com/early-human-counting-tools.html.

Saffo, P. (2007). Six rules for effective forecasting. *Harvard Business Review.*

Saffron Technologies. (2017). Retrieved from saffrontech.com/saffronresources/.

SAS. (2017). Machine learning—what it is and why it matters. Retrieved from www.sas.com/en_us/insights/analytics/machine-learning.html.

Schlangenstein, M. (2013). UPS crunches data to make routes more efficient, save gas. Retrieved from www.bloomberg.com/news/articles/2013-10-30/ups-uses-big-data-to-make-routes-more-efficient-save-gas.

Schouten, P. (2013). Better patient forecasts and schedule optimization improve patient care and curb staffing costs. Retrieved from www.beckers hospitalreview.com/hospital-management-administration/better-patient-forecasts-and-schedule-optimization-improve-patient-care-and-curb-staff ing-costs.html.

Shuttleworth, M. (2009). What is the scientific method? Retrieved from explorable.com/what-is-the-scientific-method.

Taylor (2016). Battle of the data science Venn diagrams. Retrieved from http://www.kdnuggets.com/2016/10/battle-data-science-venn-diagrams .html/2.

Value Proposition (n.d.). Wikipedia. https://en.wikipedia.org/wiki/Value _proposition.

Wolfram, S. (2010). Making the world's data computable. *Stephen Wolfram Blog.* Retrieved from blog.stephenwolfram.com/2010/09/making-the-worlds -data-computable/.

Woodford, C. (2016). Speedometers. Retrieved from www.explainthatstuff .com/how-speedometer-works.html.

CHAPTER **2**

The People
of Analytics

Developing talent is business's most important task—the sine qua non of competition in a knowledge economy.

Peter F. Drucker

WHO DOES ANALYTICS?

Some experts may relegate the land of analytics to the chosen few—the mathematicians, statisticians, and computer scientists who develop sophisticated algorithms. I disagree. That is the realm of data science and indeed a sophisticated and rewarding field. My view is that almost anyone can "do" analytics. It is true that the level of education and quantitative training can prepare you for using advanced methods, but analytics is a team sport. Decisions are made throughout the organization and what often gets overlooked is the fact that two distinct processes are in action: the decision lifecycle and the analytics lifecycle. As Figure 2.1 shows, this linkage informs how the analytics needs of the organization are to be serviced.

Problem solving is not a unique endeavor—we do it every day. While some are better than others, the skill can be learned, developed, and coached. Some would suggest that data scientists are on one end of the spectrum and business users on the other, with the citizen data scientist sitting in between (Figure 2.2). Gartner defines a citizen data scientist (Moore, 2017) as "a person who creates or generates models that use advanced diagnostic analytics or predictive and prescriptive capabilities, but whose primary job function is outside the field of statistics and analytics."

If we consider analytics as a decision-supporting discipline, then the "deep data science" activities comprise a relatively small (albeit important) percentage of the people who make up the analytics community in an organization. Thus, a more flexible model is needed that doesn't alienate business users or minimize the importance of having true data scientists on the team.

I view the organization and its resources as an ecosystem.[1] As such, it's important to think about the resources that are critical

---

[1]Note: this concept of analytics as an ecosystem is shared by others, see for example (Fattah, 2014).

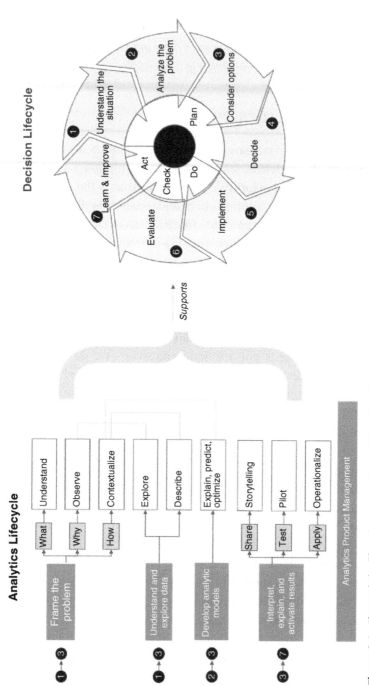

Figure 2.1 The analytics lifecycle supports the decision lifecycle.

40

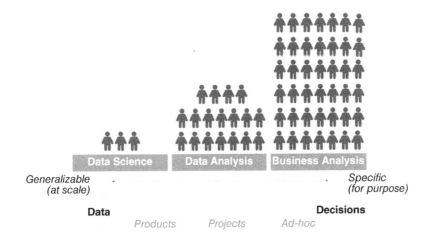

Figure 2.2 Using data to support decisions includes a variety of roles

to developing and sustaining an analytics capability. The remainder of this chapter will outline the people side of this equation, and Chapter 3 will explore the broader concept of an analytics "capability."

ROLES PEOPLE PLAY

Part II of this book will move from the general discussion of analytics—what it is, who does analytics, and why—to the specifics of tasks and processes found in analytics. First, however, it is useful to talk about who does the work of analytics.

There is little agreement on a universal set of **analytics roles and titles**. This is, in part, due to the organizational mindset that "we are different." Another aspect is the fact that it is unlikely that two organizations, even in the same industry, have the same analytics strategy or maturity level. The scope, data maturity, experience, and resources inform the structures used to house analytics professionals. Furthermore, organizations are composed of individuals who have different competencies and come from diverse, and sometimes nontraditional, backgrounds.

Teams that provide analytics services often develop by way of evolution, not selection. This means that existing job descriptions at many organizations can be poor representations of the analytics work that is required. Similarly, traditional analytics job families rarely exist that would provide clarity to one's career development, nor do they display interrelatedness between all analytics roles.

However, there are some general patterns that can serve as a guide. To that end, Figure 2.3 illustrates a standard set of job families for analytics and describes the roles and responsibilities needed for a full-service analytics product team.[2]

It should be noted that these job families have unique career growth trajectories. This framework can be useful in making hiring,

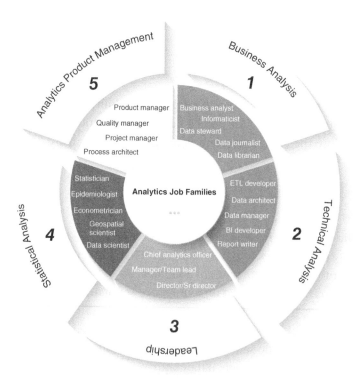

Figure 2.3　Five job families for analytics

---

[2]Note: This particular analytics competency model was developed by the company I founded, ThotWave, and serves as a useful model here. www.thotwave.com/healthcare -analytics-competency-model-talent-development-program/.

talent retention, and professional development decisions. But for general purposes, these distinctions can help frame the processes and participants in the analytics processes discussed in Part II.

Job Families for Analytics

In my experience as a consultant, educator, and manager of analytics teams, five job families have been identified that cover the various roles and responsibilities needed to perform the Analytics Lifecycle. Each job family has a different set of competencies that define the ideal set of knowledge, skills, behaviors, and disposition (Figure 2.4).

Nine domains of competency are critical for analytics success at the organizational level (Figure 2.5). Remember that this is a general model, but note that the unique characteristics of an organization, its

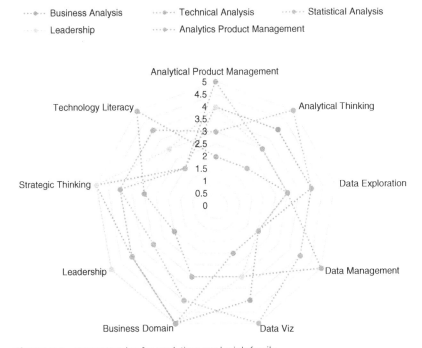

PROFICIENCY IN ANALYTICAL COMPETENCIES BY JOB FAMILY: ALL

····•··· Business Analysis ····•··· Technical Analysis ····•··· Statistical Analysis
····•··· Leadership ····•··· Analytics Product Management

Figure 2.4 Competencies for analytics vary by job family.

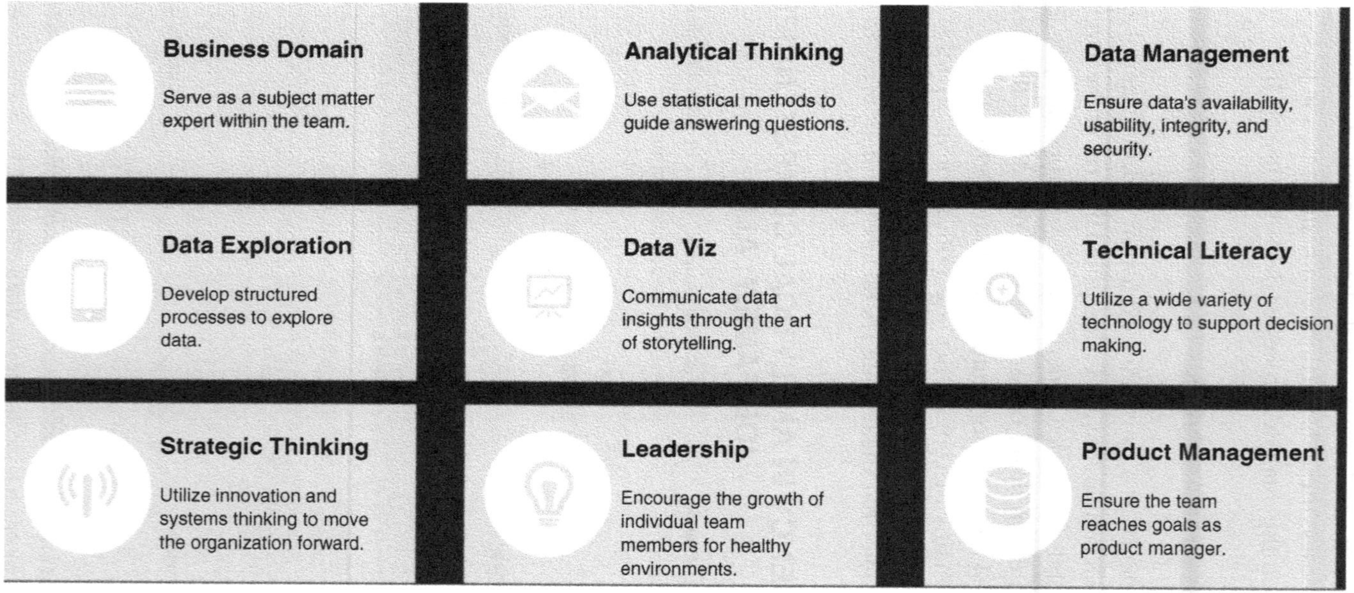

Business Domain

Serve as a subject matter expert within the team.

Analytical Thinking

Use statistical methods to guide answering questions.

Data Management

Ensure data's availability, usability, integrity, and security.

Data Exploration

Develop structured processes to explore data.

Data Viz

Communicate data insights through the art of storytelling.

Technical Literacy

Utilize a wide variety of technology to support decision making.

Strategic Thinking

Utilize innovation and systems thinking to move the organization forward.

Leadership

Encourage the growth of individual team members for healthy environments.

Product Management

Ensure the team reaches goals as product manager.

Figure 2.5   The knowledge domains for analytics. (The Analytics Competency Model)

culture, and mission will likely influence the importance of individual elements within this design. In my advisory work, this reference model works well for most organizations

Each of the five job families discussed below differs with respect to the specific competencies needed within the nine domains presented here. There is no analytics unicorn (Olavsrud, 2015), and no one person will have proficiency in all domains of knowledge. Note, in the following job families, I intentionally do not have a title called data scientist, as my intention is to clarify, rather than confuse the point that analytics is a product of data science and that the term *data scientist* refers to a myriad of roles.

Business Analysis

Business analysis refers to the ability to achieve organizational goals by combining business knowledge, business and operational workflows, and data analysis within a continuous improvement mindset. Within this family, roles may have a technical emphasis or focus on information synthesis. All functions require strength in requirements analysis and quantitative skills (either in the analysis or management of data). Core competencies include a strong command of business workflow, knowledge management, feasibility assessment, data-driven change leadership, and business impact assessment. Typically, specific business analysis roles have other functions that overlap with the statistical analysis, technical data analysis, or analytics product management job families.

Business Analysis Common Job Family Titles

- *Business analyst*—An analyst who is tasked with understanding business change needs, assessing the business impact of those changes, documenting requirements, and analyzing and visualizing business data as part of a communication strategy with relevant stakeholders.

- *Informaticist*—One who captures, communicates, and uses data and business or domain knowledge to drive the development, maintenance, optimization, and appropriate usage of information technology.

- *Data librarian*—A specialist in knowledge management who organizes, documents, and curates information regarding the body of data and analytics products in use by the business.

- *Data journalist*—A writer who interprets, critiques, and reformulates data and analytics results such that they can be put into the context of a business story for nontechnical stakeholders.

- *Data steward*—The person who manages and oversees a particular domain of business data to ensure that data consumers have high-quality data elements that are created and made accessible in a consistent, predictable manner.

Statistical Analysis

Statistical analysis is the core capability of analyzing data for insights and solutions that address business challenges. Typically, this is done using advanced knowledge of statistics, data visualization, and some algorithmic programming. Roles in this job category are expected to be highly consultative with business owners across the enterprise as they produce information to be consumed by wider audiences including senior leaders, researchers, frontline operational staff, and even external parties such as partners, customers, or patients. Core competencies include exemplary analytics thinking, visualization, and storytelling. Specific roles that may be more technical and include a data-programming component will overlap the skills emphasized in the technical data analysis job family.

Statistical Analysis Common Job Family Titles

- *Statistician*—Uses data engineering, mathematical, statistical, and programming skills to extract sound insights from a wide variety and volume of business data.

- *Geospatial scientist*—Uses geographic information systems to analyze business data that can be tied to concepts of location and space as they change over time.

- *Intelligence Analyst*—Performs a variety of simple and complex statistical activities to provide business entities with insights to maintain, improve, or transform business activities.

- *Research Analyst*—Carries out a variety of simple and complex data analysis tasks in support of research that seeks to answer a question related to the organization.

Technical Analysis

Technical analysis spans a variety of professional roles where data and data products are cleaned, manipulated, modeled, and transformed into the substrate that can be leveraged by those who seek insight from enterprise data. While tools to accomplish this come and go, the ability to adopt new methods quickly and to move between tools is essential for the modern analytics team. Roles in this job family understand the implications of technology frameworks on the ability to organize, retrieve, and share data insights. Core competencies include data wrangling, data profiling, tool agility, and systems thinking.

Technical Analysis Common Job Family Titles

- *Business intelligence architect/developer*—Develops the framework for organizing the data, information management, and technology components used to build enterprise systems for both reporting and the socialization of analytics results.

- *Data architect*—Recommends and initiates the creation of data structures, data models, relationships, attributes, values, and schemas; understands the implications of architectural design on different arms of the business.

- *Data manager*—Manages and maintains data based on a complete understanding of enterprise relationships, business definitions, and business usage profiles; ensures that information is organized, maintained, and stored in a manner that facilitates business enablement and intelligence.

- *Data engineer*—Develops programmatic solutions in response to technical needs such that they meet requirements and design specifications. Technical in nature, these roles often sit in IT and can also be referred to as ETL developer, data analyst, or data integrators.

- *Report writer (and dashboard builder)*—Analyzes, provides specifications for, and composes a variety of reports, dashboards, and scorecards for business entities.

Analytics Leadership

The leadership job family includes both line managers and director-level leaders who guide and manage analytics teams. They assist the organization in consuming data and analytics products to impact business decisions. They bring together the business, quality, technical, and analytics interests of the enterprise to drive collaboration, best practice sharing, and deployment of shared intellectual assets. Leaders must have significant knowledge of business culture as well as workflows. They also need exemplary capabilities in design thinking, data-driven decision making, analytics evangelism, and the maintenance of strategic alignment.

Leadership Common Job Family Titles

- *Manager/team lead*—Line manager of analytics and data product teams; responsible for aspects of project prioritization, team dynamics, and professional development. May also serve as an individual contributor to teamwork products.

- *Senior manager*—Line manager who directly oversees analytics staff, including groups under team leads; responsible for broad aspects of team culture and harmonizing professional development strategies.

- *Analytics executive*—Director level and higher organizational leaders who take strategic business goals and matches those to the needed capabilities of the data and analytics teams.

Analytics Product Management

The project management job family is a catch-all to describe those roles that focus on developing, managing, and enforcing processes around products, projects, and portfolios. These jobs are essential to the Analytics Lifecycle and govern many of the processes that are core to turning insights into action. Program or project managers will scope projects, maintain project plans, set team priorities, and even mentor teams in effectively using suitable processes. Some individuals serving in this role also manage small groups. They typically also have strong business domain knowledge and excel at consensus building as part of aligning projects to organizational strategy. These managers increasingly use agile methodologies in team development activities.

Analytics Product Management Common Job Family Titles

- *Product manager*—Owns the analytics or data product and ensures that it is deployed, maintained, updated, and reevaluated in alignment with organization needs for insights; responsible for delivery, managing scope, cost, and schedule of data products. This is also referred to as a portfolio manager in some cases.

- *Program manager*—Uses well-known project management methodology to support projects and project portfolios so that they meet their goals; supports the management of scope, cost, schedule, and escalation when deviations arise. Depending on the scale of their responsibilities, they may be referred to as program managers or project managers.

- *Process architect*—Identifies current process state, elicits attributes, documents all details, and facilitates stakeholder consensus regarding new business process designs; identifies impact and linkages between data products, user behavior, real-world workflow, and business policies.

- *Quality manager*—Responsible for ensuring that analytics products are developed using best practices for quality assurance; also tasked with the maintenance and durability of the analytics product and its overall lifespan of usefulness.

CRITICAL COMPETENCIES FOR ANALYTICS

Chapter 1 included a discussion of building organizational capabilities, which were defined as what can be accomplished because of the collective competencies of the people in the organization. In Chapter 3 we will elaborate on this concept of organizational capabilities. Here, I wish to begin the discussion of the general competencies needed but a detailed discussion of competencies is the focus of Chapter 12.

In analytics circles, there is a great deal of focus on what people need to be good at. Opinions range from deep mathematical skills to computer science and statistical modeling. While specific methods and technologies are necessary, the unsung heroes of analytics are actually those who excel at problem solving, critical thinking, story-telling, and collaboration. Unfortunately, soft skills are hard to codify on one's resume and even more challenging to assess when hiring. Organizations often fall back to the tangible, testable attributes of a person—what she knows, rather what she is capable of achieving.

In a paper titled "The Elusive Data Scientist" (Nelson & Horvath, 2017), (shown here in Figure 2.6) one of my colleagues and I noted four areas around which we measure analytics talent:

1. Technology
2. Business domain
3. Methods
4. Soft skills

 ANALYTICS COMPETENCY

Analytics competency relates to the knowledge, skills, abilities, and disposition required to turn data into actionable interventions successfully.

The Elusive Data Scientist

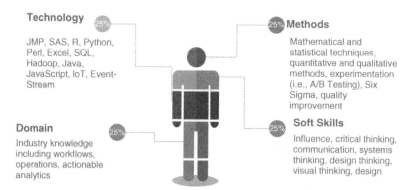

Technology 25%

JMP, SAS, R, Python, Perl, Excel, SQL, Hadoop, Java, JavaScript, IoT, Event-Stream

Domain 25%

Industry knowledge including workflows, operations, actionable analytics

25% **Methods**

Mathematical and statistical techniques, quantitative and qualitative methods, experimentation (i.e., A/B Testing), Six Sigma, quality improvement

25% **Soft Skills**

Influence, critical thinking, communication, systems thinking, design thinking, visual thinking, design

Figure 2.6 The elusive data scientist combines competencies in technology, data, business domain, and methods.

Knowledge, skills, and *competencies* are words used without precision when people speak about talent development. But for this discussion, it is important to clearly define these terms so that the process of aligning analytics to desired organizational capabilities is evident. With this in mind, several concepts are relevant:

- *Knowledge area*—the body of information that a person has acquired that enables them to perform competently in an individual job function or business area.
- *Skill*—an ability, based on one's knowledge, to perform an activity that can be readily measured through assessment; skills are specific learned activities that are necessary but not sufficient to fulfill a role.
- *Competency*—the collective knowledge, skills, and behaviors that afford an individual the ability to do something successfully.
- *Ability*—the capacity to perform a specific activity at a point in time.
- *Proficiency*—a specific level of achievement that is attainable given a competency.

I advocate a shift away from measuring people using technical skills to an approach that looks at proficiency in a whole range of analytics competencies. For example, people can be measured by their technical expertise in languages (such as SAS, R, Java, Python), but an alternative approach is to look for depth in their capacity to perform the job successfully. We will discuss this in more detail in Chapter 12.

Beyond the current discussion of the "soft skills" of analytics, I discuss the detailed competencies required for analytics professionals across each of the five job families in Chapter 12.

Tools and Templates @ www.analyticslifecycletoolkit.com

Analytics competencies across five job families.

Styles of thinking can influence how one approaches (and solves) a problem, but it can also be important to consider when working with others that the way that we think (perceive, make sense, judge, decide) may not be the way that others think. Analytics, after all, is about influencing action (i.e., interventions) through scientific, fact-based strategies.

Stephen Few, a visualization expert, summarized the types of thinking as applied to analytical thinking. In an article, Few suggested a curriculum he titled "A Course of Study in Analytical Thinking" to address the competency gap he saw with analytics professionals. Specifically, he outlined nine different types of thinking that analysts need in their arsenal:

1. Whole-brain thinking
2. Critical thinking
3. Logical thinking
4. Scientific thinking
5. Statistical thinking
6. Systems thinking
7. Visual thinking
8. Ethical thinking
9. Data sensemaking

Everyone interested in analytics should not only read his article (Few, 2015) but also consider how to nurture analytics staff and broaden their perspectives.

In this context, I think it is important to examine some of the nontechnical competencies to look for when evaluating proficiency (Figure 2.7). We will touch on a few of these here:

1. Analytical thinking
2. Problem solving
3. Critical thinking
4. Systems thinking

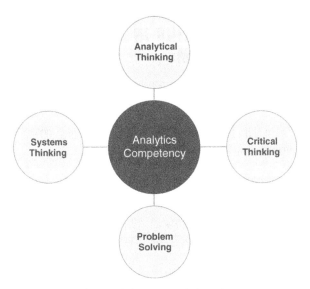

Figure 2.7 Key competencies needed across analytics roles

Analytical Thinking

Analytical thinking is a broad concept that refers one's ability to scrutinize information and evaluate the component parts in an attempt to evaluate their strengths and weaknesses. People who are analytical thinkers will break problems down, brainstorm multiple solutions to the problem, reconcile data discrepancies, weigh the pros and cons of various solutions, and utilize testing and validation to confirm or reject solutions. Analytical thinking is used throughout the analytics lifecycle and especially in categorizing the type of problem we are facing. As we will see throughout this book, accurately assessing the problem space and correctly assigning the analytics method or methods that can be used to solve the problem is a critical skill. In the example shown here (The Bat and Ball Problem), we note that it is easy to make misattribution and assume that it is one type of problem unless we engage in analytical thinking.

ANALYTICAL THINKING IN ACTION: THE BAT AND BALL PROBLEM

A commonly used exercise that demonstrates analytical thinking is expressed in the form of a word problem:

"A bat and a ball cost $1.10 in total. The bat costs $1.00 more than the ball. How much does the ball cost?"

Studies have shown that the majority of people get this answer wrong. The answer is not $0.10 but rather $.05, as shown by simple algebra:

$$x + (\$1.00 + x) = \$1.10$$
$$\$1.00 + 2x = \$1.10$$
$$2x = \$1.10 - \$1.00$$
$$2x = \$0.10$$

Then solve for x:

$$x = \$0.05$$

Check your work:

$$x + (\$1.00 + x) = \$1.10, \text{ so}$$
$$\$0.05 + (\$1.00 + \$0.05) = \$1.10$$

Problem Solving

A variety of techniques can be used to frame and solve problems. Traditionally, organizations have used reductionist methods to analyze problems. That is, they break down (or reduce) a problem to its constituent parts and analyze the elemental parts, describing them using the properties that help distinguish them from other parts.

For example, in trying to figure out why our car won't start, we begin by considering the factors (electrical, fuel, engine) that might be contributing to the problem. From there, we come up with a set of potential options that might help us understand our predicament (Figure 2.8).

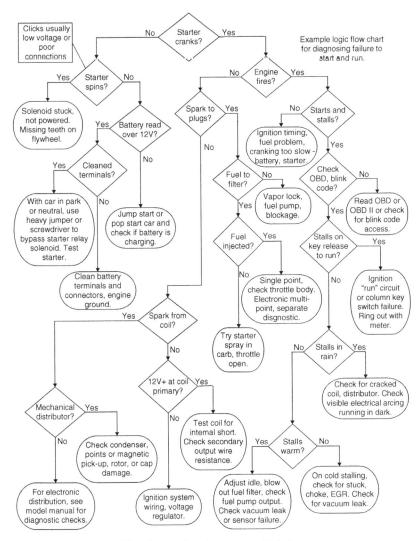

Figure 2.8 Decomposition diagram for why a car won't start
Source: *Copyright 2008 by Morris Rosenthal www.ifitjams.com*

This style of problem solving is often used in management consulting to solve complex business and organizational problems. McKinsey and Boston Consulting Group, for example, popularized the use of various visual models that can be used to dissect a problem or synthesize the results such as the Issue Tree, MECE Principle, Pyramid Principle, and the BCG Matrix. These models will be addressed specifically in Part II in the context of the Analytics Lifecycle.

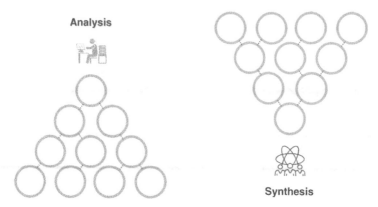

Figure 2.9 Analysis and synthesis are two processes used in problem solving.

These tools are examples of two processes in action: *analysis* and *synthesis*. In analysis, something is broken down into its parts or components. Synthesis, on the other hand, is the opposite (Figure 2.9). That is, separate elements or components are combined to form a coherent whole (or system).

In analytics, it is common to iterate between the synthesis (systems thinking) and analysis (reductionism) in a number of areas of the analytics lifecycle:

- Problem definition and understanding
- Data discovery, relationships, and insights creation
- Interpolation and generalizability
- Evangelism, testing, and prototyping

A generalized view of this as applied to analytics can be seen in Figure 2.10. Note this figure is an adaption of Vijay Kumar's innovation planning model from his work on deploying design thinking for innovation (Kumar, 2012).

Problem solving takes a certain "stick-to-it-iveness" to find a solution without stopping at the easy potential answers. It is easy to throw out theories about why something might be broken, but it requires discipline to follow a structured approach to problem solving. Curious analytics professionals who demonstrate this discipline and utilize processes such as the analysis-synthesis, **DMAIC**, or other methodologies are problem solvers. Let's examine the analysis-synthesis process.

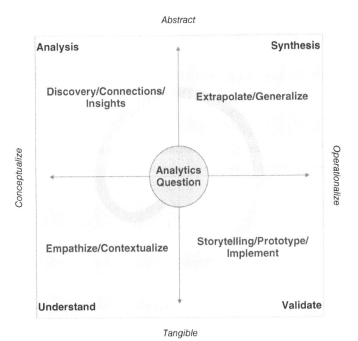

Figure 2.10 Analytics innovation planning model

 DMAIC

DMAIC is a data-driven improvement strategy rooted in Six Sigma. DMAIC is an acronym for Define, Measure, Analyze, Improve, and Control.

Analysis

Analysis generally includes three steps:

1. Take an issue and break it down into its constituent parts; this process isolates the parts and decomposes them into mutually exclusive, collectively exhaustive elements.

2. Analyze the parts as individual elements in isolation.

3. Recombine these different components into the original system where it is described in terms of the properties of the individual elements.

The benefit of this approach is that it isolates areas of focus, so you don't have to "eat the whole elephant" but rather, focus on high-priority issues. The limitations of the reductionist approach can be found in the fact that it necessarily deemphasizes the relationships and interconnections present in the system. That is, the relationships between elements of a system are considered in isolation and thought to be merely the sum of its parts.

This approach is suitable for situations in which there is little interconnectivity or interdependence within the system being examined. However, in complex systems such as fraud detection, patient adherence to medication, or forecasting retail sales, the phenomenon cannot be divorced from the system in which it operates since it is defined by the relationships and dependencies themselves.

Synthesis

More complex issues may require the use of the synthesis perspective, in which the first step is to understand the system of which the object of interest is an element, examining the interconnectedness and dependencies that exist between elements of the system.

> Synthesis is defined as the combination of components or elements to form a connected whole.

This paradigm focuses on the relationship and dependencies found within a system and is used to describe an entity in the context of its relationships within the entire system of which it is a part.

Note: Later in this chapter, we will discuss the concept of systems thinking, which is related to synthesis.

Like analysis, there are three stages of reasoning in synthesis:

1. Identify the system or whole in which the object of interest lies.

2. Create a broad outline of how the whole system functions.

3. Try to understand how the parts are connected and functioning.

It is important to note that analysis and synthesis are the two primary frames of reference or paradigms that can be used to describe something. The reason we discuss the two paradigms of reasoning is that we often don't explicitly consider how we are thinking about a problem in the natural course of working. That is, we may drift between analysis and synthesis without realizing it.

For most people, it's easy to think about the specifics (the tactics of a problem) and to focus on the detailed steps of decomposition, analysis, and reconstitution, or the mechanics of the technology. The risk of not explicitly shifting our thinking and exercising our critical thinking skills is that we subject ourselves to unnecessary risks, which can lead to blind spots in our analytics approach. These trouble spots can be seen in the areas of business analysis, data exploration, analysis, results in dissemination, and even in the operationalization of analytics.

Tools and Templates @ www.analyticslifecycletoolkit.com

Practice Sheet: Analysis and Synthesis.

Critical Thinking

As discussed above, analytical thinking refers to our ability to scrutinize and break down facts and considerations into their strengths and weaknesses. Critical thinking is a complementary but slightly different way of approaching the world; it involves the use of mental models to overcome lazy or unconscious biases in our thought processes—forcing us, for example, to think about the problem more actively. Amos Tversky and Daniel Kahneman (Tversky & Kahneman, 1974) first talked about the built-in biases or heuristics that we use to ease everyday decision making. Later, Kahneman elaborated on this work in his best-selling book *Thinking, Fast and Slow* (Kahneman, 2013).

Kahneman describes two systems at work: System 1 refers to the automatic, unconscious thinking (rule of thumb or heuristic) that occurs in response to everyday stimuli. System 2 thinking is the slower, more thoughtful process that occurs when we consider something critically.

We use critical thinking across all of the best practice areas of the analytics lifecycle but it can be particularly useful in data sense-making in hypothesis generation. As Few suggests, "Critical thinking recognizes the ways in which our minds often mislead us and seeks to correct those thinking flaws…Data sense-making requires the necessary skills of critical thinking, which are by no means common sense" (Few, 2015).

As humans, we are perfectly imperfect. Across disciplines (including such fields as neuroscience, cognitive psychology, and behavioral economics), we note that there is growing evidence of our fallibility and how this affects our thinking. Examples include logical fallacies (logical connections that are not real), false assumptions, delusions (believing ourselves without questioning, even in the face of contradictory evidence), and the neuroscience of perception and memory. While we may see, hear, and experience things, our brains do not record those directly, but rather perception is the process of constructing a reality that we understand and fits the rest of our constructed narrative. That is, we confabulate information based on what we attend to, beliefs, motivation, egos, and emotions. Furthermore, what we think and experience becomes a memory. Our memories are further constructed, altered, and integrated. Research studies have shown that our memories are often a poor reflection of what really occurred. Often, we don't recall memories as much as we reconstruct and update them, altering the information every time we access it as our brains seek to fill in the gaps.

As analytics professionals, there are a number of limits to how our brains work including making mental shortcuts (or heuristics), logical fallacies, unexamined biases, and false assumptions. To combat these limitations, we can utilize the learned skills of logic and critical thinking to help us evaluate the world around us.

Critical thinking is the mode of thinking where we intentionally seek to improve the quality of our thinking (including our assumptions, premises, conclusions, and arguments) by deftly taking charge of the structure of our thinking and applying intellectual standards on them.

To think critically means to:

- Examine all of the facts that you are assuming or that you think are true.
- Examine your logic to ensure that it is not flawed or biased in some way.

- Understand your own motivations and how they might be influencing your thinking.

- Invest in the process rather than the outcome or conclusion. If we are not tied to the solution but the rigor of our process, then we are open to a myriad of outcomes based on a defensible and robust process.

- Thinking through the implications of a belief to ensure that your beliefs about the world are compatible with each other.

- Open yourself to scrutiny by allowing yourself to be questioned by others and consider their perception. This also allows you to verbalize your assumptions, premises, and conclusions that make up the whole of your argument.

- Know your limitations. We all have different experiences, education, and perceptions. Careful consideration of how your argument is being shaped by your limitations is essential.

- Be comfortable with uncertainty. While most business executives want an answer, we all need to understand that analytics and the models that we produce are inexact at best.

Examples of Critical Thinking in Analytics

In my conversations with analytics leaders, critical thinking is one of the most important skills necessary in analytics. Here are some examples of critical thinking for analytics:

- A critical care nurse would use critical thinking skills to analyze the readmission rate score (produced from analytics) for her patient and decide what factors contributed to the score, which ones are most impactable, and what course of action should be considered.

- A data analyst would use critical thinking skills to evaluate which data would be most useful for understanding the current performance of a marketing campaign.

- A statistician would review the evidence and use critical thinking to make sense of the model results and help create recommendations around what interventions are needed to improve manufacturing operations.

How Can We Improve Our Critical Thinking Skills?

**Tools and Templates @
www.analyticslifecycletoolkit.com**

Train-your-brain: Do critical thinking exercises.

While scientific skepticism is often introduced in middle and high school science classes, most of us don't get the opportunity to fully develop critical thinking skills beyond on-the-job (OTJ) training. Just like a concert pianist, critical thinking is a learned skill. We don't come out of the womb knowing how to do it but it requires practice and feedback.

My advice on how best to develop your critical thinking skills can be found in the following habits:

1. *Question.* Question yourself by thinking about your thought process. What are your motivations? What haven't you considered? What must be true for this to be true? What are some alternative explanations? What are your beliefs and emotions? It is important to surround yourself with others who will help you think better by asking you tough questions. We often consider questioning of our peers or from supervisors as threatening but we will get better if we open ourselves to scrutiny—of our process and our logic.

2. *Practice.* We only get better at something by regularly exercising our critical thinking skills. Consider a problem someone has already solved and sketch out the argument (e.g., mind map). What were their assumptions? What were the premises? Did the logic follow from the premises? What alternatives did they consider? Also, practice with others either as a team or as individuals on real world problems. There are numerous design thinking or innovation contests. Alternatively, tackle a problem your organization is facing but be sure to find a coach or mentor who can challenge you along the way. Practice without feedback is akin to serving in tennis without seeing where the ball ended up.

3. *Learn*. Become a life long learner. As Charlie Munger and Warren Buffett suggest, if you want to outsmart people who are smarter than you, temperament and life long learning are more important than IQ (Sellers, 2013). We learn through observation, through questioning, and through doing. While there is no possible way that we could learn everything, we can exercise our curiosity by asking the fundamental question, "why?" For me in my own learning, I find it necessary to consider whether I am learning about something (to know of) or learning to do something. Critical thinking requires the latter.

4. *Reflect*. An essential part of learning is through active reflection of what you learned. Mortimer Adler in his book *How to Read a Book* (Adler & van Doren, 1972) identifies four levels of reading that most of us don't consider. In higher-order reading, we consider, reflect, compare, and analyze. For critical thinking, consider the use of an analytics journal (see Chapter 7 for additional detail) or learning portfolio (columbiasc.edu/faculty/learning-portfolio/) as a way to capture your learning experiences.

Systems Thinking

Systems thinking is a management discipline that concerns an understanding of a system by examining the linkages and interactions between the components that comprise the entirety of that defined system.

William Tate in *The Search for Leadership: An Organizational Perspective* (Tate, 2009)

Most of us have worked with others in a business or personal context and noticed that some people just think differently. For example, some of us need to get the lay of the land—a holistic view—before diving into the details. Other people are very detail-oriented and must work their way up to the high level by first examining the details. The fact is that we think differently, and everyone's thinking patterns are different.

There is no right way to think. Many of us are taught to break a problem down into its component parts and then analyze them separately. But in doing this, we may be susceptible to blind spots if we ignore the relationships between the focus of our analysis and the environment in which they operate.

Learn More

To learn more about how Pixar sees the relationship between the environment (world) and the character, take a look at this video: www.khanacademy.org/partner-content/pixar/ storytelling/we-are-all-storytellers/v/video-4-world-character.

Similarly, in the context of analytics, it is important to note that the creation of data (i.e., the digital footprint of people, processes, and technology) operates within an environment that is a system.

Systems thinking ("Systems Theory," 2017) is an approach to problem-solving that takes into consideration the context and content of the surrounding system (Figure 2.11).

 SYSTEMS THINKING

Systems thinking is the process of reasoning known as synthesis or holistic thinking, and is defined by the belief that the parts are intimately connected and explicable only by reference to the whole.

When we consider the dependencies and interconnectedness within the system, we can effectively solve complex problems—even when the system is large and has many interrelated components such as the patient journey through the various data touchpoints found in health care.

> *Systems Thinking is one of a Data Scientist's most essential tools. The ability to tell a story from huge amounts of "Big Data" is only possible if you understand the system. (Coleman, 2011)*
>
> Howard Elias, EMC president and chief operating officer,
> Information Infrastructure and Cloud Services

Often, we see the dynamics of a system as too complicated and prefer decomposition while others view everything as a system and

Figure 2.11 Cultural alignment—patient-centered care

are often criticized for not being tactical enough to quickly address the components of a problem. This natural tension between analysis and synthesis can also be seen in the differences between Lean Six Sigma and Systems Design (Higgins, 2017). One organization that appears to have realized the benefits of combining multiple perspectives (such as systems thinking and Lean Six Sigma) is Harley Davidson (see sidebar).

Harley Davidson Combines Systems Thinking and Continuous Improvement

Dantar Oosterwal, the former head of the new product development at Harley Davidson Motor Company, used systems thinking in conjunction with continuous improvement programs like Lean Six Sigma to modernize their product development strategy. This new mindset resulted in an accelerated product development cycle that improved the average number of new models released to the market by over 600 percent between 1996 and 2007. In his book,

(Continued)

(Continued)

Oosterwal emphasized just how important systems thinking was in continuous improvement programs by stating that "with a focus on tools and techniques there may be a monetary improvement, but the change they usher in will not become embedded as part of the system; the change will just become another fine program" (Oosterwal, 2010).

CHAPTER SUMMARY

In the field of analytics today, we have the opportunity to impact the trajectory of organizations, the lives of people, and the world around us. We all know of the analyst who creates the stunning visualization or in-depth analysis of a phenomenon but fails to ask the "so what?" question. The linkage of the data to the environment is a critical-thinking skill and much-needed competency in analytics.

Analytics strategy involves aligning the aspirations of the analytics team with the overall organization's strategy. That linkage is critical so that there is clear line of sight between the "data and technical" efforts that you undertake and the business context in which you will operate.

In practical terms, strategy is the game plan. Note that strategy is not something to do at the beginning of a planning cycle only to be forgotten once the realities of everyday operation consume us. As in business, there must be a clear linkage between strategy and execution. A 2006 survey conducted by Palladium (founded by Harvard Professors Kaplan and Norton) shared a striking statistic—only 25 percent of companies said they performed as well as, or better than, the average of their industry peer group when it came to linking strategy with execution. This means that 75 percent of organizations were less than or equal to being average! In the January 2008 *Harvard Business Review* article "Mastering the Management System," Kaplan and Norton tackle this issue directly, describing an integrated process for linking strategy and operations" (Kaplan, 2008).

REFERENCES

Adler, M. J., & Van Doren, C. L. (1972). *How to read a book* (rev. and updated ed.). New York: Simon and Schuster.

Coleman, F. (2011). Data analytics—systems thinking. *Dell EMC—Big Data*. Retrieved from infocus.emc.com/frank_coleman/data-analytics-systems-thinking/.

Fattah, A. (2014). Going beyond data science toward an analytics ecosystem: part 1. Retrieved from www.ibmbigdatahub.com/blog/going-beyond-data-science-toward-analytics-ecosystem-part-1.

Few, S. (2015). A course of study in analytical thinking. Retrieved from Perceptualedge.com: perceptualedge.com/articles/visual_business_intelligence/a_course_of_study_in_analytical_thinking.pdf.

Higgins, M. (2017). Increase lean Six Sigma's power with TOC and systems thinking. Retrieved from www.isixsigma.com/methodology/lean-methodology/lean-six-sigma-toc-systems-thinkin/.

Kahneman, D. (2013). *Thinking fast and slow*. New York: Farrar, Straus, and Giroux.

Kaplan, R. S., & Norton, David P. (2008). Mastering the management system. *Harvard Business Review, 86*(1), 62–77.

Kumar, V. (2012). *101 design methods: a structured approach for driving innovation in your organization*. Hoboken, NJ: John Wiley & Sons.

Moore, S. (2017). Gardner says that more than 40% of data science tasks will be automated by 2020 [Press release]. Retrieved from www.gartner.com/newsroom/id/3570917.

Nelson, G. S., & Horvath, M. (2017). The elusive data scientist: real-world analytic competencies. Retrieved from support.sas.com/resources/papers/proceedings17/0832-2017.pdf.

Olavsrud, T. (2015). Don't look for unicorns. Build a data science team. *CIO.com*. Retrieved from www.cio.com/article/3011648/analytics/dont-look-for-unicorns-build-a-data-science-team.html.

Oosterwal, D. P. (2010). The lean machine: how Harley-Davidson drove top-line growth and profitability with revolutionary lean product development. New York: AMACOM.

Sellers, P. (2013). Warren Buffett and Charlie Munger's best advice. *Fortune*. Retrieved from http://fortune.com/2013/10/31/warren-buffett-and-charlie-mungers-best-advice/.

Systems Theory. (2017). *Wikipedia*. Retrieved from en.wikipedia.org/wiki/Systems_theory.

Tate, W. (2009). *The search for leadership: an organisational perspective*. Axminster: Triarchy Press.

Tversky, A., & Kahneman, D. (1974). Judgment under uncertainty: heuristics and biases. *Science, 185*(4157).

UK Healthcare Strategic Plan. Retrieved from ukhealthcare.uky.edu/strategic-plan/foundation/.

CHAPTER 3

Organizational Context for Analytics

Innovation is the lifeblood of an organization. Knowing how to lead and work with creative people requires knowledge and action that often goes against the typical organizational structure. Protect unusual people from bureaucracy and legalism typical of organizations.

Max De Pree, American businessman and writer

ORGANIZATIONAL STRATEGY AND ANALYTICS ALIGNMENT

Most leaders today recognize the importance of alignment. That is, the vision, mission, values, and strategies must be coordinated and communicated through the enterprise. In the context of analytics, the strategy—that is, the specific analytics game plan—is directly related to achieving the mission of the organization.

Strategy is a word that is often misused and ill-defined. Simply put, strategy is a set of integrated choices that helps position a firm for future success. Analytics strategy defines a specific game plan for how the leadership team will use data analytics to help the organization compete. Explicitly setting the analytics strategy helps with communication, creates a sense of purpose, and details the requirements for the **analytics capabilities** and resources along with the management systems that are needed.

Analytics alignment to the enterprise means creating clarity in our intentions (see Figure 3.1):

- *Purpose*—Why are we doing this?
- *Strategy*—What is our game plan? What do we want to accomplish? What will we do and not do? What is our unique advantage?
- *Organizational capabilities*—What aspects do we need to be good at?
- *Resources*—What is required in order to deliver on those capabilities?
- *Execution and measurement systems*—What systems or oversight and management are required to keep us on track?

69

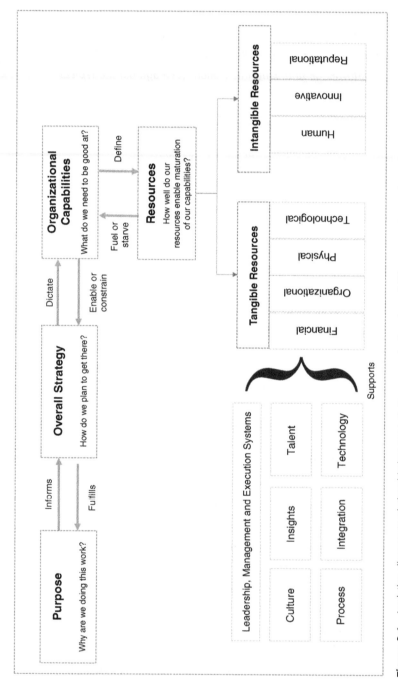

Figure 3.1 Analytics alignment: relationship between strategy, organizational capabilities, resources, and management systems

Purpose

Purpose is the North Star for an organization—a beacon that guides the enterprise and provides a standard trajectory. The rationale for having an analytics function in an organization typically includes:

- To support the information needs of leadership
- To gain competitive advantage through the use of advanced analytics
- To evangelize the use of data in everyday decision making

There is no right or wrong answer as organizations seek to find their analytics true north; however, having a strategy does inform the possible set of options to get there. The purpose of an analytics function should directly support the organization's goals.

Tools and Templates @ www.analyticslifecycletoolkit.com

Questions to guide your analytics strategy.

Strategy

If the mission statement articulates the organization's purpose and the vision statement gives a picture of the organization in the future, the **strategy** is the set of choices that will be used to get there.

For example, if an organization views its competitive advantage in the information it can exploit, then the strategy should be focused on the game plan to achieve analytics superiority. That is, moving beyond the standards of consistent, usable data to exploit the predictive and **prescriptive power of analytics**.

 PRESCRIPTIVE ANALYTICS

Prescriptive analytics refers to an advanced technique in which the correction or course of action is "prescribed." It goes beyond predictive analytics, which help us understand what is likely to happen, to instead outline specific interventions based on the predictions.

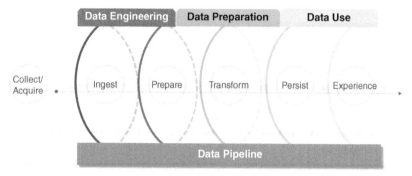

Figure 3.2 Data pipeline supports the Analytics Lifecycle

The analytics function becomes an analytics product factory—servicing both ad-hoc requests as well as creating innovative and reusable data products (see Figure 3.2).

If, on the other hand, an organization is intent on democratizing the use of data for better, well-informed decisions and not building a grand data science strategy, then the approach to data storage, data management, metadata management, and data exploitation will be markedly different in that the focus will be on managing data to support more tactical decisions. Most business leaders don't want to give up anything and usually want to do both, but this comes with a price. The cost of governance and active management is not insignificant. It may well be that a game plan for this latter type of strategy is to outsource model development (data science) and focus its internal energy on data quality and data governance. The organization can always build on these latter capabilities once it masters the former.

Note that when working through the strategy, three fundamental principles apply:

1. Strategy is the creation of a unique and valuable position, involving a different set of activities.

2. Strategy requires you to make trade-offs in competing—to choose what to do and what not to do.

3. Strategy involves creating "fit" among the company's activities.

As shown in the next section, this fit means evaluating your analytical aspirations given your current tangible and intangible resources.

Organizational Capabilities

An organization's capabilities are often expressed in terms of resources (e.g., tangible and intangible resources such as human, physical assets, financial, information, and intellectual), but it is also important to consider the intangible assets. That is, the way of doing business, the way the organization thinks about and addresses challenges, the way it evolves and innovates. In the context of analytics, **capabilities** refers to what can be accomplished as a result of the collective competencies of its people. Analytics organizations need to be good at many things (see Figure 3.3).

Organizational capability refers to those skills that are required in order to be successful (both effective and efficient). However, recognizing the requisite skills is necessary, but not sufficient, for realizing the organization's goals. Capabilities are aspirational.

For example, an organization may want to be good at machine learning (assuming that it aligns with the analytics strategy), but present realities suggest that this may be something that matures over time.

As Jonathan Trevor and Barry Varcoe suggest in their *Harvard Business Review* article "How Aligned Is Your Organization" (Trevor & Varco, 2017), "It is a reckless leadership team that commits to a business strategy without knowing whether they can achieve it."

Figure 3.3 Culture and competencies of the modern analytics organization

Resources

It is difficult to talk about organizational capabilities without considering the resources that support the intentional realization of those capabilities. Those resources include the human element, organizational and communication structures, culture, best practices, and processes. Aligned resources are measured by the degree to which the resources are optimally configured to influence and drive outcomes.

While the human element is only one of the critical resources needed for analytics, it is perhaps one of the most important, even before a sound data foundation as we will see in the next chapter. As Norm Smallwood and Dave Ulrich suggest, "Organizational capabilities emerge when a company delivers on the combined competencies and abilities of its individuals" (Smallwood & Ulrich, 2004).

Measurement and Management Systems

Finally, in discussing the strategically aligned analytics function, it is important to reflect on the management and measurement systems in an organization. As noted earlier, strategic alignment means clarity of purpose, strategic objective, defined capabilities, and the resources needed to deliver.

Many projects fail without operational planning (management and measurement systems) for major initiatives such as an analytics strategy effort. Long-term strategy must be linked to day-to-day operations, aligning strategy with operating plans and budgets while focusing on those process improvements that are most critical to the strategy. Practically, this means that business operations must account for and build operational impacts into their workflows and workload. Work streams should account for impacts to the Analytics Lifecycle, data governance, and quality processes.

> *Just because something is obvious doesn't make it easy. Real strategy lies not in figuring out what to do, but in devising ways to ensure that, compared to others, we actually do more of what everybody knows they should do.*
>
> David Maister, *Strategy and the Fat Smoker* (Maister, 2008)

This plays out in organizations that recognize the need to develop the capability for mature data governance, yet fail to do what everyone knows has to be done—talk to each other, collaborate, break down fiefdoms, and so on.

People are always busy—responding to requests, diving into data, creating models—yet they often fail to focus on the outcomes. The sidebar (How Google Uses OKRs) is a summary of how Google transformed itself from focusing on activities to outcomes. In analytics, this becomes especially important as it is easy to get caught up in activities rather than focusing on outcomes.

How Google Uses OKRs

One of the reasons that Google has been so successful in both innovating and in execution is a purposeful strategy designed to accelerate the time to execution by having people focus on the outcomes over activities. Originated at Intel by Andy Grove and later popularized by John Doerr at Google, OKRs—objectives and key results—is based on the belief that people work better when there is alignment to achievable outcomes. Rick Klau, a Partner at Google Venture, talks about how Google manages work (Klau, 2012) and looks at the website re:Work from Google (Google, 2017) where Google shares best practices and templates for implementing OKRs.

Google has been evangelizing a method that elevates the tactics of their organization to focus more on the outcomes they intend to achieve—they refer to this as OKRs (objectives and key results), and this is the engine behind the strategy—the linkage between strategy and execution.

OKRs is a powerful goal-setting methodology that creates clarity of purpose, increases focus on what matters, connects everyone's work to the organization's top objectives, drives company-to-employee and cross-functional alignment, helps all employees (and volunteers) understand that their work has meaning, and ultimately improves performance and results in all types of companies. It is the next generation goal-setting process and system, an evolution of S.M.A.R.T. goal methodology (Specific, Measurable, Aligned, Relevant, Time-based), and MBO (Management by Objectives) ("OKR Goals—Objectives and Key Results—Focused Overview"). These traditional goal-setting practices have been used successfully since the early 1950s, but the OKR process is different from these methods in that it adds two important aspects critical for today's rapid-paced work environments: (1) cascading alignment of goals, and (2) breaking up an objective into smaller steps (the three to five key results).

Here are some useful definitions and guidelines:

Objective—a statement of what is to be accomplished (the "what")

- Objectives should be focused on outcomes or results, not activity.
- Timelines must be set quarterly.
- Objectives should be qualitative (key results should quantify the objective).
- The primary objectives must be connected to or cascade down to the team or individuals on the team so that they can identify their supporting objectives and align them to the goals of the CEO, analytics executive, or manager.

Key result—the measurement of how the analytics objective will be achieved

- Results must be measurable, either by metrics or milestones.
- Metrics must be quantifiable with a number such as units, dollars, or percentages (e.g., "generate 1,000 likes").
- Milestones are not typically quantifiable, but are nevertheless a measure of what has been accomplished, such as "deploy a predictive model" that can be judged as either complete or incomplete.
- Milestones may be stated such that they are shown to contribute to an overarching objective such as "increase our marketing results."

ORGANIZATIONAL CULTURE

In the context of people and organizations, it is important to discuss the role that culture plays in analytics success.

Cris Beswick, Jo Geraghty, and Derek Bishop (Beswick, Geraghty, & Bishop, 2015) define culture as:

> the combination of leadership style, values, behaviors, attitudes, and working practices of an organization's people together with the formal and informal infrastructure which makes it stick.

In my experience as a consultant and educator, I find organizational culture fascinating. As a friend once said, "Every organization has one, but they aren't always good!"

Culture and leadership go hand in hand. In the context of data analytics, culture is manifested in five dimensions:

Data-centrism—The organization uses fact-based processes and data-derived insights for both decision-making and business solutions. Analytics maturity is recognized to mean placing data products in the hands of frontline staff and business partners to drive decisions.

Innovation—People are encouraged to try new things, brainstorm, and aspire to creative, big-picture thinking to solve current and future problems. People need to be allowed to make mistakes and learn.

Learning—The organization commits to continuous investment in staff competency development. Leadership language and staff behavior follow established norms and expectations for professional improvement.

Service—The staff has an intrinsic desire to proactively address customer problems and "delight" them through the delivery of data products. Service and "doing the right thing" are valued over policy and organizational charts.

Team engagement—Individuals within the analytics teams engaged in solving problems, strive to improve, and have a shared sense of purpose, trust, and commitment to the mission.

In my consulting work, we use a culture survey to help frame the opportunities and recommendations from an analytics maturity assessment (you can access this tool from the companion web site). The dimensionality of culture can be seen in Figure 3.4.

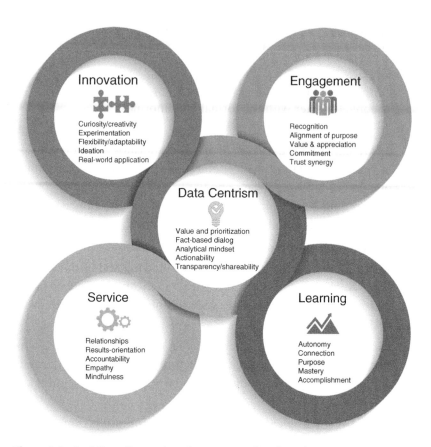

Figure 3.4 Analytics culture and readiness rests on five dimensions

---

Tools and Templates @
www.analyticslifecycletoolkit.com

Analytics Culture Survey.

Culture is important because it creates the environment for a learning organization. It allows people to be safe, it tries new things, it fails fast, and it innovates. If the culture is so rigid and people fear getting anything wrong, they will be afraid to try new things. They didn't have permission to fail. While the word *fail* might be construed as a bad thing, I think it is important to convey the acceptance of leadership when things don't always go right.

"If you're not failing every now and again, it's a sign you're not doing anything very innovative."

Woody Allen

Failure is how we learn and we need to encourage learning new things.

Analytics functions often face a dual challenge—how to ensure the speed, robustness, and repeatability demanded by customers, and at the same time innovate. Unfortunately, organizations often regress to an operational function and lose sight of their creative, innovative side. Some organizations intentionally organize to support these two very different mindsets.

Innovation and the Design of Experiments (DOE)

While machine learning and advanced analytics methods may seem exciting, you should not overlook the role of experimentation in innovation. The design of experiments (DOE) merits mention as one of the more strategic applications of analytics, even though the learnings aren't "operationalized" in the way predictive models or forecasts are. However, DOE is often the fastest way to learn from data, and the learnings are potentially much more valuable than the incremental gains of improving a predictive model or forecast. DOE is often the place where the learnings result in patents or the learnings save millions of dollars—even with one experiment. To learn more about DOE, take a look at explorable.com/design-of-experiment.

One word of caution regarding the notion of data-centrism—that is, the predilection of an organization to use facts in all of its decision making. Some teams lose their personality and sense of soul if everything is always about the numbers. One of the dangers of data-centrism is that it encourages us to believe that no matter what the problem, it can be solved with data. Organizations are messy, and we need rational thinking and sometimes experience and insight to help keep us on the rails.

For an interesting perspective on this, see the article "The Data Centric Revolution: Seven Warning Signs of Appliosclerosis" (McComb, 2015) as well as one from Rob Preston, who starts his article "Let Data Put You out of Business" (Preston, 2015) with "Data pisses me off!"

ORGANIZATIONAL DESIGN FOR ANALYTICS

In analytics, some common organizational structures are in use, ranging from a centralized analytics function to decentralized, with hybrid centers of excellence models in between. Much has been written about the pros and cons of various structures, but you might want to start with these resources for additional reading:

- "An Introduction to the Six Organizing Models for Analytics Teams" from the International Institute for Analytics (Analytics, 2015)

- "Organizational Models for Big Data and Analytics" by Robert L. Grossman and Kevin P. Siegel (*Journal of Organizational Design*) (Grossman, 2014)

- "Building an Analytics-Driven Organization" from Accenture (Accenture, 2013)

- "Organizing Your Teams for Modern Data and Analytics Deployment" by Mark A. Beyer from Gartner (Beyer, 2017)

Determining the most optimal structure for any particular organization has as much to do with its intent (purpose) and processes as it has to do with heritage and culture.

Organizations are made up of people, the roles that they perform, the structures that organize their relationships, and the processes they perform (Figure 3.5). Operations include operational and organizational (management) processes, the latter ensuring that the organization is appropriately focused and administered (World Customs Organization, n.d.).

As analytics often leads to change and impacts nearly every corner of the organization, the appropriate organizational design that fits with the culture of the organization is an essential component of analytics success.

Every change effort has some implication—whether large or small—for the organization's structure, people, and processes whether it arises from a strategic merger, a business process outsourcing effort, or a technology implementation program. It is critical to purposefully align the organizational structure for the maximal impact needed to achieve

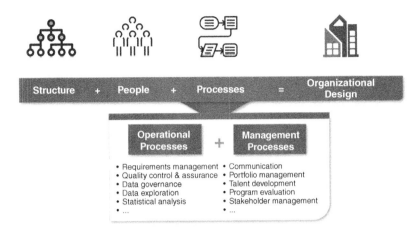

Figure 3.5 Organizational design is a function of structure, people, and processes

future state capabilities. The structure then serves as a framework in which specific roles, jobs, and teams are defined and configured.

The goal of organizational design is to answer the question: How do we need to be organized for the analytics to work? The design encompasses all the building blocks of business—formal and informal structures, internal processes and systems, relationships, people, and knowledge.

While there are a number of facets of organizational design, Jay Galbraith provides an excellent perspective in his seminal work around the "Star Model" (Galbraith & Nathanson, 1978). The model outlines five categories of design policies which, when combined, can help determine how best to design effective organizations.

In the Star Model, design policies fall into five categories (Figure 3.6):

1. Strategy determines direction.

2. Structure determines the location of decision-making power.

3. Processes have to do with the flow of information; they are the means of responding to information technologies.

4. Rewards provide motivation and incentives for desired behavior.

Figure 3.6 Galbraith's Star Model for the design of organizations

5. The selection and development of the right people—in alignment with the other policies—allow the organization to operate at maximum efficiency.

Organizations must be designed to reflect not only where the company is now relative to strategy, philosophy, and the value propositions for its customers, but also where it will need to be to achieve a competitive advantage in the future.

Thoughtful and purposeful organizational design is important in order to:

- Ensure that the organizational structure supports the analytics strategy and the leadership objectives.
- Create roles, jobs, and teams that will enable the operational change.
- Allocate work activities efficiently.
- Prepare employees to take on new responsibilities through clarity of vision and efficiency of communication channels.
- Deliver on the promise of analytics (improved outcomes, value, creation).

WHICH ORGANIZATIONAL DESIGN IS BEST?

PwC, the management consulting juggernaut, found in its 2014 Strategy+Business survey that 42 percent of executives felt that their organizations were not aligned with their strategy, and that parts of the organization resisted it or didn't understand it. In an article titled "10 Guiding Principles of Organization Design" (Neilson, 2015), PwC outlined eight elements of organizational design, summarized in Table 3.1.

As I said above, there is no one right solution for every organization, and the right structure for today will likely change over time as technology, customer experiences, and shifting roles will demand fluidity. In my work, I have found three common organizational designs dominate. However, I propose a list of capabilities that are required of any organization wishing to deliver on the promise of analytics for their organization. You will note that this model that considers the analytics customer experience and management of analytics products or outcomes as central figures in the capabilities needed for any analytics organization.

Centralized

Centralization is chosen when the enterprise-wide queue of requests for data and analysis needs to be centrally managed, which helps both in measuring ROI and targeting projects to those individuals with the right skills.

Table 3.1   Eight Elements of Organization Design

Formal	Informal
Decisions—how decisions are made	**Norms**—How people instinctively act or take action
Motivators—how people are compelled to perform	**Commitments**—How people are inspired to contribute
Information—how the organization formally processes data and knowledge	**Mindsets**—How people make sense of their work
Structure—How work and responsibilities get divided	**Networks**—how people connect beyond the lines and boxes

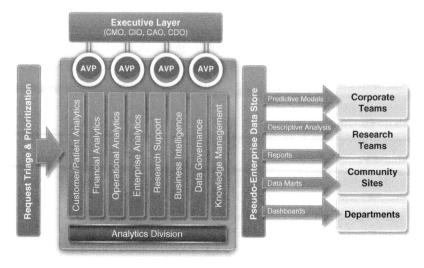

Figure 3.7 Centralized organizational structure for analytics

Figure 3.7 is a composite of some typical analytics organizations. Some directors or AVPs report up to someone in the executive layer. That may be a chief analytics officer or may have dual reporting lines into different C-level leaders.

The massive queue of requests is taken in and triaged according to the service line needed. In this way, services can be provided to specific business departments as well as to enterprise-facing corporate needs.

This model ensures a healthy relationship with data governance. While the governance structure may not formally reside here, there should at least be a shared reporting relationship.

Benefits

Co-locating all of the analysts allows them to learn from each other and moves them out of silos. This has significant ramifications for staff engagement, and also allows management to ensure that analytics activities relate to the strategic goals of an enterprise.

Proponents of this model have noted that it helps prevent duplicate or very similar work from being done twice. Data management times are reduced in that all of the business definitions are shared among the analyst team, and data can be harmonized and "analysis-ready" before it gets to them. Processes can be codified, and service level agreements are usually written to ensure that all departments understand their working relationship with analytics and what to expect from the team.

Centralization allows leaders to inject consistency into the tools, training, and career development of analysts. This has been reported to have a beneficial impact on staff morale.

Finally, another advantage is that if you are getting a vast new domain of data (IoT, edge analytics, omics, mobile, etc.), you can start to strategize how to handle data management and analytics on that new resource.

Drawbacks

While centralization has worked well for some organizations, it is not for everyone. One of the biggest challenges might be the culture and history of an organization. Moving nearly all analysts into one location could be seen as stripping departments and divisions of control and autonomy. Depending on the viewpoints of the organization, this may be an impossible task.

At the same time, it is critical for the analysts to maintain a deep connection to the departments so as to fully understand their needs, especially if their analytics problems align tightly with strategic goals.

This, then, is an issue of communication, and organizations such as Carolinas Health System have chosen to have their analysts physically work directly with business units about 20 percent of their time.

> *I think the biggest lesson learned is that prior to creating this new infrastructure, work was being done in a very siloed fashion across the organization, but now that we have committed to actually consolidating analytics in one area, enterprise-wide, things have worked much more efficiently. Focusing on an effort as big as this from a centralized perspective is really key.*
> Vice president for Advanced Analytics, Carolinas HealthCare System

Another potential issue is that executive needs could serve to overpower departmental needs given their direct access to the analysts.

Their "just do it" commandments can be a distraction, and despite best efforts, I have seen this happen at organizations I have worked with.

Centralization often has the stigma of being anti-innovation, as one cannot always plan for the effort that discoveries may need. This is a particular challenge for groups with a substantial, well-funded research presence. If they are accustomed to having strong relationships with analysts embedded in business units and this helps their research, there will be a political, gravitational pull away from the centralization of analytics teams.

Decentralized

Now let's examine the decentralized model (Figure 3.8) and those who use it.

This is a mosaic of all the decentralized organizations I have personally examined, but the common thread is that each business unit has its own analytics group and they go to a shared, external resource to obtain the data they need for their work. This may be a data warehouse or a data lake, as has been described, since the volume of data coming in can exceed the time needed to model it.

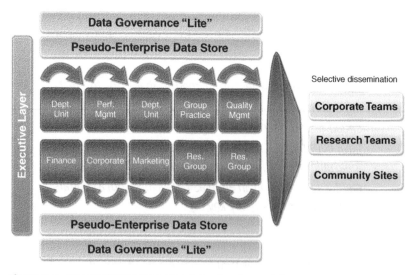

Figure 3.8 Decentralized organizational structure for analytics

An IT group will apply transformations to data to harmonize it for analysts, and this is typically done in a way that incorporates data governance, although it may be a lightweight form of governance so that the ability of individual groups to use their own business definitions remains.

Results are disseminated per the mandate of each functional group; that is, some can be shared across the organization, published in the case of research, or used just for internal business unit consumption.

The strength of this model is that the analytics are closely tied to the business units and the individual groups retain autonomy in business definitions and analysis styles. Therefore, many very large organizations with a strong research presence have chosen this model. Often, in places where analytics has a long, rich history, centralization is just not politically possible, or even desirable.

Benefits

The benefits of the decentralization model include that it is well-suited for very complex organizational structures as it allows the most flexibility. With analysts deeply embedded in business units, they steep in workflow knowledge that helps in designing questions and interpreting results.

Another advantage is that each department or division can choose whatever tool they want to use to analyze data without being under the yoke of corporate policies. Similarly, these units can define their own analytics approaches. Some may have entirely different analysis philosophies depending on what is standard to their field.

A strong point of decentralized models is that they are known for fostering much innovation. In fact, several companies such as those in health care have developed spin-off companies that sell their analytics models or approach to analytics via data management, analysis, and consulting services.

Drawbacks

Decentralization is not without its challenges. This is not the best model for all organizations and best suits those with a long history of data collection and analysis predating the enterprise data warehouse.

Analysts embedded in different divisions will not be communicating as often as if they were co-located. This can cause pockets of tribal knowledge to grow in business areas that are not part of a larger knowledge management strategy.

Thus, change management can become a huge barrier. That is, if something fundamental in the upstream data sources changes, how do you communicate this satisfactorily to all analytics groups? With a decentralized model, it is always possible to have an unrealized pocket of analysts out there somewhere.

Without top-down management, you might have issues where very similar work is being done in distinct silos and thus get duplication of effort as well as inconsistency in reports depending on the data assumptions made. Depending on how this bubbles up to executives, it only serves to add confusion.

Without a centralized home for analytics, the training, tool use, and processes can be all over the place for analysts. Some may have a sensible career path progression ahead of them, while others may not.

You may also encounter *tool bloat;* that is, an organization buying analytics tools without considering more viable alternatives given what is already owned.

These risks can be managed if leadership is aware of them at the onset, but by choosing to remain decentralized in an environment thirsty for data and more analysts, all of these problems will likely occur.

Center of Excellence

The last model is a center of excellence (COE), which is a blend of the other two approaches (Figure 3.9). Many organizations are moving to this model as they recognize the need for more consistency in data management, tools, and processes, while the number of analytics consumers increases.

Once again, this is a mosaic view. A center of excellence creates a home for analytics in an organization, with most analysts embedded within the business. It is usually led by a senior leader who has in-depth industry knowledge and a strong IT vocabulary and perspective. A COE structure has a substantial role in data governance, shared

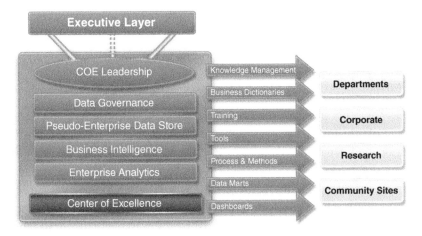

Figure 3.9 Center of excellence organizational structure for analytics

oversight and authority over the architecture of the data warehouse, enterprise business intelligence teams, and usually a small enterprise analytics team.

The COE's primary deliverables are codified processes for training, tool usage, and knowledge management. The COE sets down the best practices to be followed by all analysts across the organization. BI and analytics COE staff can push out rules to standardize the look and feel of reporting, and even act as drop-in consultants to embedded analysts within business units.

Benefits

The advantage of this model is the fact that an analytics community is created—it gives a home for analytics even if staff are geographically scattered.

It also allows individual departments to have some autonomy as they are blending resources and socializing best practices, consistent training, tool usage, but not combining budgets.

Organizations that are successful in building a COE have outstanding knowledge management approaches so that data about the business is socialized for all.

Organizations taking on this approach should make a concerted effort to ensure that mentoring programs are set up and that participation is part of one's expected job results. This helps ensure that the community of analysts develops even if the workers are geographically distributed.

Drawbacks

Like the other models presented, the COE is not without its challenges.

Role confusion can occur when enterprise analytics competes with embedded department analytics, and there can be disagreement about how the projects for staff members are prioritized or operationalized when sharing the same resources. This is where service-level agreements with departments or divisions can be beneficial; but of course, that means that leadership effort must be spent to negotiate, draft, and regularly update these agreements.

COEs don't solve the issue of vendor bloat that is seen in the decentralized paradigm; that is, when every divisional group chooses their own tools, you may lose advantages in volume purchases.

The COE model is relatively new and can take a lot of arm twisting, depending on the organizational culture, as some amount of centralization is necessary. Strong leadership must be in place to ensure that the best practices are not just codified, but are employed.

The Analytics Organization

As you will see throughout this book, my bias heavily sways my perception of what is truly needed for analytics success. Specifically, I believe that the customer experience should weigh heavily in how we organize and the capabilities needed to deliver analytics products and services.

If we organize around the (analytics) customer journey, you will note that this changes how people perceive what we do to include their purpose and mission—a critical component of strategy. Unfortunately, we have historically aligned our organizations around how we think about data and systems rather than how customers think about their problem. For example, while it might make sense for the CIO to organize around technologies such as data management, business intelligence, data governance, and security, the customer experience may suffer since the separate functions often don't know what the underlying problem might be. What could be perceived of as a "data issue" could be related to security, the client tools or technology, governance, or general systems failure.

Give your BI team a problem to solve, and the solution will be a report. It is better, in my opinion, to organize around the customer journey and align the structure (teams, departments, divisions, project teams) in a way that centralizes the focus on the customer, where a "hub person" takes the lead. In modern medicine, this approach is used to facilitate care across a variety of specialties and ensures a patient-centered experience. In analytics, the "analytics concierge" serves to understand, frame, and prioritize the problem and then consults with experts on potential approaches. This fits nicely with the best practice areas outlined in this book.

The analytics concierge is far more than a traditional business analyst in that they have a very wide understanding of the business, operation tactics, visualization methods, problem solving techniques, internal business systems and related data, and analytics possibilities.

They serve the customer to understand their challenges and bring in analytics, technical, or other resources as needed to triage the problem all the way through to the end result. This model is depicted in Figures 3.10 and 3.11.

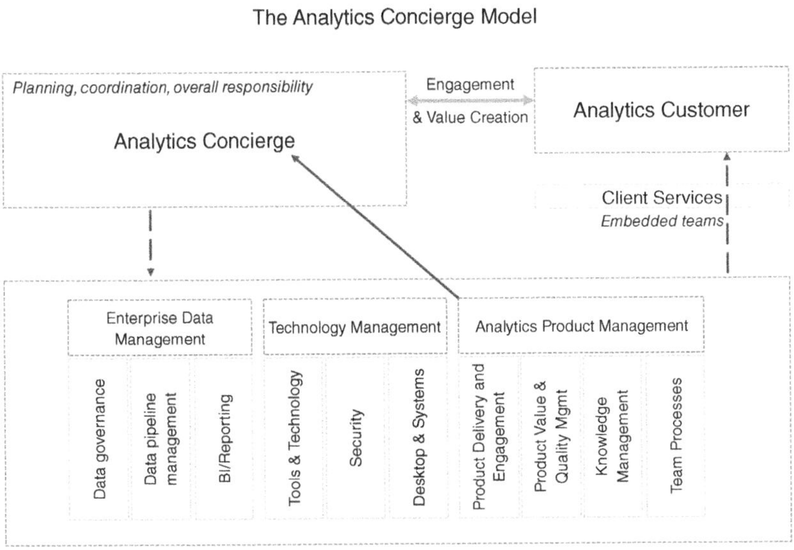

The Analytics Concierge Model

Figure 3.10 The analytics concierge model

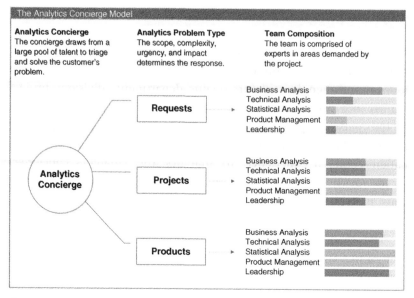

Figure 3.11 Staff configuration in the analytics concierge model

CHAPTER SUMMARY

Analytics strategy involves aligning the aspirations of the analytics organization with the overall organizational strategy. That linkage is critical so that there is clear line of sight between the "data and technical" efforts that you undertake and the business context in which you will operate.

In practical terms, strategy is the game plan. Note that strategy is not something done at the beginning of a planning cycle only to be forgotten once the realities of everyday operation consume you. As in business, you need to ensure that there is a clear linkage between strategy and execution. A 2006 survey conducted by Palladium (founded by Harvard Professors Kaplan and Norton) shared a striking statistic where only 25 percent of companies said they performed as well as, or better than, the average of their industry peer group when it came to linking strategy with execution. This means that 75 percent of organizations were less than or equal to being average! In their January 2008 *Harvard Business Review* article "Mastering the Management System," Kaplan and Norton tackle this issue directly, describing an "integrated process for linking strategy and operations" (Kaplan, 2008).

There is no perfect organizational structure for analytics, but making the right choice depends on strategic, cultural, business, and technical factors that influence the design of an analytics function. Ultimately, what matters is ensuring **organizational alignment** with business objectives and structures that facilitate the most efficient use of the resource available to the organization. Finally, recognize that it is important to organize around the (analytics) customer needs.

REFERENCES

Accenture. (2013). Building analytics driven organization. Retrieved from www.accenture.com/us-en/~/media/Accenture/Conversion-Assets/Dot Com/Documents/Global/PDF/Industries_2/Accenture-Building-Analytics -Driven-Organization.pdf.

Beswick, C., Geraghty, J., & Bishop, D. (2015). *Building a culture of innovation: a practical framework for placing innovation at the core of your business*. London and Philadelphia: Kogan Page.

Beyer, Mark A. Organizing your teams for modern data and analytics deployment. Retrieved from www.gartner.com/doc/3645917/organizing-teams-modern-data-analytics.

Galbraith, J. R., & Nathanson, D. A. (1978). *Strategy implementation: the role of structure and process*. St. Paul, MN: West Pub. Co.

Google. (2017). re:Work. Retrieved from rework.withgoogle.com/guides/set -goals-with-okrs/steps/introduction/.

Grossman, R. L., & Siegel, K. P. (2014). Organizational models for big data and analytics. *Journal of Organizational Design, 3*. Retrieved from www .jorgdesign.net/article/view/9799.

International Institute for Analytics. (2015). Six organizing models for analytics teams. In International Institute for Analytics (Ed.). Retrieved from iianalytics.com/analytics-resources/six-organizing-models-for-analytics-teams.

Kaplan, R. S. & Norton, David P. (2008). Mastering the management system. *Harvard Business Review, 86*(1), 62–77.

Klau, R. (Producer). (2012, 7/20/17). How Google sets goals. Retrieved from https://library.gv.com/how-google-sets-goals-okrs-a1f69b0b72c7.

Maister, D. H. (2008). *Strategy and the fat smoker: doing what's obvious but not easy* (1st American hardcover ed.). Boston: Spangle Press.

McComb, D. (2015). The data centric revolution: seven warning signs of appliosclerosis. Retrieved from tdan.com/the-data-centric-revolution -seven-warning-signs-of-appliosclerosis/19166.

Neilson, G. L., Estupiñán, J., & Sethi, B. (2015). 10 principles of organization design. *strategy+business, 79*(Summer 2015 | Issue 79). https://www.strategy-business.com/article/00318?gko=c7329.

OKR Goals—Objectives and key results—focused overview. Retrieved from https://www.atiim.com/okr-goals-objectives-and-key-results.

Preston, R. (2015). Let data put you out of business. Retrieved from www.forbes.com/sites/oracle/2015/05/27/let-data-put-you-out-of-business/#12fe94871e8a.

Smallwood, N., & Ulrich, D. (2004). Capitalizing on capabilities. *Harvard Business Review (June)*.

Trevor, J., & Varco, B. (2017). How aligned is your organization? *Harvard Business Review* (February 7).

World Customs Organization (Ed.) (n.d.). Strategic organization design and job profiling. In WCO Framework of principles and practices on customs professionalism. Retrieved from clikc.wcoomd.org/pluginfile.php/30120/mod_label/intro/Section%20II_EN.pdf.

CHAPTER **4**

Data Strategy, Platforms, and Architecture

Not having a data strategy is analogous to allowing each person within each department of your organization to develop their own chart of accounts and use their own numbering scheme.

Sid Adelman, Data Warehousing Expert (Adelman, Moss, & Abai, 2005)

nalytics relies on data. While this may seem like an obvious point, it is worth repeating here. Regardless if you are making a decision, solving a problem, investigating a new venture, or considering how to defend against potential threats, you will use facts to help frame the problem, determine its impact, understand the realities, and act as a basis for investigating possible solutions.

How much data is required? Do we need a data warehouse? Should we structure our data in an enterprise data warehouse, data mart, or data lake? Ultimately, many of these questions should be answered by a data strategy and careful alignment of the resources required to meet the aspirational goals of your analytics capability.

In this chapter, a number of these questions will be discussed in the context of a **data strategy**. Note that I distinguish here between the overall strategy for an analytics organization (discussed in Chapter 3) with data strategy. Data strategy in this context refers to how an organization decides what data they will collect and actively manage. In this chapter, I frame the discussion about data strategy in a similar way that we talk about business strategy—underscoring how it needs to be tightly linked to business goals.

DATA STRATEGY

Strategy is a term used in everyday conversation. Everyone seems to understand the word as "something important" or "not tactical." Despite its common usage in our vocabulary, I would argue that strategy is perhaps one of the most misunderstood words used in business, and the implications to the organization can be seen in various ways:

- Inability to respond to emergent questions
- Poor customer satisfaction around analytic products
- Massive backlogs of data requests
- Analytic staff turnover

In business strategy, we talk about the components of an organizational statement—mission, values, vision, and strategy—as a way to help ensure alignment between who we are, the values by which we operate, and the strategies that we use to accomplish our goals. These organizational statements outline the fundamental positions of the company that guide our everyday work and keep us focused on our goals.

Every analytics team should have a strategy statement that not only describes why they exist and who they want to be but also outlines how they intend to achieve those objectives. By articulating their strategy, the team sets down a flag to say not just who they are but who they are not, which can be an incredibly helpful compass when rationalizing potential project opportunities. Furthermore, analytic teams should have a plan for how they intend to measure success and whether their business strategy is working. When such plans don't exist, which is very common, the entire strategic planning process is undermined, and staff understandably start to question its value.

There is a strong relationship between the lessons that we learn in business strategy and data strategy. In business (or organizational) strategy, we define elements that articulate our purpose (mission) and paint a picture of the future (vision) as our foundational goals. The strategy is the set of choices that will be made to get there. Similarly, data strategy is the integrated set of choices that we use to position our firm for analytic success. Data strategy is the guide we use to support decisions on what data we choose to pursue, manage, use, and govern.

Data Strategy Statement

As mentioned in Chapter 3, the strategy statement articulates the organization's mission, purpose, and vision, and details a specific game plan.

The key to the development of a data strategy statement is to provide clarity around what you intend to do. The strategy statement includes three parts: objective, scope, and advantage.

- Objective: It begins with a definition of the ends that the data strategy is designed to achieve—that is, the **strategic objective**. This is a single, precise objective that will drive the organization over the next five years or so and has enough clarity that there is no room for misinterpretation.

- Scope: Next, the **scope** outlines the boundaries of operation for the organization (or what data to actively pursue). Typically, the scope identifies the analytic stakeholder, as well as analytic products or service offerings. One way to visualize this is to think of all the potential analytic functions that might be provided by others in or outside the organization. Boundaries of scope may fall on **customer segments** (internal customers), data domain (subject), the sophistication of analysis, or operational analysis versus discovery and innovation (client service versus project management).

- Advantage: Finally, **advantage** is the unique edge of the analytics organization that makes it distinctively different and capable of delivering value. There are two parts to the advantage statement—the first is the customer value proposition and the second is the set of unique activities that position the organization to deliver on that value proposition.

For analytics teams, the advantage could come in the form of analytics sophistication, breadth or depth of data, the speed of transformation from data to insights, and so on.

In sum, the strategic statement is a clear statement outlining the organization's objective, where it will operate, what value it creates for the customer, and what set of activities it will perform to achieve differentiation.

Mission
Why we exist

Values
What we believe in and how we will behave

Vision
What we want to be

Strategy
What is our game plan

Execution & Measurement Plan
How we will implement and monitor

Strategy:

Data & Analytics Strategy
1. Organizational Capabilities (future state)
2. Business Process Alignment (processes)
3. Organizational Design (roles, jobs & teams)
4. Knowledge & Skill Assessment
5. Performance Management
6. Talent Management
7. Training and Knowledge Management

Figure 4.1 Relationship between corporate strategy and the analytics function

Figure 4.1, adapted from Collis and Rukstad (Collis, 2008), outlines the relationship between the mission, values, vision, strategy statement, and the execution and measurement approach for an organization's business strategy.

So, with the general strategy statement in mind, the data strategy parallel would include a strong understanding of what we want to accomplish, then defines the boundaries of what we intend to include in the data strategy, and concludes with our advantage. The following sections outline a framework that can be used to develop your plan; it borrows liberally from business strategy development.

Strategy versus Implementation

> *Just because something is obvious doesn't make it easy. Real strategy lies not in figuring out what to do, but in devising ways to ensure that, compared to others, we actually do more of what everybody knows they should do.*
>
> David Maister, *Strategy and the Fat Smoker* (Maister, 2008)

The data strategy development process is designed to create a plan for the use of corporate data as a vital asset for strategic and operational decision making. Through my consulting experience, I know that investing in a formal data strategy frames the organization's intentions for the inevitable data issues that will crop up in any enterprise. These include issues around data quality, metadata management, access and data sharing, performance, ownership, provenance, maintainability, usability, security, and privacy.

The data strategy involves aligning the aspirations of your analytics organization with the overall organization's strategy. That linkage is critical so that there is a clear line of sight between the "data and technical" efforts that you undertake and the business context in which you will operate.

STRATEGY DEVELOPMENT PROCESS

Just as in business strategy development, some approaches can be used to develop your data strategy. Figure 4.2 is based on years of consulting experience with customers, and I have found this to work well. Note, however, that an agile approach is utilized so these stages are iterative and not a series of sequential steps. This process is based heavily on the philosophy of design thinking.

Design thinking is a user-centered process that begins with understanding the user. That is, we prioritize the needs of the analytics consumer (end-user) and not the development desires of a product

Figure 4.2 Analytics strategy development process

creator. Typically, the users are beneficiaries of a well-executed data strategy. The process leverages the collective expertise of the key stakeholders and establishes buy-in among the participants in the data strategy process—not just the IT folks responsible for managing the data platforms (SAS, Hadoop, Oracle, Teradata, Netezza, etc.). Design thinking encourages innovation by exploring multiple avenues for the same problem and getting to feasibility much more rapidly.

Relating these stages to data strategy is one way to think about how an organization might create the same alignment between data strategy development and the execution of a data roadmap. Table 4.1 highlights the critical steps in linking data strategy to implementation.

The following information will explore this methodology by first discussing what should be included in the data strategy and then walking through a practical example.

DEVELOPING A DATA STRATEGY ROADMAP

What should be included?

While there is no perfect answer, the following roadmap elements are common; but the template or format you choose should follow these guidelines:

- Use whatever form you can create quickly and easily.
- Be sure that it has collaboration features that allow for commenting on drafts by multiple collaborators.
- It should serve as a living document with changes noted and approved so that you have a history of your strategy's evolution.
- It should be accessible in a form that people can digest (e.g., executives, business users, and employees) so everyone knows where it is, what is current, and what is ahead on the roadmap.

There are many opinions about the best place to start when formulating a data strategy. In taking a pragmatic approach, you might ask, "What information is essential for us to achieve breakthrough performance in our organization?" Since your data strategy is built to support organizational objectives, this should be prioritized based on how these data can help move the needle on your strategic initiatives.

Table 4.1 Six Stages for Data Strategy Execution

Process Area	Deliverables/Milestones	Description of Activities
Develop the Strategy	▪ Approved data strategy statement ▪ Analytics organization mission and vision (who is served and for what value) ▪ Design Thinking workshops (empathize, define, ideate, prototype, test)	Your analytics organization must be able to state exactly what business you're in, identify the key issues you face, and determine how best to compete to support the organization in achieving the best possible outcomes. Developing the data strategy uses goes beyond traditional business strategy activities such as mission, values, and vision statements; external competitive, economic, and environmental analyses; and methodologies. Utilize the business strategy to map your data strategy to the vision, mission, and strategic goals of the organization. In addition, you should develop measures of success that align to the organization's KPIs. Using these as inputs, the data strategy statement outlines the purpose, scope, and advantage, the organization should provide clarity around what you intend to do as an analytics organization.
Create the Roadmap	▪ Approved and funded data strategy roadmap (plan for execution)	Once the data strategy plan is outlined, then you must translate the mission, vision, and strategy into an execution and measurement plan. This is where you articulate the strategic objectives, measures, targets, initiatives, and budgets that will ultimately guide action and resource allocation. It is critical to describe the data strategy, measure the plan, identify plans of action, evaluate potential risks, and mitigation strategies. Once detailed, that serves as input to funding and staffing and leadership decisions. Traditional business strategy uses tools such as OKRs (see the reference to Google in Chapter 3), balanced scorecards, and other measurement approaches.
Align the Organization	▪ Change management plan ▪ Data governance plan ▪ Stakeholder management and communications plan	As you begin the execution of your data strategy, it is imperative to link it to the strategies of individual business units engaged as stakeholders in the process. If you are developing an enterprise data strategy, that would mean the individual business units or divisions. If the data strategy is for a service line or unit, then the stakeholders would be those affected (either positively or negatively).

Table 4.1 (Continued)

Process Area	Deliverables/Milestones	Description of Activities
Align the Organization		You must utilize strong change management methods to ensure alignment, motivation, engagement, and action so that you can optimize strategy execution. Use both formal and informal methods to ensure alignment through a formal communications process, and by linking employees' personal objectives and incentives to strategic objectives impacted by the data strategy.
Execute the Plan	▦ Analytics and data lifecycle workflow ▦ Quality processes	Many projects fail when they omit the operational planning for major initiatives such as a data strategy effort. You must link long-term strategy with day-to-day operations, aligning strategy with operating plans and budgets while focusing on those process improvements that are most critical to the strategy. Practically, this means ensuring that the business operations account for and build operational impacts into their workflows and workload. Work streams should account for impacts to the Analytics Lifecycle, data governance, and quality processes.
Monitor and Learn	▦ Measurement plan and results	As with most things, sustained execution requires a commitment to monitoring performance results once a strategy has been developed, planned, and implemented, so that you can determine if the strategy is being properly executed. It requires monitoring and learning about problems, barriers, and challenges. This process integrates information about operations and strategy into a carefully designed structure of management review meetings.
Test and Adapt	▦ Lessons learned ▦ Knowledge management plan ▦ Best practices evolution	Learning organizations become very good at testing fundamental strategic assumptions to determine if you, indeed, do have the right strategy. This involves testing and adapting the strategy, using internal operational data and new external environmental and competitive data—thus launching a new cycle of integrated strategy planning and operational execution.

Unfortunately, one of the challenges that people face is that "they don't know what they don't know." The folks supporting the IT side of the data often frame their questions around "What are your requirements?" The business folks typically ask, "How can data best help us, and what information is available?" or "What questions should I be asking?" Thus begins a pattern of "who's on first" riddling that cycles endlessly due to lack of a common language.

That's why an agile approach based on design thinking can spur a dialog based on empathy and problem definition. We often look to the business processes that support strategic objectives and ideate around what the processes would look like if access to data weren't a problem. Blue sky thinking can often break the chains of traditional **requirements analysis**. A recognition that data supports the analysis of important decisions that, in turn, support the organization's movement toward achieving breakthrough performance is often lost on those who push data into their data lakes and warehouses.

> *Recognize that data is the lifeblood of your organization and treat it accordingly.*
>
> Michael A. Schiff, Data Management Consultant

A typical data strategy includes the following perspectives, along with the principal questions that should be addressed.

Scope and Purpose

- What data will we purposefully manage? What data is out of scope?
- What information do we need to run our organization versus data that is required to grow our business or meet our strategic objectives?
- What are we trying to achieve?
- How do we measure success for our data strategy?
- How much is our data worth?

The data strategy must complement the business strategy. Analytics organizations should develop a mission statement that articulates their identity and reason for existence. This not only serves to define what is in scope but also helps to clarify what is out of scope.

Also, establishing clear expectations for how an organization will measure progress against its data strategy is key. Metrics can include data service level metrics (for data systems and data quality), agility in supporting strategic decisions or operational metrics, or milestone achievement against the plan.

Early on, you should begin to catalog key challenges or risks, and define a communication plan to support the anticipated design decisions. Map the customer journey to understand and prioritize where processes are broken.

When looking at priorities, ask yourself, "What is the value of a key field such as an address?" What incremental revenue can we expect? Putting a value on data helps to make data management a continuous improvement process and supports the value that you are creating through these efforts.

Trap: Do not fall into the trap of accepting "all data" in answer to the question of what data is needed. Successfully managing data consumes resources, and there is a limited supply of resources for any organization.

Data Collection, Standardization, and Cleansing

- How frequently does data need to be updated?
- What are the data archiving and summarization requirements?
- What data do you need where and when? Today and in the future?
- Where is your database of record for different data, and do you require a single customer view?
- How do you integrate data silos? What data transfers are necessary, and how frequently?

This stage is often where things go wrong. The need to connect the dots means data connections are becoming as important as data collections. This is your opportunity to create a clear definition of the types of data or information needs that are required and translate those into a prioritized list. It is no longer sufficient to develop data warehouses and data marts that are domain specific. Architects must consider the complete customer, patient, or product journey.

You cannot have data standardization without also considering data integration. This means that not only data redundancy has to be addressed but also **master data management**. If working at the departmental level, a master data management strategy may be out of reach. So you'll need to advocate to leadership why this is a critical enterprise tool and minimally operate at the level that you can affect.

 MASTER DATA MANAGEMENT (MDM)

Master data management (MDM) refers to an approach used by organizations to ensure that there is consistency and uniformity of data across the enterprise. While supported by technology, MDM is not a tool.

Data Architecture, Virtualization, and Integration

- Where do you need real-time data, and what specific data should be real-time?
- How should data be shared between the various data silos?
- How do you access, share, and manage data?
- Should data services be cloud based, such as software as a service (SaaS) or in-house solution?
- How should data be modeled?

While there are a tremendous number of data integration tactics, tools, and technology, in your data strategy you should be asking yourself more technically agnostic questions, such as what data should reside in what format and how often it should be loaded. What should be the data's source, and how much history must be retained? It is rarely practical or necessary to have all data available in real time in one place. Similarly, cloud-based storage solutions may look attractive, but without a sound data strategy, these solutions can turn into a solution without a problem.

For example, for nearly two decades people have been espousing the concept of a **virtual data warehouse**. This means that data could be accessed without first moving it into a data warehouse. Although some of the benefits include access to real-time data and reduced storage costs, one overwhelming risk is that data from multiple sources is often inconsistent or inaccurate, which can have deleterious effects on operational systems.

Similarly, some data needs to be available on-demand, while other data might not be as time critical. How and where you store the data should be based on sound requirements. A data strategy should consider what needs to be archived and where to archive it.

Your data strategy must also answer the question of whether to store data on the premises or in the cloud. As organizations move data to the cloud and/or use SaaS applications, it is important to consider a "worst case scenario" should you suddenly be cut off from your data—for example, from a massive hacking, ransom-ware, or a system-wide outage for your cloud storage provider (like the Amazon Storage Services outage). Furthermore, make certain you retain all rights to your data and ensure that you have timely backups in your possession.

In recent years, people have been talking about the merits of data lakes (and data swamps) as an alternative to modeling data using traditional technical methods (e.g., logical data model, entity relationship models, physical database designs, etc.). Regardless of what database design schema you ultimately choose for storing the data, you should still create business data models for understanding the semantics and the business rules of the data first, or else it will be impossible to standardize the data.

Data Insight and Analysis

- How should you facilitate data exploration?
- How will you develop, deploy, and manage analytic results?
- Will you be providing self-service access to data or develop a provisioning team?
- How will analytic leadership learn about what's working in the data strategy?
- How should you foster collaboration on data throughout the organization?

While it should not have to be said, the goal of the "data" exercise is not to end up with the most data. Rather, the purpose is to put data to work for your organization to drive decisions, improve performance, and drive innovation. If data is the lifeblood of an organization, then analytics is the heart, pumping insights to every corner of the system. Asking yourself questions like, "So what? What will we do with the results if we had them? How will this change our processes or workflows?" is critical.

Data Governance and Data Quality

- Who owns the data?
- Who will provide strategic leadership around the data strategy?
- Who is responsible for data stewardship? For data quality? For educating users? For managing security?
- Who ensures that the data architecture will be updated as evolving data types and needs arise?
- Who will decide who gets what level of access? Who can change, copy, move, or delete data?
- Who gets to bring in new data?
- What level of data quality is practical?
- What is the cost of cleaning data?
- How will we measure data quality?

Data governance is just one part of an overall data strategy. In data governance, tough questions must be answered about roles, responsibilities, approvals, and workflows to ensure that the data is well managed. This cascades from the overarching rules of engagement down to who owns the data elements, value lists, and verification strategies (e.g., should addresses be checked against postal databases during data entry). Questions are addressed here about how often a value must be updated when it changes and what the legal requirements are, for example. Although many organizations have devoted considerable effort to governance initiatives concerning customer, master, and financial data, data governance should apply to all data assets. It should be noted that data governance is not a tool or a technology.

A data strategy is one of the crucial components of a strategic plan for enterprise-wide data governance and of analytics in general. It is my belief that instituting enterprise-wide data governance is a business responsibility supported by IT. This responsibility starts with data ownership and extends to data stewardship. The data owners are usually the originators or primary users of the data. Data stewards are responsible for enforcing standards and data governance policies, and for managing business rules. While they do not have the authority to set policies or to create business rules, data stewards are accountable for performing data audits and resolving data disputes.

A critical part of any data governance program is a related concept around data quality. The data strategy addresses the definition of what you mean by "high" and "low" quality data in an objective manner. How you communicate, raise awareness, and garner support for data quality issues across the organization is part of data governance. Tactically, the data quality and governance process will address questions such as who is responsible for data quality; who will identify, evaluate, and diagnose data quality problems; and who is responsible for outlining the processes by which we validate our data integration and transformation processes.

While quality is an important concept, it should be noted that it is important to evaluate the cost of cleansing data. Not all data may be worth its cleaning costs. Determining the cost of poor data quality for your organization allows prioritization of cleaning efforts. From a practical standpoint, we know that incentives often drive behavior. As such, for data governance to succeed, we need to enlist support from those most affected—whether it be influential departments such as finance or those with the most opportunity to affect customers. Defining a data governance roadmap has dramatic implications for shaping an organization's culture.

Metadata Management

- What metadata should be managed? Who should define business metadata and technical metadata?
- Who is responsible for raising awareness and managing metadata?

- Who is responsible for capturing and maintaining metadata?
- How can we exploit metadata once we have it?
- What tools and systems generate metadata?
- What tools will expose metadata for business use?

Metadata is one vehicle for achieving data standardization and integration. Metadata is contextual information about IT assets such as data, processes, and programs. Metadata components for data assets include business definitions, domains (valid values), data formats (type and length), business rules for creating the data, transformation and aggregation rules, security requirements, ownership, sources (operational files and databases), timeliness, and applicability. While many companies talk about metadata and can demonstrate the data they collect, not many companies capture these components, and those that do don't always make effective use of it. Metadata should not be a dirty word and left as a documentation exercise. Nor should all decisions surrounding metadata strategy be punted to a vendor of a tool. Rather, metadata should be the map that people use to navigate the data across the enterprise.

Access, Distribution, Privacy, and Security

- Who can access data, and what level of detail can they see? Does that vary by country or location?
- How should data be protected, and should it be encrypted?
- How will we determine responsibility for security and privacy?
- Who will own (and what process will be used) to establish security and privacy procedures?
- What is the process, and how often will we audit our security policy?
- How will we address regulatory issues that may be highly domain relevant?

Perhaps one of the more contentious areas in any data strategy is who should get what access to which data. It is in the data strategy that you outline how you decide what methods will be used to manage, monitor, and improve the access, distribution, and security aspects of data. In today's business environment, it is no longer appropriate to lock people out of data. Rather, you need to adopt a tone of data democracy in which the collective organization can use data. Obviously, there are some limits to that where personal, private, or confidential data are concerned.

The data strategy should outline the process for how to determine users' need for data and to define the standards for what data to distribute when, where, and to whom. As with most things, you should also monitor, measure, and report the cost to distribute data and assign responsibility for administrative activities related to distribution so that we understand the full value of your efforts and can support prioritization.

You may face several global issues related to where and how data can be accessed across borders. For example, some countries place restrictions on data that can be collected or transmitted as if there were a virtual "customs" gate for data. Make sure your organization, or your cloud vendor, is not inadvertently violating governmental restrictions as data passes through international lines.

Furthermore, you are accountable for the data that can be displayed. For example, the US government and various state regulations regulate the use, storage, and display of Social Security numbers. Further, in 2016, the European Union passed the General Data Protection Regulation (GDPR). The GDPR was the most comprehensive regulatory response, and was designed to do three things:

1. Harmonize data privacy laws across Europe.

2. Protect and empower all EU citizens' data privacy.

3. Reshape the way organizations across the region approach data privacy.

With continued **digital disasters** such as those experienced by Equifax and others, scrutiny will continue to drive increased measures to protect data. Furthermore, I anticipate the evolution of protection methods such as **blockchain** as a way to protect data assets such as those used in analytics and will need to solve the issues of data at rest as well as those in transit (for example, event stream).

BLOCKCHAIN

Blockchain refers to a technique for storing data in which the keys to unlocking the data can be found in a ledger. In the context of analytics, blockchains may be used to store sensitive data and the keys (or blocks) are secured by cryptography.

Data Retention

- How long should we keep the data?
- What data will we keep?
- Who determines our policies for the maintenance and archival of historical data?

Most organizations place little effort on a strategy to determine what analyses and data sources may no longer be needed for on-demand access. Managing and protecting data comes with a cost; just because it is easy to capture and store massive amounts of transactional data, should you? Could those resources be put to better use?

One of the common tactical issues to address is the level of detail that should be retained. That is, what level of granularity should be kept, in what format, and what should the service level agreement entail? You may design a strategy around keeping detailed data for some weeks or months and then retain lightly summarized data for several months or years. Legal and regulatory implications should be reflected in any retention plan.

Nonetheless, make sure that you retain data at the level required to meet current and anticipated needs. There should be different strategies for data that has a clear business purpose versus data that merely has a potential to be useful at some point.

Performance and Service Level Agreements

- Who is responsible for creating the requirements for performance?
- Who is responsible for determining the requirements for availability?

Finally, your data strategy should outline how you intend to manage service-level agreements—that is, what performance is expected, implicitly or explicitly. The data strategy should address how the provider will perform capacity planning of data, network, and security infrastructure. Also, you should discuss how you intend to monitor, measure, and report on how your **data systems** are performing and what process will be used to manage service level agreements.

AN AGILE APPROACH TO DEVELOPING YOUR DATA STRATEGY

While this list may seem overwhelming, you can use these questions to guide the development of your data strategy and address the components that are most pressing for your organization. Make your data strategy a living document and fill out the details over time. To that end, you should have a plan for what items you intend to address over what period so that key stakeholders understand what the destination looks like and what stops you will make along the way.

Tools and Templates @ www.analyticslifecycletoolkit.com

Document your data strategy.

You will likely need to address many other questions as you go from strategy to execution, even though they may not be critical to the data strategy itself. Additional topics would likely include tools and technologies, data standards, the Analytics Lifecycle model to be used, and testing of data theories. You may have questions like, "How will we address new data sources in the future? How will we manage the software selection process, and what are our criteria for software selection? Will we sell our data, and if so, why and how?" If you need to develop a data strategy in the future, start thinking about these questions now.

One of the challenges with the model outlined above is that it doesn't specify whether an organization is designing its data strategy for the first time or refining it. As a practical matter, the agile approaches for working through these stages (for an overall analytics strategy or the supporting data strategy) should utilize design thinking best practices. Do NOT fall into the trap of traditional software development lifecycle practices where the artifacts are captured in a manner analogous to planning a trip to the moon (e.g., capture requirements; get sign-off; develop a design specification; get sign-off; design the software; get sign-off; create testing plans; get sign-off; execute testing; get sign-off; go through change management procedures; get sign-off; etc).

DATA STRATEGY SUMMARY

The focus of this topic has been to outline the components of a data strategy. This is an essential activity that helps to ensure alignment between who you are, the values by which you operate, and the strategies that you use to accomplish your analytics goals. Think of your data strategy as the fundamental positions that you hold as a data-driven organization, which should help guide your everyday work and keep you focused on your analytical goals. A data strategy is an essential and fundamental building block for all IT initiatives, regardless of whether they are operational or decision-support-based in nature.

A well-defined data strategy can help you achieve many factors that can contribute to your success in the analytic organizations:

- Align all areas of an organization toward a single-minded "data" purpose that everyone understands.
- Serve as a focal point for individuals to identify with the organization's purpose and direction.
- Guide daily activities by providing a consistent, clear message regarding what is important.
- Determine priorities and support decision making.
- Motivate those participating in the organization so they know why they are there and why they are doing the things they are doing to support the data-driven efforts.
- Establish the guiding principles by which they will operate.

- Clarify the purpose of the data efforts to external stakeholders.
- Articulate where people will and will not spend time.
- Provide a basis, or standard, for allocating organizational resources.
- Establish a general tone or organizational climate.
- Facilitate the translation of strategic objectives into organizational structure, capabilities, team organization, team composition, and work processes around data.

I believe that a data strategy should be aligned with and support the organization's strategic drivers, including increasing revenue and value, reducing cost and complexity, and ensuring survival by mitigating risk and enforcing constraints. These recommendations apply no matter the industry. Every initiative that you spend resources on, including data-related initiatives, must serve these fundamental drivers.

PLATFORMS AND ARCHITECTURE ANALYTICS

People often confuse analytics with the technologies that enable them. A myriad of hardware and software vendors offer "technology" solutions to support the Analytics Lifecycle, including:

- Data storage
  - Databases
  - On-premise and cloud-based data stores
  - Data federation and data virtualization
  - In-memory data fabric
  - Data appliances
- Data management
  - Data integration and ETL tools
  - Data governance
  - Data encryption and masking
  - Master data management
  - Data quality

- Analysis and presentation
  - Search and knowledge discovery
  - Stream analytics
  - Data mining
  - Text mining (NLP, NLG)
  - Statistics
  - Machine learning
  - Artificial intelligence and cognitive computing
  - Visual analytics
  - Data visualization

It's easy to confuse the **data pipeline** and the associated technical architecture with the Analytics Lifecycle. Figure 4.3 depicts how the data pipeline supports the Analytics Lifecycle.

ANALYTICS ARCHITECTURE

The **technology** used in support of the Analytics Lifecycle is fairly widespread. There are hardware solutions, appliances, software "stacks," platforms, and solutions for nearly every aspect of the current and evolving landscape of the analytics ecosystem. When looking at the appropriateness of one solution over another and how much technology is needed for the task at hand, the question often arises—what is the best choice? As my friend and former professor often says, "The best option is often one that doesn't involve technology at all."

Despite the choices of technologies, platforms, and **architectures**, there is no simple answer as to what you need to support any organization's analytics capability. As shown in Figure 4.4, some factors to consider include:

- Scope (breadth and depth)
- Complexity of decisions
- Urgency and impact

Let's look at each of these and discuss how each of these factors informs the technology landscape required for analytics.

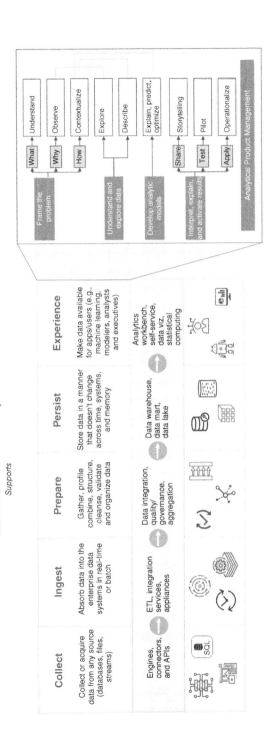

Figure 4.3 Relationship between the data pipeline and the Analytics Lifecycle

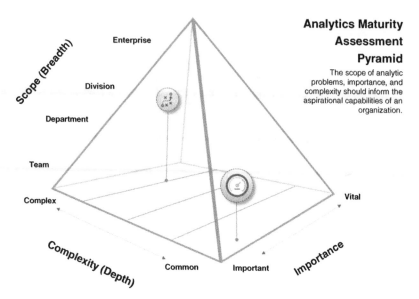

Figure 4.4 Analytics maturity assessment pyramid

Scope: Business Scale and Lifecycle Support

Scope, in this context, is both the breadth and depth of the Analytics Lifecycle processes as well as the scale of business functions that need to be supported. The number and types of users (data scientists vs. **data champions**) will inform the extent of the architecture.

 DATA CHAMPION

Data champion was coined by ThotWave (Hovarth & Nelson, 2016) as a way to describe those that participate in the Analytics Lifecycle and champion the use of data throughout an organization.

Highlighted earlier in this chapter was the relationship between the data pipeline and its corresponding technologies used in support of the Analytics Lifecycle. The selection of technologies for an organization wishing to support the entire lifecycle will look dramatically different from an organization that is supporting a subset—say, statistical hypothesis testing. In the latter case, a desktop version of a statistical analysis software package may suffice. In the first instance, an enterprise architecture may be necessary.

Complexity of Decision

Another factor to consider is whether the analytics capability is in support of novel problems (the land of innovation) versus extracting efficiencies out of well-known, established processes.

In decision theory, these are referred to as programmed and non-programmed decisions. A **programmed decision** is one that is fairly structured or that recurs with some frequency, or both. A **nonprogrammed decision** is unstructured and occurs much less often than a programmed decision. Often, these get translated into a distinction between automated analytics versus discovery analytics with the latter serving as the foundation for the organization's innovation or discovery capabilities.

As shown in Figure 4.5, everyday problems might be thought of as those that are relatively operational and solvable utilizing basic techniques (dashboards, visual analytics, quality root cause, statistical process control techniques, etc.); others may require more in-depth statistical exploration and testing.

As David J. Snowden and Mary E. Boone describe in their *Harvard Business Review* article (Snowden & Boone, 2007) we (as leaders) need to tailor our approach to decision making to fit the circumstances they face.

Understanding Complexity

Snowden and Boone define the characteristics of complex systems that make it challenging for leaders to solve. Complexity, by definition, means that there may be multiple "right" answers and we, as leaders, must sense, categorize, and respond for simple problems, but for complicated systems, we must "sense, *analyze*, and respond." They cite a number of characteristics of a complex system:

- Large numbers of interacting elements
- Nonlinear interactions

Percent of problems

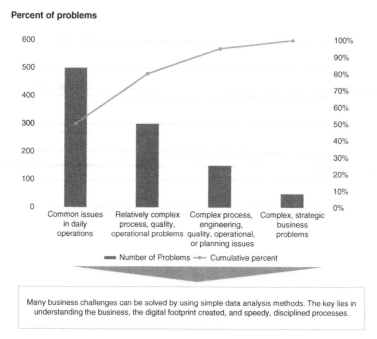

Many business challenges can be solved by using simple data analysis methods. The key lies in understanding the business, the digital footprint created, and speedy, disciplined processes.

Figure 4.5 Percent of problems by differing complexities

- Dynamic system
- Continually evolving system
- Difficult to predict (Oosterwal, 2010)

Urgency and Impact

Finally, as it relates to the factors to consider when determining the appropriateness and scale of an enterprise analytics architecture, the relationship of technologies is important to the urgency and impact of a decision.

With regard to the urgency of a business decision, note the following constructs:

- **Crisis**

  A crisis is an emerging challenge that needs to be addressed quickly and with high accuracy. It is both important (critical to the success or sustainability of an organization) and urgent (must be dealt with immediately). The business could be in crisis; for example, consider Johnson & Johnson's 1982 incident where seven people died in the Chicago area after taking cyanide-laced capsules of Extra Strength Tylenol (Moore, 1982). More recent examples including Target Department stores' response after they were hacked and Chipotle's reaction to an E. coli outbreak across their chain.

▨ **Noncrisis**

We all face noncrisis problems in our everyday work. A noncrisis problem is a challenge that "may" be important and require resolution, but will not send the organization into a death spiral if not addressed immediately. Examples of a noncrisis problem might be declining revenue or customer churn.

▨ **Opportunity**

An opportunity problem is one in which the organization is either shoring up its defenses (e.g., regulatory, reputational, or financial risk), or, as the name implies, taking advantage of new opportunities.

The data required for each of these problem spaces are slightly different in that noncrisis analytics depends on highly curated, stable data—what is often referred to as a **data for purpose**. In contrast, crisis problems rely on the ability to integrate high-quality data from unanticipated sources. In other words, no one sat down and drew out a data model for the unexpected questions that would be asked. Opportunity problems are often characterized by a combination of the two: highly curated as well as unanticipated data.

Note that each of these problem types inform requirements for a data and analytic architecture in different ways. In the *Journal of International Humanitarian Action* (Qadir, 2016), Junaid Qadir and his colleagues outlined a taxonomy for crisis analytics that includes some of the enabling technologies required for a successful platform. Note the multidisciplinary and wide-ranging data sources (Figure 4.6).

Qadir et al. point to the need to harness the power of nontraditional data sources that include the following:

▨ Data exhaust—the natural data byproduct of everyday processes

▨ Online activity—user-generated data from interactions (e.g., emails, comments) and the web (search engine and social media activity)

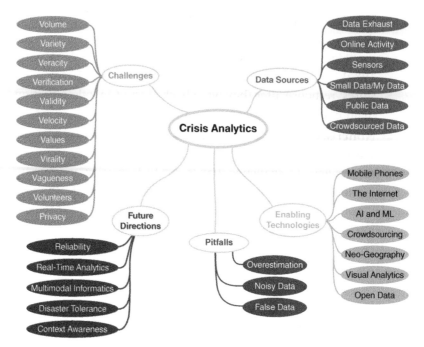

Figure 4.6 The dimensions of crisis analytics
Source: *Qadir, Junaid; Ali, Anwaar; Rasool, Raihan ur; Zwitter, Andrej; Sathiaseelan, Arjuna; and Crowcroft, Jon (2016). Crisis analytics: big data-driven crisis response.* Journal of International Humanitarian Action 1(12).

- Sensing technologies—IoT and smart-objects
- Public data—including open source and open data
- Crowsourced data—curated and democratized data

DATA FOR PURPOSE OR POTENTIAL

It is probable that most data and analytics architectures are designed to deal with noncrisis problems. Despite the strategic nature of opportunity or crisis type problems, we put energies into those things that we can anticipate, then gather requirements, model, and productionize. Over the last several years, there has been a push to distinguish between data for purpose and **data for potential**.

When we talk about purpose in this context, most people think of "known" requirements—that is, we understand the target uses for the data and structure the data accordingly. Potential means that we don't yet have a clear idea of how we might use the data, but it could be interesting.

Architecturally, the data strategies that are used for both types are very different. Data for purpose is stored in nice, neat databases with columns and rows, referential integrity and highly routinized processes for access, integration, cleansing, enrichment, and storage. In the case of data for potential, we don't know what we don't know—that is, we are "consciously ignorant."

> *Thoroughly conscious ignorance is the prelude to every real advance in science.*
> Stuart Firestein in *Ignorance: How it Drives Science* (Firestein, 2012)

By allowing the curious among us to play with the unknown **data exhaust** and giving them an analytics sandbox, we are apt to discover novel interactions that may not only lead to new insights but better prepare us to respond quickly to the crisis and the opportunity problems.

Janssen Research Depends on Diversity

While completing my master's degree at the Fuqua School of Business at Duke University, I had an opportunity to invite Paul Stang, PhD, and Patrick Ryan, PhD, to present at our analytics conference. Patrick heads up Epidemiology Analytics at Janssen Research and Development. One of the most impressive parts of their talk was when they described how they assembled their team. Instead of the traditional "analytics" roles like biostatisticians, medical professionals, and data jockeys, they created a team comprised of psychologists, behavioral economists, writers, artists, and engineers.

This is not unlike many of the evolving innovation centers (Nelson, 2016), which seek to embrace multidisciplinary perspectives in order to create, design, and revolutionize entire industries.

CHAPTER SUMMARY

Whether you are trying to address a crisis of epic proportions or ensure that your analytic engine has enough fuel to power its engine, analytics relies on data. The efficiency and effectiveness of an organization can often be measured in how well it manages its critical information assets. As outlined in this chapter, being intentional about your purpose and approach to managing data is essential—that is, create a data strategy! It will serve you well as you purposefully decide what to manage and what can be left on the side.

We often look to technologies to answer the question of what our data strategy should be. That is a mistake. Data architectures, platforms, and technologies should be built in support of the organization's current and aspirational capabilities.

What is essential in any data architecture is the consistent, reliable, valuable flow of data to serve the organization—that is, the data analytics pipeline. I see the "pipeline" as a natural evolution of the Corporate Information Factory (Inmon, Imhoff, & Sousa, 2000).

As Michael Li suggests, "reproducibility, consistency, and productionizability let data scientists focus on the science" (Li, 2015).

REFERENCES

Adelman, S., Moss, L. T., & Abai, M. (2005). *Data strategy*. Indianapolis, IN: Addison Wesley.

Collis, D. J., & Michael G. Rukstad. (50th Anniversary McKinsey Award Winner for Best Article in Harvard Business Review, 2009.). (2008). Can you say what your strategy is? *Harvard Business Review, 86*(4).

Firestein, S. (2012). *Ignorance: how it drives science*. Oxford; New York: Oxford University Press.

Horvath, M. P., & Nelson, G. S. (2016). We need data champions in healthcare. Retrieved from info.thotwave.com/download-the-we-need-data-champions-in-healthcare-research-summary.

Inmon, W. H., Imhoff, C., & Sousa, R. (2000). *Corporate information factory*. Retrieved from www.netlibrary.com/urlapi.asp?action=summary&v=1&bookid=56348.

Li, M. (2015). Three best practices for building successful data pipelines. *Data*. Retrieved from www.oreilly.com/ideas/three-best-practices-for-building-successful-data-pipelines.

Maister, D. H. (2008). *Strategy and the fat smoker: doing what's obvious but not easy* (1st American hardcover ed.). Boston, Mass.: Spangle Press.

Moore, T. (1982). The fight to save Tylenol. *Fortune.* Retrieved from fortune.com/2012/10/07/the-fight-to-save-tylenol-fortune-1982/.

Nelson, G. S. (2016). Using design thinking to solve hospital readmissions. Retrieved from www.thotwave.com/blog/2016/12/05/2753/.

Oosterwal, D. P. (2010). The lean machine: how Harley-Davidson drove top-line growth and profitability with revolutionary lean product development.

Qadir, J., Ali, A., ur Rasool, R., Zwitter, A., Sathiaseelan, A., & Crowcroft, J. (2016). Crisis analytics: big data-driven crisis response. *Journal of International Humanitarian Action, 1*(12).

Snowden, D. J., & Boone, M. E. (2007). A leader's framework for decision making. *Harvard Business Review.* Retrieved from hbr.org/2007/11/a-leaders-framework-for-decision-making.

PART II

Analytics Lifecycle Best Practices

CHAPTER **5**

The Analytics
Lifecycle Toolkit

Innovation and best practices can be sown throughout an organization—but only when they fall on fertile ground.

Marcus Buckingham

ANALYTICS LIFECYCLE BEST PRACTICE AREAS

Analytics involves more than just assembling a group of data scientists and analysts. Analytics leaders must be concerned with a sphere of activities to achieve their business goals. Product managers, project managers, process architects, business analysts, quality managers, and technical developers are all key contributors to achieving analytics success. Organizational capabilities must include the following elements, each of which comprise the Analytics Lifecycle. Each capability is an analytics best practice that will be further described in this and subsequent chapters:

- *Problem framing*—To support ideation through the clear articulation of a problem, translation of that problem into a question that can be answered by data, investigation of potential root causes, and the effective prioritization of problems to be solved.

- *Data sensemaking*—To identify and acquire the data that is required to answer a question, then harmonize, rescale, clean, and prepare the data for analytics; also to explore and characterize the data to assess its utility in addressing our business question.

- *Analytics model development*—To use a variety of techniques including data visualizations, descriptive and inferential statistics, and advanced analytics; to support data storytelling to solve existing problems or anticipate the unexpected.

- *Results activation*—As analytics and data insights leave the "laboratory," to champion the results through understanding and action; to anticipate the challenges and consider how the results can be acted upon and operationalized.

- *Analytics Product Lifecycle management*—To view analytics models as *data products* requiring design, implementation, testing, and

130

deployment as professional **responsibilities**; to product manage, which includes the proactive management of knowledge
and of change, as well as quality processes, project execution,
program evaluation, and team oversight.

Figure 5.1 depicts the Analytics Lifecycle in terms of the activities
that generally occur and the level of effort typical for creating an analytics product.

As Figure 5.1 shows, the Analytics Lifecycle begins with a definition of the fundamental question or problem and continues through
data exploration, analysis, and results activation. The loop is closed
when analytics insights are operationalized into the business workflow
in some way. It is important to understand that each phase of analytics
is not a rigid, sequential step. You may need to extract and explore data
before going back to refine the question. Similarly, you may experience
false starts or discover blind spots in your theories; or, detailed exploration and analysis can reveal that you do not have the right data. But
by closely following this process, you can prevent failures in the operationalization stage caused by a missed requirement or poorly formed
business questions.

ANALYTICS AS A PRODUCT OF DATA SCIENCE

Chapter 1 included a discussion of the difference between analytics and
data science, and the use of analytics to address particular challenges
within an industry or problem space. If the analytics data product is the
outcome of analytics, and in general, of data science, then what should
evolve is both truth and understanding. Analytics helps us to know
truth and understand the context—that is, the process, organization,
and environment.

Analytics helps us uncover facts known to be true. That is, we
use data as well as the best practices and processes outlined here to
empirically test theories through data analysis, to ensure their reliability through validation and testing, and to benefit from them by
operationalizing their insights.

We achieve understanding through these lifecycle processes in an
effort to describe, explain, predict, and prescribe.

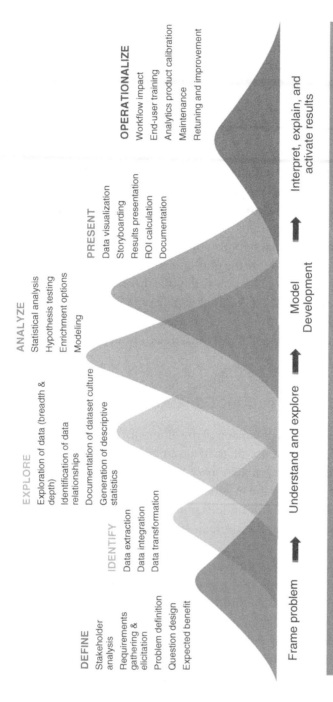

DEFINE
Stakeholder analysis
Requirements gathering & elicitation
Problem definition
Question design
Expected benefit

IDENTIFY
Data extraction
Data integration
Data transformation

EXPLORE
Exploration of data (breadth & depth)
Identification of data relationships
Documentation of dataset culture
Generation of descriptive statistics

ANALYZE
Statistical analysis
Hypothesis testing
Enrichment options
Modeling

PRESENT
Data visualization
Storyboarding
Results presentation
ROI calculation
Documentation

OPERATIONALIZE
Workflow impact
End-user training
Analytics product calibration
Maintenance
Retuning and improvement

Frame problem → Understand and explore → Model Development → Interpret, explain, and activate results

Analytics Product Lifecycle Management

Figure 5.1 Analytics Lifecycle

GOALS OF ANALYTICS

Up to this point, I have generally referred to the purpose of analytics as one of "problem solving." However, analytics can be used to achieve one or more of the following objectives:

- *To solve a problem*—Applied analytics is concerned with the discovery of solutions to practical problems, and we measure success by its immediate utility or application. In the Analytics Lifecycle, the emphasis is usually on speed and explanatory value.

- *To support a narrative*—Analytics professionals often use techniques to directly support a story, such as confirming a hypothesis or visualizing a relationship. The outcome is of primary benefit to emphasize accuracy and reliability, and not necessarily the repeatability of the process.

- *To understand a phenomenon*—We often embark on an analytics project to understand a phenomenon more fully in the most general and parsimonious way possible. Techniques such as visual analytics or exploratory data analysis can support the discovery of these relationships.

- *To discover something new*—Analytics can be used to tell us something that we didn't already know. We can trace this objective back to its heritage in data mining; it often takes advantage of new analytics methods or unstructured and unorganized data, and it is often focused on innovation-type endpoints. Curiosity and inquisitiveness motivate the discovery about the relationships and associations.

In each case, the attention differs in how the results are to be used. However, while the analytics methods used will likely vary based on the purpose, the discussion of the Analytics Lifecycle as a generalized **methodology** or framework remains the same (see Figure 5.2).

It should be noted that other objectives are intentionally missing here, such as monitoring a process, guided exploration, or looking up a value. For an in-depth discussion of the broader description of the uses specifically for data visualizations I recommend reading Stephen Few's perspective on this topic (Few, 2012).

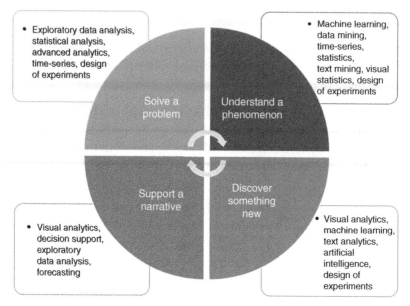

Figure 5.2 The motivation for analytics

Certainly, these objectives are relevant to business intelligence and data visualization in general, but are not considered the realm of analytics.

SCALE AND SCOPE OF ANALYTICS PRODUCTS

It is worth noting that not all analytics products require the same diligence, quality assurance, level of effort, or management oversight. The factors that determine such scrutiny are often the same as those previously discussed in Chapter 4, including scope, complexity, and urgency.

Four types of analytics "deliverables" are outlined here to serve as a heuristic for planning different types of analytics (or data) products.

■ *Simple ad-hoc requests*—Those that take less than a day to resolve; typically, these requests are made in support of previous inquiries or to explore a potential problem and provide support.

■ *Complex ad-hoc requests*—These products are usually more involved but require a deeper understanding of the problem in order to find and transform data or to prepare results for presentation; these applications range in effort from a day to a week.

■ *Special projects*—Unlike ad-hoc requests, data projects are one-time projects that have a life (a beginning and an end) but require planning, coordination with other teams, and the integration of new or novel data. Data projects are considered "one-off" initiatives and, while they may eventually become data products, the focus is scaled accordingly.

■ *Products*—Analytics data products are primarily research and development activities that go through the entire lifecycle with the intention of supporting decisions as a production-ready deliverable. Usually, these are part of an automated process or integrated into a business workflow.

Table 5.1 includes examples of each type of **analytics projects/ products** and their characteristics.

Note that throughout this book, the term **analytics product** is used as the general term for the output or deliverable of the Analytics Lifecycle. Where appropriate, the terms *problem, project,* or *request* will also be used.

HOW THE ANALYTICS LIFECYCLE TOOLKIT IS ORGANIZED

Subsequent chapters of this book will outline each of the five best practice areas—one per chapter. Each will feature a description of the best

Table 5.1 Types of analytics "project types"

Category	Level of Effort	Level of Automation	Oversight/Testing
Simple ad-hoc request	Hours	Low	Self-check
Complex ad-hoc request	Hours to days	Low	Peer review
Special project	Weeks	Low to medium*	Team review
Analytics data product	Months	High	Formal validation

* Note that special projects may evolve into future data products.

practice area, why it is important, and who is involved. It will include the following:

- **Processes**—what you need to do and why it is important.

- **Roles**—responsibilities that can be assigned to an individual with the required skill sets and that are associated with processes and deliverables.

- **Tools and templates**—deliverables, brainstorming tools, worksheets, and plans that are produced as a result of working through the process.

Furthermore, as each of the best practice areas are discussed, I will highlight examples, tips, key points, case studies, and further reading where appropriate.

A Word on Processes

Before diving into the best practice areas, I want to share my perspective on process. For many people, even the mention of the word *process* raises the proverbial "hair on the back of your neck." I share your concerns. Many consider processes (as well as policies and procedures) as a reason to stop thinking about how to improve something. Moreover, it also gives the connotation of following rules without thinking critically about their value.

A process is defined as "a collection of interrelated work tasks initiated in response to an event that achieves a specific result" ("What Is a Process?" 2016). We have all seen processes that stifle creativity, or worse, waste time when they are ignored or circumvented. The perception of process done poorly is often accompanied by the reality that organizations don't allow it to continuously improve.

I would ask you to suspend judgment on the "I hate process" stance and consider the benefits. Adam Smith, the Scottish economist, coined the term "process"; and he found that by creating a process and assigning the steps to individual specialists, productivity increased. Furthermore, he suggests in the *Wealth of Nations* (Smith, 1776) that the division of labor also stimulates innovation as well. By allowing for individuals to exercise "the whole force of the mind" to an area of focus, people naturally strive to reduce the amount of effort they must expend and therefore come up with incremental improvements. Over time, different people add to the body of improvements, adding even more to the productivity gains. Smith concludes that "(t)hese different improvements were probably not all of them the inventions of one man, but the successive discoveries of time and experience, and of the ingenuity of many different artists."

In my experience, the Analytics Lifecycle processes described in this book have positively impacted the speed, agility, and reliability of analytics products and dramatically improve the value of analytics for organizations.

In the Analytics Lifecycle, we use process as a necessary division of labor because the task isn't just in one person's head anymore. While a data champion or data scientist might be creative in how to approach the problem, we need to learn from those experts and not try to control them or force them to use our method. Processes are designed to be improved—but before we can improve, we must first capture the essence.

As analytics processes become core to your business, I hope you will agree that whatever your business does at its core, best practices and processes should be in place to make your business scalable, efficient, and effective.

Analytics Lifecycle Best Practice Areas, Processes, and Tools

As Figure 5.3 shows, the Analytics Lifecycle Toolkit is organized into five best practice areas:

- Problem framing
- Data sensemaking
- Analytics model development
- Results activation
- Analytics Product Lifecycle management

Tables 5.2 through 5.6 summarize the key activities found within each of the five best practices.

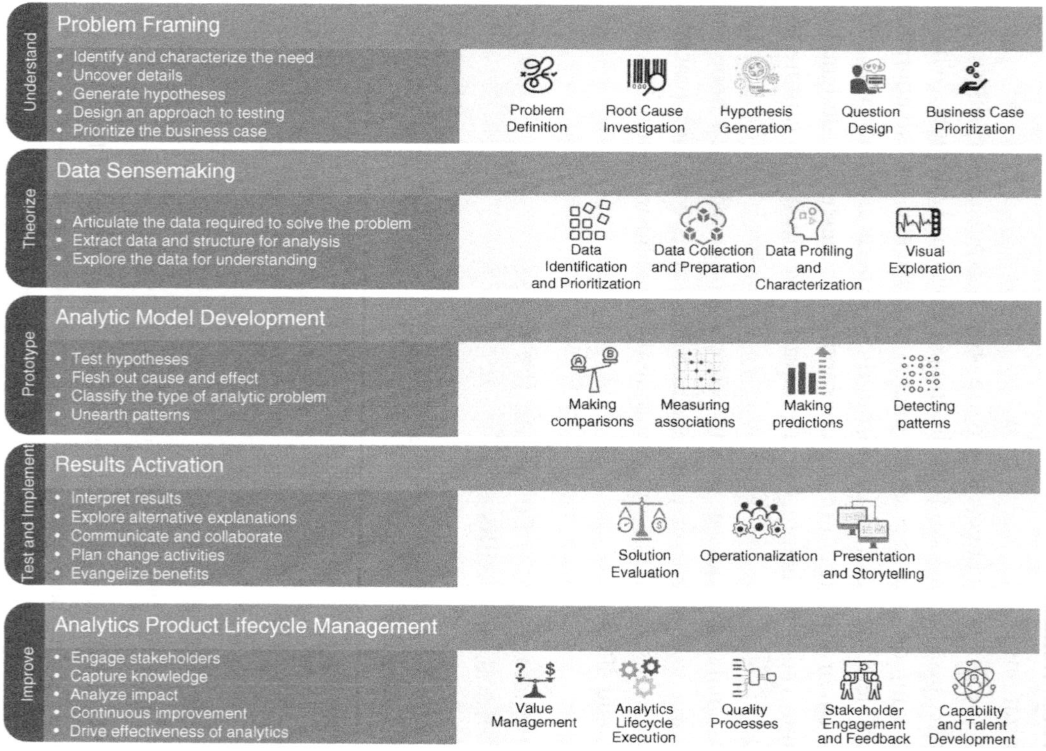

Problem Framing

Understand

- Identify and characterize the need
- Uncover details
- Generate hypotheses
- Design an approach to testing
- Prioritize the business case

Problem Definition · Root Cause Investigation · Hypothesis Generation · Question Design · Business Case Prioritization

Data Sensemaking

Theorize

- Articulate the data required to solve the problem
- Extract data and structure for analysis
- Explore the data for understanding

Data Identification and Prioritization · Data Collection and Preparation · Data Profiling and Characterization · Visual Exploration

Analytic Model Development

Prototype

- Test hypotheses
- Flesh out cause and effect
- Classify the type of analytic problem
- Unearth patterns

Making comparisons · Measuring associations · Making predictions · Detecting patterns

Results Activation

Test and Implement

- Interpret results
- Explore alternative explanations
- Communicate and collaborate
- Plan change activities
- Evangelize benefits

Solution Evaluation · Operationalization · Presentation and Storytelling

Analytics Product Lifecycle Management

Improve

- Engage stakeholders
- Capture knowledge
- Analyze impact
- Continuous improvement
- Drive effectiveness of analytics

Value Management · Analytics Lifecycle Execution · Quality Processes · Stakeholder Engagement and Feedback · Capability and Talent Development

Figure 5.3 The five best practice areas in the Analytics Lifecycle Toolkit

Table 5.2 Best practice area: Problem framing

Process	Key Activities
Problem definition	▪ Identify and characterize the business problem/need.
	▪ Manage the problem definition and impact.
	▪ Support the justification for effort.
	▪ Reformulate problem statement as an analytics problem and/or technical requirements.
	▪ Identify assumptions related to the problem and proposed solution.
	▪ Refine the business and analytics problem statements.
Root cause investigation	▪ Utilize brainstorming techniques and effectively use divergent thinking processes to uncover potential cause-and-effect relationships.
	▪ Classify requirements appropriately and determine feasibility.
	▪ Apply root cause analysis to requirement definitions.
Hypothesis generation	▪ Generate (and manage) testable hypotheses.
	▪ Validate expected results and key requirements information with stakeholders.
	▪ Generate testable theories and validate their reasonableness.
	▪ Shadow workflows that are not understood.
	▪ Conduct primary and secondary research as needed to understand potential sources of the issue.
Question design	▪ Utilize the FINER criteria (Car, 2013) to evaluate whether a problem can be translated into a question that can be answered.
	▪ Convert a question into a proper study design.
Business case prioritization	▪ Prioritize requirements based on business value, cost to deliver, and time constraints.
	▪ Validate that solution design meets the business need.
	▪ Define the capabilities needed to support solution.
	▪ Manage the metrics related to solution implementation and success.

DESIGN THINKING FOR ANALYTICS

Design thinking is a human-centered approach to innovation that draws from the designer's toolkit to integrate the needs of people, the possibilities of technology, and the requirements for business success.

—Tim Brown, CEO of Ideo

Table 5.3　Best practice area: Data sensemaking

Process	Key Activities
Data identification and prioritization	▪ Articulate the data required to solve the problem. ▪ Reconcile the difference between the data we can get versus data that we want. ▪ Trace back the business and operational workflows reflected in the data. ▪ Articulate the provenance and governance assumptions of the data.
Data collection and preparation	▪ Extract data from large, structured data stores. ▪ Extract data from unstructured data sources. ▪ Integrate data from multiple sources. ▪ Ensure privacy and protection of data. ▪ Utilize a variety of methods to cleanse and/or enrich data. ▪ Map results back to business and operational workflows. ▪ Model the data appropriately for the type of analysis needed.
Data profiling and characterization	▪ Identify relationships in the data. ▪ Perform exploration of unknown data. ▪ Profile datasets. ▪ Develop and execute a structured process to describe the aggregate trends, features, and culture of a data set. ▪ Generate descriptive statistics, frequency analysis, and distributions of data (aka, exploratory data analysis – EDA). ▪ Identify and investigate outlier data. ▪ Develop theories that might address the problem.
Visual exploration	▪ Utilize a variety of programmatic and menu-driven visualization tools to examine associations. ▪ Utilize principles of good design to craft visuals appropriate to their type. ▪ Create graphics that help express the context and insight of the data.

What Is Design Thinking?

Chapter 1 defined analytics as "a comprehensive, data-driven strategy for problem-solving." As part of the analytics playbook, we have a number of tools that we can utilize as we tackle challenges. I consider **design thinking** as one of our most durable and sensible tools. Design thinking utilizes elements such as empathy and experimentation to arrive at innovative solutions.

Table 5.4   Best practice area: Analytics model development

Process	Key Activities
Making comparisons	▪ Determine appropriate statistical tests and utilize them in basing conclusions. ▪ Apply a wide variety of statistical models, processes, routines, and measures to compare two or more groups. ▪ Compare and contrast features of categorical and numerical data sets using appropriate tests. ▪ Apply quantitative measures to describe the properties of a sample of data. ▪ Define and apply statistical significance, confidence intervals, effect size, and hypothesis testing. ▪ Differentiate between categorical versus continuous data and the appropriateness of various testing strategies used for making inferences.
Measuring associations	▪ Utilize visualization methods to examine relationships between different types of data. ▪ Distinguish between an explanatory and response variable and their role in tests of association. ▪ Describe the types of tests used in measuring associations including those in parametric and non-parametric testing. ▪ Relay the difference between an association and a cause-and-effect relationship.
Making predictions	▪ Identify the two classes of prediction models. ▪ Enumerate the types and methods of supervised and unsupervised methods used for prediction models. ▪ Relate the type of prediction problem being asked back to the methods available in statistics, data mining, and machine learning. ▪ Recognize common analytics methods such as predictive models, cluster analysis, neural networks, and machine learning.
Detecting patterns	▪ Classify the types of problems that we can solve using pattern recognition. ▪ Describe the various classification approaches. ▪ Illustrate the difference between feature selection and feature extraction. ▪ Describe the difference between classification and discrimination.

There have been tremendous shifts in our thinking and agility over the past 20 years. We have moved from waterfall methods in software development to those more agile and responsive to customer needs. Markets have shifted from mass marketing approaches that blasted product messaging to those that consider the personal preferences and tastes of individuals. Even my real estate broker uses lifestyle profiles

Table 5.5 Best practice area: Results activation

Process	Key Activities
Solution evaluation	▪ Conduct data/analytics output interpretation.
	▪ Coach and mentor stakeholders.
	▪ Perform business validation of the model.
	▪ Compare results from various models.
	▪ Explore alternative explanations.
Operationalization	▪ Incorporate a set of analytics and insights into business workflow such that a continual, positive benefit is seen and the organizational learning paradigm is realized.
	▪ Create model, usability, and system requirements for production.
	▪ Deliver production model.
	▪ Support the business process change.
	▪ Support the implementation of the model.
	▪ Assess actionability and impact to operational workflows.
	▪ Document and communicate findings (including assumptions, limitations, and constraints).
Presentation and storytelling	▪ Communicate effectively with various audiences.
	▪ Create data visualizations that convey meaning.
	▪ Deliver report with findings.
	▪ Evangelize value of analytics/business benefits.
	▪ Socialize analytics results, advances.

and targets her advertising to specific personas that fit that lifestyle. We move from products to experience (Rose, 2013).

In analytics, we should make decisions, deliver products, and design experiences around what our customers want rather than how we are organized or what we consider important or interesting. Design thinking enables us to design solutions (solve problems, create opportunities) that start with empathy. I view design thinking as a way to get out of our own heads and forget our preconceived notions about what someone wants or needs, instead forcing us to define problems from the user's perspective.

In organizations, we must resist the temptation to find, build, and deploy solutions without first understanding the context in which the problem exists or how a solution will fit in to their work.

Table 5.6 Best practice area: Analytics Product Lifecycle management

Process	Key Activities
Value management	▪ Strategic alignment. ▪ Develop and support a collaborative product management culture. ▪ Analytics evangelism. ▪ Evaluate the business benefit of analytics over time.
Analytics lifecycle execution	▪ Analytics prioritization. ▪ Utilize project management principles to define, execute, and manage project activities. ▪ Develop and establish project goals and milestones. ▪ Implement project standards and procedures. ▪ Monitor and analyze project costs. ▪ Estimate project work. ▪ Manage capital and expense reporting.
Quality processes	▪ Improve the way in which data is governed. ▪ Create and follow quality management plans. ▪ Promote continuous improvement. ▪ Follow robust testing and quality processes. ▪ Utilize a risk-based validation approach. ▪ Participate in peer reviews of both code and data products. ▪ Document and improve quality principles. ▪ Track model quality and durability. ▪ Recalibrate and maintain models.
Stakeholder engagement and feedback	▪ Analyze impact of change. ▪ Support training and communication activities. ▪ Manage change. ▪ Promote processes for managing change and measuring the impact of decisions ▪ Promote a culture of sharing and collaboration.
Capability and talent development	▪ Manage resources and evaluate performance. ▪ Manage portfolio of projects with available resources. ▪ Manage talent development. ▪ Provide performance improvement coaching. ▪ Manage conflict. ▪ Demonstrate leadership and influence with the team and with external stakeholders. ▪ Assess lessons learned. ▪ Catalog data assets and ensure that metadata is accessible and usable.

Design Thinking Takes the User Journey into Account

The myriad participants, perspectives, and incentives make a solution impossible without consideration of that system in total. Most organizational processes are characterized by highly coordinated activities and require a multidisciplinary approach to problem understanding and problem solving. In design thinking, we exercise our minds by documenting the user persona and the user journey in ways that help us empathize with them along their route, so that the problem definition is clear, as well as what we must consider along the way.

Five Steps in Design Thinking

Design thinking can have direct implications for both the design of products (e.g., analytics models, reports, findings) and how they are operationalized (experienced as part of their work), as well as how data-consumers experience our services (analytics project triage, prioritization, and conveyance of status). Design thinking is a human-centered approach to both problem seeking and problem solving. As we will see later in this book, both **problem seeking** and **problem solving** are central to analytics as a problem-solving strategy.

Problem Seeking

The process of hypothesis generation and open-ended inquiry revealing patterns and associations; the synthesis of issues to define questions that can be answered with data.

Problem Solving

The practice of using scientific processes such as hypothesis-based testing to evaluate the application and reliability of an underlying phenomenon.

Design thinking offers a five-step process (Figure 5.4) that can be used iteratively to support the application of analytics products and services:

1. Empathize
2. Define

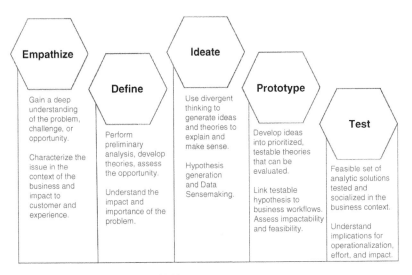

Figure 5.4 Five steps in design thinking

3. Ideate

4. Prototype

5. Test

Sometimes, different people also include a final, sixth step of implementation.

Note that I am not trying to suggest that the five steps used in design thinking correspond to the five best practices of analytics as outlined in this book. Rather, I view the design thinking processes as a complementary approach to how we should design analytics products and services. Specifically, I believe the best opportunity for delighting analytics customers is to adapt tools and techniques from a variety of methodologies, including strategic innovation, design thinking, experience design, **lean startup**, product thinking, and **agile** methods, as depicted in Figure 5.5 (Ries, 2011).

Throughout this book, we will align the analytics **best practices** to the various stages of design thinking to anchor these concepts. As shown in Figure 5.6, the analytics follow an iterative cycle. Here, we have expanded the five steps traditionally found in design thinking to frame our conversation around the iterative nature of analytics

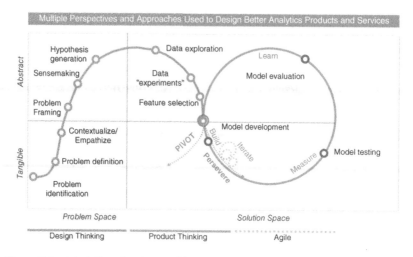

Figure 5.5 Adaptation of various toolkits (such as design thinking, product thinking, and agile methods) can enable better analytics solutions
Adapted from Nordstrom's Innovation Lab

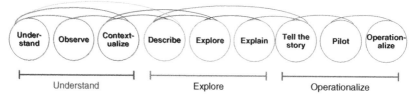

Figure 5.6 Design thinking processes applied to analytics

processes. As we go through each of the five analytics best practices, I will highlight where the best practice fits in this iterative model.

CHAPTER SUMMARY

The Analytics Lifecycle contains five best practice areas that are used throughout the design, development, and delivery of analytics products. While not every analytics project (problem, project, product) will exercise each of these areas in the same manner, they provide a framework for ensuring that analytics projects deliver value and the effort appropriate to their outcome.

REFERENCES

Few, S. (2012). Use-based types of quantitative display. *Visual Business Intelligence Newsletter*, January/February/March 2012. Retrieved from www.perceptualedge.com/articles/visual_business_intelligence/types_of_quantitative_display.pdf.

Ries, E. (2011a). Case study: The Nordstrom Innovation Lab. Retrieved from http://www.startuplessonslearned.com/2011/10/case-study-nordstrom-innovation-lab.html.

Smith, A. (1776). *An inquiry into the nature and causes of the wealth of nations.* London: W. Strahan and T. Cadell.

What is a process? (2016). *Enterprise Process Support.* Retrieved from its.syr.edu/eps/services/process/what_is.html.

CHAPTER 6

Problem Framing

We accomplish what we understand. If we are to accomplish something together, we need to understand it together.

—Ron Jeffries

PROCESS OVERVIEW

The best practice of problem framing is based upon understanding and prioritizing business needs and ensuring that potential solutions solve the problem that was originally posed without creating new ones. This broad-based systems perspective requires planning, feasibility determination, information gathering, business case preparation, and risk assessment.

I intentionally refer to this best practice as problem framing rather than the broader term **business analysis**. While the profession of business analysis has been around for decades, its origin has roots in software development; and not unlike the software development lifecycle, business analysis in analytics requires specialty skills that range from business planning to the quantitative and qualitative methods used in advanced analytics (at least an awareness of options). In addition, this best practice area relies on the soft skills of interviewing (for requirements elicitation), fact-based problem solving (analysis/synthesis), storytelling, knowledge management, negotiation, influence, and case study methods.

WHY DO THIS?

The primary focus of analytics in general is to fully understand the needs of the organization and to identify actionable opportunities that allow the organization to meet its goals.

Organizations that excel at problem framing know the difference between the important and the urgent and demonstrate empathy by fully understanding the problem, its impact, and the value of solving the problem. They also benefit through lessons learned about what has

149

worked in the past and what's likely to work in the future. To position our analytics projects for success, we need a deliberate and intentional purpose that will help guide the analytics teams to focus on the right things with the right context in order to properly solve the right issues for the right people.

PROCESS AREAS

In analytics, the discussion of problem framing is focused on the following key processes:

- Problem definition
- Root cause investigation
- Hypothesis generation
- Question design
- Business case prioritization

The process outlined in Figure 6.1 is a representation of the scientific method applied to analytics inquiry. The method posits that we

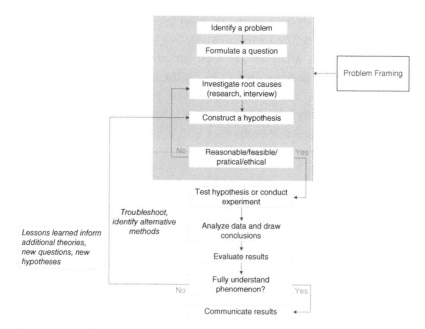

Figure 6.1 Problem framing best practice area in context

gather knowledge by purposeful examination and study. Although we can build evidence to support our theory, we can never really know something for certain, but knowledge is gained through demonstration of that evidence.

In order to support a data-driven, fact-based problem-solving approach with analytics, we will need to accurately define the problem in its simplest terms. By doing this, we set a strong foundation of framing the problem as a question that can be answered with data.

To brace your problem-solving efforts, it is important to research what was attempted previously to solve this issue or how others have addressed this problem area, not just in your company or industry, but in other domains. Seek to understand potential causes through the application of such techniques as root cause analysis, interviews, and process reviews. Armed with potential causes, you can then discuss theory generation and how to limit the possibilities down to the precious few that you can impact.

Beyond problem framing is data discovery (we refer to this as sensemaking, which you will see in the second best practice area). Here you will define the scope of the data needed to help you find a solution, and develop a plan to collect the data. You will ask, is that plan feasible? Is it reasonable to expect that the collected data will answer the business question?

Note that as we explore each of these processes, it is important to realize that you may work on multiple processes in parallel and even revisit a previous process through the elaboration of requirements. For example, during your root cause analysis, other questions may arise.

By answering these questions, you will have a well-defined problem and can move forward to developing a business question. You are then ready for the next steps of hypothesis testing and planning for generalizability—that is, translating the results back to the business in a real-world setting.

Learn More

To learn more about the profession and the Business Analysis Body of Knowledge, visit www.iiba.org/babok-guide.aspx.

Problem Definition

A problem well stated is a problem half solved.

John Dewey

As seen in the previous chapter, you can have one or more specific analytics goals in mind that may include:

- Solving a problem
- Supporting a narrative
- Understanding a phenomenon
- Discovering something new

While a number of approaches can be used to help define the question, set up analysis plans, and execute an investigation, at their core, they are all related to the basic scientific method (see Figure 6.1).

Often, when we seek to solve, understand, communicate, or discover, we want to dive in and begin exploration or start proposing solutions. Try to resist this temptation, as you cannot really find a solution to a problem that has not been defined. The reason you should focus on problem definition first is to make sure that you really understand and appreciate the problem and create a shared understanding of its impact if left unsolved. All too often, a problem is ill-formed or too general to solve and, as such, is impossible to solve if we cannot define it properly.

TIP

Be careful not to fall into the trap of either asking the wrong question (type III error) or asking a question not worth answering (type IV error).

Problem definition starts with identifying a problem, usually in the form of a symptom, such as something that has gone awry in the business. While there may be multiple reasons, it is all too easy to jump in and start twisting knobs and turning levers. Instead, you should start by fully understanding, observing, and contextualizing the problem area (Figure 6.2).

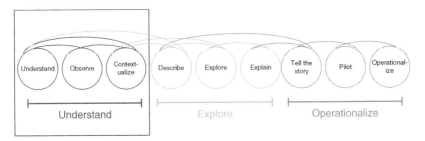

Figure 6.2 Problem framing relates to the empathy stage in design thinking

The problem area is the broad landscape of pain that is felt in the organization. What is the request, project, or product all about, and how does it impact the organization?

Specifically, you need to understand the following:

- What is the problem?
- Who does it affect?
- What is the impact of the problem, and what happens if left alone?
- What does a successful solution look like?

Problem Definition in Practice

As a practical example, consider the following challenge:

> A company that specializes in manufacturing and selling high-end motorcycles has been trying to market its new line of cruisers with limited success. In fact, it barely sells one or two per week. The head of sales blames marketing for not delivering leads while marketing blames product development for not creating products that customers want. Everyone blames sales for not creating revenue, and management is questioning the overall strategy.

What is the problem?

- There are lots of theories about what might be causing the issue but the simple truth is that the problem for the business is *a shortfall in projected revenue.*

Who or what does the problem affect?

- The problem will likely impact everyone in the company, including executives, managers, salespeople, engineers, designers, and marketing specialists. Further, external stakeholders such as vendors and customers will be affected.

What is the impact?

- The obvious impacts might include layoffs, lack of bonuses, pay cuts, or contract cancellations. However, the impacts are likely greater than the initial estimates and may have far-reaching implications, such as kids going without braces, parents having to move in with their adult children, plant closures, and more. Without overdramatizing the situation, it's important to understand that assessing impact is critical, and categorizing the types of impacts are helping in presenting the business case (without the hyperbole!). A solid business case supports the prioritization of the problem and justifies the effort spent in solving the issue.

What would success look like?

- In the short term, success can be defined as a shared understanding of the issues that cause the problem and mutual agreement on the theories that we intend to pursue. Long term, success should be measured in business results. For the shortsighted, success might mean firing the sales manager, but it's better to avoid personalizing blame and focus instead on the specific, tangible success that can be measured. In this example case, success means selling at least 15 motorcycles per week within six months of launch. It is critical to include specific and measurable success criteria. That is, define the target for improvement and a specific goal date.

Learn More

To learn more about goal setting, see this classic article on goal setting from Psychologists Edwin Locke and Gary Latham (Locke & Latham, 2002).

In addition to answering the questions above, it is also helpful to include assumptions, constraints, timelines, and dependencies. Once you bring this together, you have a *problem statement*, which is simply a way to summarize the results of your brainstorming and research and capture the essence of the problem. That is, what is the issue, who does it affect, what is the impact, and what does success look like if the issue were to be solved?

Summary and Exercise

In this process, we have explored the activity necessary to properly cast a problem in terms that everyone understands. In the case study, the Harley Davidson dealership faced a significant challenge with sales during the winter months.

Case Study: Harley Davidson Uses AI: (Power, 2017)

Read the case study and complete the problem definition table below. It is critical to stop here and do this documentation exercise. The reason is this: while you may have a good grasp of your current problem, it's likely that in a few months your memory will fade and you will need to clearly answer these questions when talking about the results to your organization's leadership or collaborators.

Toolkit @ www.analyticslifecycletoolkit.com

Download a problem statement template from the companion website.

Root Cause Investigation

We all have theories about the way the world works. Depending on your perspective, academic background, experience, and biases, you may emphasize one area at the expense of others.

As Daniel Kahneman (2013) suggests in his book *Thinking, Fast and Slow,* we tend to take the easy path.

A general "law of least effort" applies to cognitive as well as physical exertion. The law asserts that if there are several ways of achieving the same goal, people will eventually gravitate to the least demanding course of action. In the economy of action, effort is a cost, and the acquisition of skill is driven by the balance of benefits and costs. Laziness is built deep into our nature.

When working through the possible reasons for a problem, it is wise to brainstorm possibilities within categories. In its simplest form, you can draw an affinity diagram ("Affinity Diagram," 2017) as shown in Figure 6.3.

Alternatively, you can use category brainstorming to help improve the consideration of factors beyond what might come easily to you. One technique that is useful to "force" us to consider alternative theories is the use of an Ishakawa diagram, also known as a fishbone diagram because of its similarity to a fish skeleton. Table 6.1 summarizes the various types of fishbone diagrams.

Just remember, these are tools that help guide your thinking and support creative problem solving. Once you have a number of theories about why the problem exists, you can use this knowledge in your discovery processes, such as interviews, research, and preliminary data reviews.

Learn More @ www.analyticslifecycletoolkit.com

To learn more about the fishbone diagram and methods to help expand your thinking, access the resources at the companion web site.

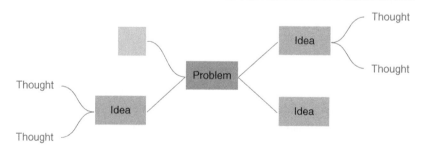

Figure 6.3 Affinity diagram

Table 6.1 Types of diagrams useful in identifying potential cause and effect relationships

Type of Diagram	Description	Example
Simple fishbone	The simplest form of the fishbone (or cause-and-effect diagram) does not have any predefined categories of causes (or affinities). This is useful in brainstorming to not predispose people in a way that limits their thinking. You start by capturing ideas, then group them and label cause categories.	
4S fishbone	This type of diagram is often found in service organizations. It organizes information about potential causes into four common categories: suppliers, systems, surroundings, and skills.	

(continued)

157

Table 6.1 (Continued)

Type of Diagram	Description	Example
8P fishbone	Similar to the 4S fishbone, this type uses 8 categories: procedures, policies, place, product, people, processes, price, and promotion.	The 8 Ps (used in service industry) Physical Evidence, People, Place, Service → Sub-cause → Service Problem Productivity & Quality, Process, Promotion, Price → Sub-cause

Man machines materials fishbone	Another variation allows you to organize potential causes of a problem into eight categories: man, materials, machine, methods, measurements, environment, management/money, and maintenance.

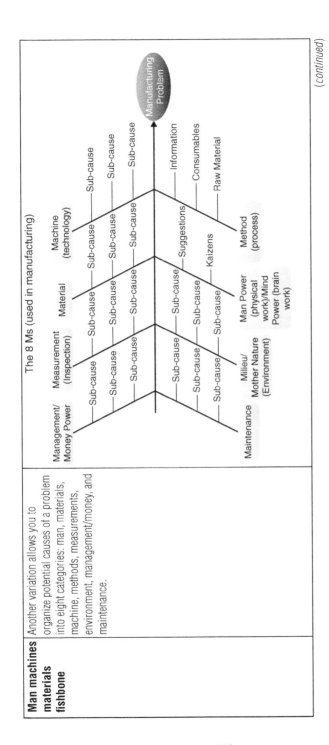

(continued)

159

Table 6.1 (Continued)

Type of Diagram	Description	Example
Design of experiments fishbone	This type of fishbone diagram allows structured brainstorming about potential factors for a response variable to help you design an experiment. You can use this diagram to organize information about potential factors of response variables into controllable, uncontrollable, held-constant, and blockable nuisance categories.	

While a number of methods could be useful with both brainstorming and documenting your efforts, I recommend using something that is easy to use, can be updated (a living document), and is appropriate for your organization (level of detail and cultural fit, etc.). In my consulting work, we have used mind maps and design thinking/brainstorming software. Figure 6.4 shows an example of using a tree diagram map to capture potential root causes.

Summary and Exercise

Root-cause analysis may seem difficult at first, as our minds tend to go blank when asked to come up with ideas. The goal of this process is to unstick our minds and shift perspectives to consider things that we may not have otherwise done.

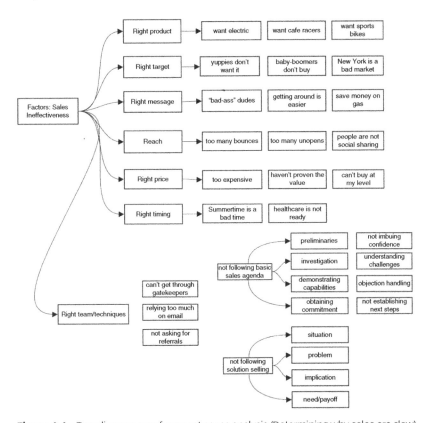

Figure 6.4 Tree diagram map from root cause analysis (Determining why sales are slow)

Table 6.2 Design thinking tools useful in analytics problem framing

	Empathize Stage	Define Stage
Deliverables	▪ Personas ▪ Empathy map ▪ List of user feedback ▪ Problems identified ▪ Problem statement	▪ Design brief ▪ Stakeholder map ▪ Context map ▪ Customer journeys ▪ Opportunity map
Tools	▪ Interview checklist ▪ Observation checklist ▪ Writing tools ▪ Flipcharts and paper (or virtual tools) ▪ Camera	▪ Drawing & writing tools ▪ Sticky notes ▪ Flipchart/whiteboard ▪ User feedback (from empathize)
Activities	▪ User interview ▪ Informal conversations ▪ Observation ▪ Shadowing ▪ Mystery shopping ▪ Picture taking ▪ Immersion	▪ Workshops ▪ Stakeholder meetings ▪ Gamestorming

Techniques in design thinking from the **empathize** and **define** phases can be useful to help understand the customer and define the problem. You will find some of the deliverables, activities, and tools useful in these processes in Table 6.2.

Empathize

During this phase we are learning about others, the end users, and the problem that we are trying to solve.

Define

Define is the convergent phase where we make informed decisions from the insights we have gained from the empathize phase. Clarity is gained from asking the right critical questions of stakeholders or team members. Here we get curious and find things out. We challenge the status quo.

Using Table 6.2, consider first the categories that you might apply to the motorcycle case study, then brainstorm with a few colleagues for 10 to 15 minutes. You can use software such as RealTimeBoard, mind mapping software, spreadsheets, sticky notes, or something as simple as a whiteboard to brainstorm the categories and the root causes within each category.

Questions to Consider

- For the motorcycle case study, which categories make sense?
- Did you find at least three potential causes of the poor sales performance within each category?

As an exercise, brainstorm a problem that you are currently facing and see how the categories for the fishbone diagram change to reflect that specific issue.

Hypothesis Generation

Approach the case with an absolutely blank mind, which is always an advantage. That way you formed no theories. You are simply there to observe and to draw inferences from your observations.

Adventure of the Cardboard Box (Doyle & Paget, 1975)

Once you have defined a problem area and have considered the potential causes (cause and effect relationships), the next step is to begin to formulate why—that is, what are your hypotheses about the relationships.

Some techniques that go beyond brainstorming include:

- *Validate expected results*—people in this stage often fail to capture the details of the current state. One of the first things you should do is characterize what you know about the data and validate it through some of the following techniques. For example, someone may describe the situation as "dismal sales performance," but equipped with data, you can put this into context. For example, you may want to show the sales performance of new product launches in the past, current sales performance of competitors that sell a similar product, or the actual performance of differentiated products during a similar startup period.

▪ *Interview stakeholders and get their feedback*—this is about understanding the perspectives of everyone involved—customers, prospects, sales, finance, marketing, customer support, quality improvement staff—anyone with a stake in the game. Capture the various perspectives of stakeholders and see if there is reliable consensus with what the expected results should be.

▪ *Shadow workflows you don't understand*—The data that you end up using in the analytics process is effectively re-summarizing the workflow that created it. You have to know how it was generated, and shadowing can be the best way. It also puts you into the head of those who generate the data and see their motivation, especially if there are work-arounds that may not be self-evident in the data.

▪ *Explore external resources*—Other resources might include online searches, published literature, experts, or user groups (or motorcycle clubs, in this case). While it may not be appropriate for this scenario, searching for similar situations can often help unblock your creative process. Remember, root-cause investigation is a divergent thinking process. Now is not the time to narrow your focus (convergent thinking). Similarly, you can look to other industries to see if there are similarities in other problem domains.

Remember, at this point, you are generating hypotheses—which is part of divergent thinking. Utilize techniques that support creating myriad ideas to generate hypotheses. In this process, use sticky notes (or a real-time collaboration tool) to state your theory. That is, we generate our ideas about how we believe the world works through statements.

While I have touched on the concept of divergent thinking, it is important to reflect on what that really means in practice. Divergent thinking embodies the emotional and cognitive processes of expanding your mindset to consider all possibilities rather than simply those that occur to you naturally. In analytics, we often find ourselves going back and forth between the problem space (what it is, how big is it, what are the effects, etc.) to the solution space (how can we solve it). That process necessarily imbues creating choices (divergent thinking) and making choices (convergent thinking). Similarly, when we seek to understand the problem, we often employ systems thinking to understand the complexity and interconnectedness of issues. Whereas, in defining solutions, we think like an entrepreneur. The perspective is illustrated in Figure 6.5.

Let's illustrate the brainstorming process by using a three-step technique that helps frame our thinking so that it creates something that can be applied to our problem:

1. Generate hypotheses about the potential causes.

2. Form the hypotheses into statements that articulate the underlying relationships.

3. Assess the risks and rewards of establishing those theories as truths.

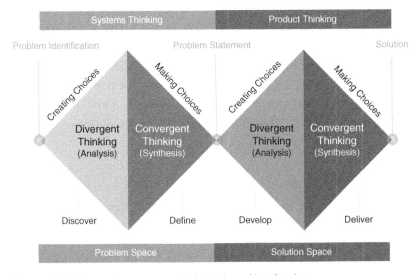

Figure 6.5 Divergent vs. convergent thinking in problem framing

---

**Toolkit @
www.analyticslifecycletoolkit.com**

Visit to access the three-step template shown here.

As an exercise, follow these three steps with the use of an example.

Step 1. Working with your team, generate hypotheses (Figure 6.6). For example, "we believe that we could attract more buyers if we ... "

- Had "new rider" classes.
- Created testimonial videos on our website.
- Advertised more on Facebook.
- Gave people a reward for referrals.
- Offered new customer discounts.
- Made it easy to get insurance.
- Sent our sales people to training.
- Bought marketing lists and engaged in outbound telemarketing.
- Provided comparisons for alternatives (electric, sports, used).

Step 2. Extract the hypotheses into the form (Figure 6.7). We believe that building this feature for persona will achieve this outcome. We will know this to be true when the we test our theory.

Step 3. Using a common set of criteria, assess the risks and rewards of each hypothesis (Figure 6.8). Here, we use a 2 × 2 matrix to evaluate the risk and impact of testing each hypothesis. Alternatives might include cost, timeline, probability, feasibility, and importance.

Learn More

To learn more about the 2 × 2 matrix and how it can be used to support decision making, visit PrepLounge, which describes the 2 × 2 matrix and the BCG matrix ("2 × 2 Matrices and the BCG matrix").

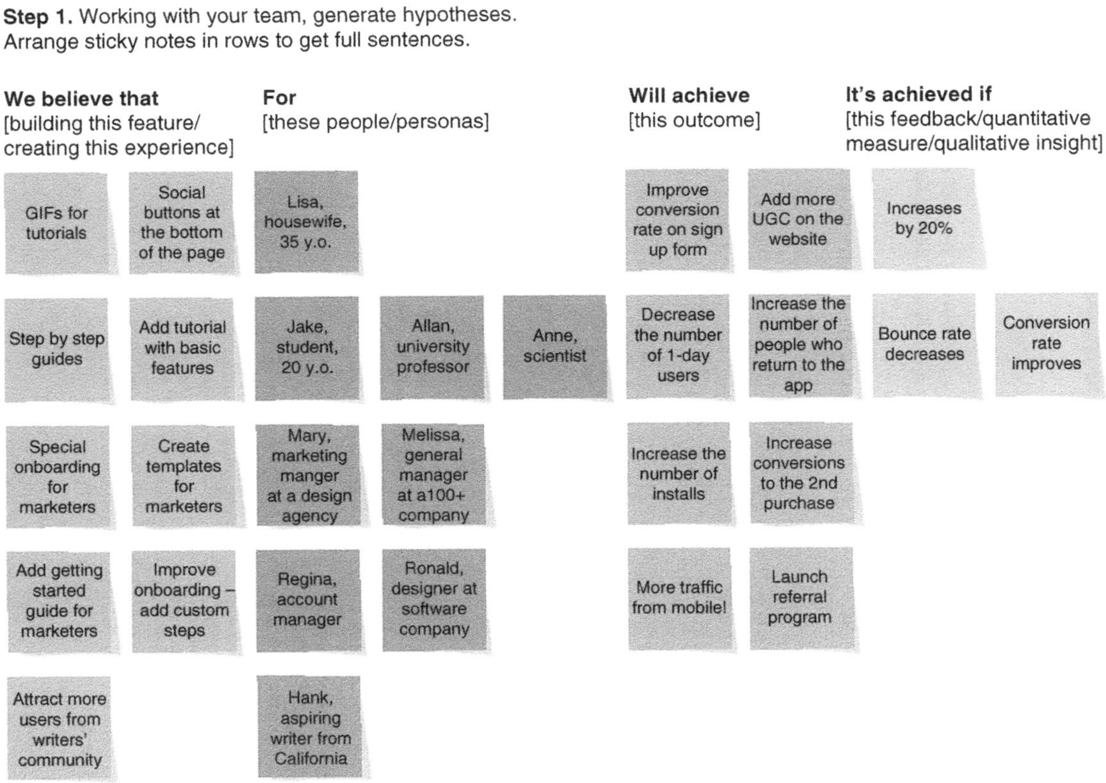

Step 1. Working with your team, generate hypotheses. Arrange sticky notes in rows to get full sentences.

We believe that
[building this feature/ creating this experience]

- GIFs for tutorials
- Social buttons at the bottom of the page
- Step by step guides
- Add tutorial with basic features
- Special onboarding for marketers
- Create templates for marketers
- Add getting started guide for marketers
- Improve onboarding – add custom steps
- Attract more users from writers' community

For
[these people/personas]

- Lisa, housewife, 35 y.o.
- Jake, student, 20 y.o.
- Allan, university professor
- Mary, marketing manager at a design agency
- Melissa, general manager at a100+ company
- Anne, scientist
- Regina, account manager
- Ronald, designer at software company
- Hank, aspiring writer from California

Will achieve
[this outcome]

- Improve conversion rate on sign up form
- Add more UGC on the website
- Decrease the number of 1-day users
- Increase the number of people who return to the app
- Increase the number of installs
- Increase conversions to the 2nd purchase
- More traffic from mobile
- Launch referral program

It's achieved if
[this feedback/quantitative measure/qualitative insight]

- Increases by 20%
- Bounce rate decreases
- Conversion rate improves

Figure 6.6 Three-step process for brainstorming in problem framing (prioritizing software features)

167

Step 2. Extract the hypotheses. Use this format: We believe that [building this feature] for [persona] will achieve [this outcome]. We will know this to be true when [quantitative/qualitative metrics]

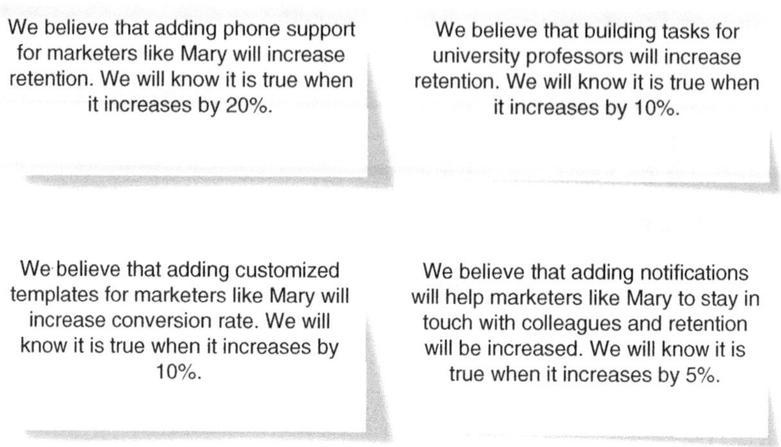

We believe that adding phone support for marketers like Mary will increase retention. We will know it is true when it increases by 20%.
We believe that building tasks for university professors will increase retention. We will know it is true when it increases by 10%.
We believe that adding customized templates for marketers like Mary will increase conversion rate. We will know it is true when it increases by 10%.
We believe that adding notifications will help marketers like Mary to stay in touch with colleagues and retention will be increased. We will know it is true when it increases by 5%.

Figure 6.7 Belief statements translated to SMART goals

Step 3. Working with your team, assess risks.
Put each card from Step 2 on the matrix.

HIGH RISK/LOW IMPACT
HIGH RISK/HIGH IMPACT
STANDARD WORKFLOW
We believe that adding notifications will help marketers like Mary to stay in touch with colleagues and retention will be increased. We will know it is true when it increases by 5%.
We believe that building tasks for university professors will increase retention. We will know it is true when it increases by 10%.
LOW RISK/LOW IMPACT
GIMMICKS & NOVELTIES
LOW RISK/HIGH IMPACT
DELIGHTFUL FEATURES
We believe that adding phone support for marketers like Mary will increase retention. We will know it is true when it increases by 20%.
We believe that adding customized templates for marketers like Mary will increase conversion rate. We will know it is true when it increases by 10%.

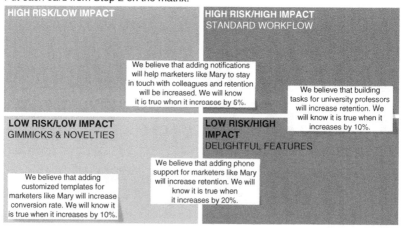

Figure 6.8 Impact and risk matrix

Table 6.3 Problem Statement Table

The problem of ...	\<What is the problem?\>
Affects ...	\<Who does this affect?\>
The impact of which is ...	\<What is the impact?\>
A successful solution will	\<What does success look like?\>
Assumptions	\<What must be true to be successful?\>
Dependencies	\<What interdependencies are required?\>
Constraints	\<What must you live with?\>

Summary and Exercise

Hypothesis generation is the process that can help us translate ideas (the how) into the why. We craft hypotheses as a way of verbalizing the assumptions about our perceptions of cause and effect.

In this exercise, complete Table 6.3 for a set of hypotheses that you have about a current problem in your organization. Remember, be explicit about what your theory is, and put it into the form outlined in Step 2. We will explore question design in the next process.

Question Design

At this point, you should have a problem statement and some clarity with respect to what might be influencing the issue, as well as some specific theories about how the world works. This leads to formalizing the problem into a proper research question. Let's start with understanding what makes a good question.

One technique for characterizing a "question" is to use the FINER criteria. That is, is the question under consideration **F**easible, **I**nteresting, **N**ovel, **E**thical, and **R**elevant?

Let's examine these one by one, returning to the case study:

- **Feasible** means the question can be answered. Questions that can't be answered often lack specificity, timing, or methods of measurement. For example, you might not have enough cases in the data to ask the question. For the motorcycle sales problem, we need to assess whether we have given this enough time, whether we have enough "true" customers (sales) to use in determining what is working, and whether we have been tracking our marketing and sales activities, market research, and prospect interviews, and the associated data assets. Even if you have the data, is the effect size large enough to matter? Everyone usually clings to the concept of statistical significance, but you cannot forget about business significance. For our case study, this question could be recast as, What would enough sales revenue look like in order to retain the new product line?

- **Interesting** means that you would find the investigation worthwhile and rewarding. I would suggest that if you could solve this issue, you and your colleagues would be heroes! As the adage goes, if leadership thinks it is interesting, it probably is (but don't forget to ask the question anyway!).

- **Novel** can be misleading, as academics often ask if there is a gap in the scholarly literature that this investigation can fill. Since this is applied research and we aren't asking the question to understand something but rather to solve an issue, novelty may seem like a strange criterion. However, in our case, what we mean is, has someone already done this investigation before? That is, is it novel to your department or organization? If so, can you partner with them or review previous findings?

- **Ethical** is an essential consideration in question design—from both the perspective of spending time on a question as well as deciding whether the "do nothing" option really should be considered. Suffice it to say that ethical means all investigations are conducted while complying with the regulations—government, academic research, etc. Moreover, ethical means doing the right thing for the right reasons and anticipating unintentional consequences or uses of data.

- **Relevant** pertains to the "so what?" questions. If you find an answer to your question, will it influence or even change some business process? In our case study, careers and livelihoods are on the line, so the project would be considered relevant.

Case Study: Consumer Protection in the Age of Big Data

In 2016, the Federal Trade Commission did a study on the uses of big data to determine whether there should be guidelines surrounding the use of big data in analytics and whether there should be protections in place for consumers (FTC, 2016). The concern, as you might expect, was whether the use of big data could serve to cause harm to individuals. While there were a number of benefits, they found that there were some negative impacts including mistakenly being denied opportunities such as lowering credit limits for consumers, or creating and/or reinforcing existing disparities, exposing sensitive information, and weakening the effectiveness of consumer choice (among others).

In this report, several recommendations are consistent with those I made above. These include asking the following questions:

1. How representative is your data set?
2. Does your data model account for biases?
3. How accurate are your predictions, based on big data?
4. Does your reliance on big data raise ethical or fairness concerns?

Potential Study Designs to Answer the Question

 TIP

A study design is a tactical plan to translate your conceptual hypothesis into a series of steps describing how it is tested.

Once you have a conceptual hypothesis, you need to translate this into operational methods for testing. In academic research, we refer to this as the study design. Common study designs might include A/B testing, surveys, qualitative research such as interviews or expert judgment, real-world evidence or observation, or experiment and trials.

The truth is, the actual measurement strategy is going to depend on the reality of what data you can actually get, so you may go through some rounds of iteration in refining your approach.

Strong study designs are important in order to determine if your hypothesis is true. A flawed design can make it difficult to draw any conclusions. The flaws can come in several forms, such as neglecting to consider and measure key variables, introducing too many interventions at once, or failing to collect sufficient data. Ultimately, your choice of study design is the process that is used to help you find an answer to your question.

Deciding on which question you end up with, other factors such as the availability of data, number of cases, or number and type of customers will influence the study design that you choose.

In our case study, our business question might be framed to look something like this:

> We believe that by examining data about our current customers we can create unique, ideal customer profiles that will help inform who is most likely to buy. Using those profiles, we can create specific targeted marketing messages. Further, these targeted messages will appeal to potential buyers and impact buying behavior. We will know this is true when sales increase by 500% (going from one motorcycle sale per week to five).

Given our hypothesis, we can simply measure pre- and post-intervention but we would never know if an uptick in sales was related to timing (seasonable effects, economic changes, warmer weather) or some external factor(s). It is advisable to have a comparison group where possible. Example comparisons might include:

- Consumers who received traditional (untargeted) content during the same time period
- Groups of consumers who received varying amounts and types of marketing content than our primary intervention group
- Consumers who received personalized calls and follow-up materials (different from the planned intervention for our target group)

2017 NFL Study on Concussions:

Over the past two decades we have seen mounting evidence that lung cancer is associated with smoking. Most researchers would argue that smoking causes lung cancer but only after a preponderance of reliable, consistent evidence that an association can be established.

- How do we know that both of these variables are not being affected by an unobserved third (lurking) variable?

- For instance, what if there is a genetic predisposition that causes people to both get lung cancer and become addicted to smoking, but the smoking itself doesn't *cause* lung cancer?

We can evaluate the association using the following criteria:

- The association is strong.

- The association is consistent.

- Higher doses are associated with stronger responses.

- Alleged cause precedes the effect.

- The alleged cause is plausible.

Finally, whatever we defer the discussion of cause and effect to, it is with proper, reproducible experimental design that we begin to whittle away and eliminate alternative explanations.

In a 2017 study (Wadman, 2017), autopsies were conducted on the brains of former US football players. In the study, 202 players were examined and 87 percent showed the diagnostic signs of chronic traumatic encephalopathy (CTE), a neurodegenerative disease associated with repetitive head trauma. That number jumped to 99 percent for former National Football League (NFL) players in the sample.

Many would immediately cite head injuries as the cause and demand that action be taken to reduce these types of injuries. However, we cannot know the definitive answer from a single study. There may, indeed, be some lurking variable that is yet unknown. A neuropsychologist from the University of North Carolina, Chapel Hill, who also happens to be a friend of mine, challenged the research for not being a true experiment. There was no control group and the study was conducted from symptomatic former players and not from those who remained free of mental problems. Just as in smoking, we need further research to eliminate these other potential causes.

In analytics, we must never forget the adage, correlation does not prove causation.

A final thought on study design: we should emphasize that the choice of study design should be right-sized with what you are trying to accomplish. For example, it may just be enough to ask whether an outcome is changing, such as brand awareness seems to be increasing or decreasing, and set up your data plan to be able to monitor this. The business goal might be to monitor and investigate further if/when a certain threshold is passed in the future. The business may want to push for further effort only when the rate falls to a level that suggests a need for process change.

Figure 6.9 summarizes various study designs often seen in use across the range of analytics problems. For each, note that the confidence in results increases as you control for factors.

Summary and Exercise

Take a business problem that you are facing and think about the ways that you could demonstrate with confidence that the results are true and not due to some external factor such as timing, novel situation, environment, or other issue.

As an exercise, specifically outline your theories and provide at least three reasons why they might not be true. Going through this

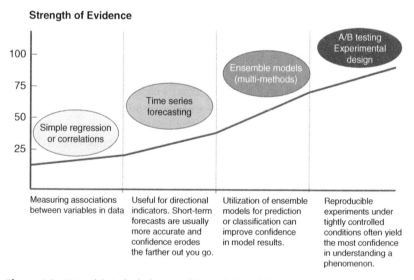

Figure 6.9 Potential study designs used in applied analytics settings

process is useful to avoid myopia, which often sets in as we limit our thinking. Hypothesis myopia occurs when you fixate on finding evidence to support just one theory at the expense of considering other explanations.

Regina Nuzzo (Nuzzo, 2015) proposed three additional techniques to help avoid the hypothesis myopia:

1. **Transparency**—this approach makes all of the data, code, and methods available such that others can reproduce the results and explore other theories. (Consider the use of notebooks as discussed later in Chapter 7.)

2. **Team of rivals**—by having others work in parallel on the same problem, the competiveness, in theory, sharpens your focus on the important elements of your analysis.

3. **Blind data analysis**—perhaps this approach has less merit in practice, but the idea is that analysts approach the data where key attributes are hidden so they don't know how close they are to desired results. The theory is that if they don't know the actual results, they will be less likely to find what they are unconsciously looking for.

Business Case Prioritization

At this point in the process, much of your background research is complete. This should help you think about the priority of the problem. That is, the effort that is put in to do this project should be proportional to its potential benefit.

This chapter has shown a full picture of how to design a problem, with a number of supporting activities that should be completed to some degree for each analysis project. At the same time, this structured approach is meant to be agile so that you can support your organization moving in the right direction while you decide just how important it is to go "down the rabbit hole" for any of these activities.

So let's ask, "Knowing *what* you know now, should this problem be solved?"

One way to do this is to use a risk assessment tool or project prioritization matrix. While there are a number of rubrics out there, what's most important is that all projects use the same one so that their priorities can be cross-compared.

Toolkit @
www.analyticslifecycletoolkit.com

Download a copy of the project prioritization matrix discussed here.

The project prioritization matrix (Table 6.4) can help you evaluate the importance, impact, and feasibility of solving a problem. Specifically, five criteria are defined here, but note that the specific criteria and the weight that you assign to analytics projects in your organization will likely be different. The criteria are those components that most commonly drive the need to change. The column titled

Table 6.4 Project prioritization matrix

Criteria	Definition	Assigned Weight	Criteria Met
Urgency	Is this a priority issue that needs to be addressed in the next 1 to 3 months (highly)? 6 to 12 months? (somewhat)	5	
Potential impact	Is it likely that addressing this critical issue will have a significant impact on one or more specific populations? Do you have a reason to believe you can be successful?	4	
Resources and feasibility	Are resources (funds, staff, expertise) either readily available or likely to be obtained? Are there resources external to your organization to leverage?	3	
Organizational readiness	Is this a critical issue identified as important by the organization? Is there momentum and desire to act on the results?	2	
Integration	Is there an opportunity to build on existing work? Will this duplicate effort elsewhere? Will this save time on other projects in the future?	1	
15–22	23–35	36–45	0
Low	Medium	High	Total Score

"Criteria Met" is then used to score the criteria on a scale from 1–3 where 3 indicates that the criteria is fully met.

The **business case** is the process within problem framing that positions the choices (generated hypotheses) that you have against alternatives. Earlier, we discussed some of the tools that can be used to help build the case, including the prioritization matrix and the 2 × 2 matrix.

 BUSINESS CASE

The business case is a justification for a proposed project or undertaking on the basis of its expected benefit.

Ultimately, the effort and scrutiny that goes into the business case rests on the shoulders of the problem statement, question design, potential options, and competing priorities. The business case should be a concise description of the problem and should be articulated in one or two sentences at most. It should describe

- What the project does
- How it impacts the strategic business objectives of the organization

It can also be used as a motivational tool that explains:

- Why the project is worth doing now
- The consequences of delaying or completely forgoing the project

While we often want to get into the details of the problem, it should be noted that you need to be able to synthesize this into something that you can use to present the case to management for prioritization. Figure 6.10 shows two tools that can be useful to present the prioritization.

Toolkit @
www.analyticslifecycletoolkit.com

Access these templates from the companion website.

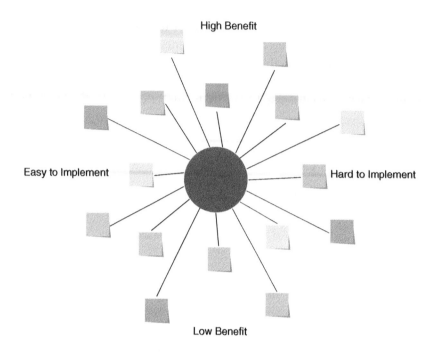

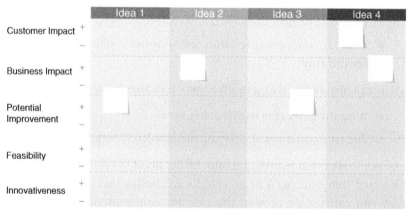

Figure 6.10 Visual presentation of the relative priorities for a project

The business context, assumptions, constraints, history, and the interactions or dependencies are important considerations that should be included in the business case; however, you will need to get to the essence of the issue.

With that said, I am a firm believer in being agile at this stage. You may invest several hours, weeks, or even months of work, and while you don't want to shortchange the business case, you certainly don't want to "boil the ocean" with documentation. Time and effort spent developing the case, outlining the scope, documenting assumptions, and providing supporting materials are based on the basic assumption that they are commensurate with the eventual benefit.

Ultimately, you need to answer the why, what, how, and who that are necessary to decide if it is worthwhile to continue a project. Given that problems are rarely in short supply and analytics professionals are typically stretched thin, appropriately right-sizing your business case effort can ensure the following:

- Important projects are prioritized (not just pet projects or those with the "loudest voice").
- The business will realize some benefit (although it is not likely that all analytics projects will turn into positive results).
- Stakeholders share the same understanding of the problem, the potential solutions and the plan of attack for what to explore further.

The business case is a structured process that integrates best practice decision making, program management, and risk management. It progressively builds an analytics case by identifying:

- The core problem
- The consequences of not addressing it
- Benefits to be gained by investing in its solution

The approach breaks the activity development process into phases that have decision gateways. As you will see in subsequent best practice areas, we will refer back to the business case and the problem statement many times to prevent any divergence from your targeted outcomes.

 TIP

Analytics problems can be applied to a variety of requests, projects, or products. Be sure to scale the effort appropriately for the problem impact.

Summary and Exercise

Effective prioritization of a project can benefit decision makers who must ultimately choose to fund your project over someone else's project or effort. Organizations face tradeoffs every day. Consider an analysis project that you are working on and complete the exercise below. Note that categories have been provided, but you can replace our evaluation criteria with your own.

Toolkit @
www.analyticslifecycletoolkit.com

Download a copy of the project prioritization matrix discussed here.

CHAPTER SUMMARY

> *Don't waste your time trying to control the uncontrollable, or trying to solve the unsolvable, or thinking about what could have been. Instead, think about what you can control and solve the problem you can solve with the wisdom you have gained from both your victories and your defeats in the past.*
>
> David Mahoney

The majority of activities in the problem framing best practice area involve laying the groundwork for an analytics project to be successful. Recognize, however, that these processes are to be considered throughout the Analytics Lifecycle, as each best practice will help refine the problem, the question, your theories, and your business case.

We have defined our problem, created a hypothesis that we intend to test, and detailed our success criteria. We also need to measure, monitor, and report on whether the analytics product was successful in achieving its desired outcomes.

At some point, we need to assess the performance of and value delivered by an analytics solution. This will be addressed in a future chapter.

Barriers to successful realization of analytics value can include:

- Competencies (lack of knowledge, skills, abilities, disposition)
- Data (availability, governance, quality)
- Technology
- Methodological and process
- Leadership and culture

This process depends heavily on the ecosystem of things going well. However, some best practices for solution evaluation include:

- **Problem definition:** Ensure that the problem is well defined, and that you know what the expected outcomes are and how you intend to measure success (operational measures).
- **Talent development:** Current competencies may not be sufficient to execute on the vision. Analytics requires ongoing talent development strategies.
- **Innovation:** Technology and methodological innovations are often required where there is little or no prior experience.
- **Measurement:** When measuring outcomes, both quantitative and qualitative assessments are necessary; go beyond statistical significance and look for real-world significance.
- **Change management:** Transforming a process, operations, or an organization necessarily involves change; expect change and build change management into the process.

We will explore the barriers to enabling change more fully in Chapter 11 and discuss talent development strategies in Chapter 12.

Learn More

The International Institute of Business Analysis has developed a comprehensive Business Analysis Competency Model that outlines the knowledge, skills, abilities, and personal characteristics required of the business analyst.

To learn more, visit the International Institute of Business Analysis to review the IIBA Business Analysis Competency Model ("IIBA Business Analysis Competency Model," 2016).

TOOLKIT SUMMARY

Best Practice Area:	Problem Framing	
Purpose:	What is the intent of this best practice area? The purpose of problem framing is to understand the problem, the challenge, or the opportunity we face and to create a foundation for its successful investigation and resolution.	
Key Competencies:	Knowledge, skills, abilities, and disposition	
What do we need to be good at?	▣ Business analysis ▣ Requirements gathering ▣ Business case development ▣ Critical thinking ▣ Divergent thinking	▣ Analysis and synthesis ▣ Data forensics ▣ Problem investigation ▣ Interviewing/ questioning
Inputs	Processes	Outputs
▣ List of identified problem(s) ▣ Stakeholder map ▣ Relevant structured and unstructured data ▣ Interviews/ questionnaire response	▣ Problem definition ▣ Root-cause investigation ▣ Hypothesis generation ▣ Question design ▣ Business case prioritization	▣ Problem statement ▣ User feedback ▣ Fishbone diagram (root causes) ▣ Opportunity map ▣ Project prioritization/ business case

	What should we know as a result of this best practice?
	▪ What is the problem?
	▪ How big is the problem?
	▪ Who does it impact?
Key Questions:	▪ Is it worth solving?
	▪ What might be causing the problem?
	▪ What data would be useful to understand the issue?
	▪ How should we plan to investigate this?
	▪ Should we continue?

REFERENCES

2x2 Matrices and the BCG matrix. *BootCamp Articles.* Retrieved from www.preplounge.com/en/bootcamp.php/case-cracking-toolbox/structure -your-thoughts/2x2-matrices-and-the-bcg-matrix.

A 35-year odyssey. *American Psychologist, 57*(9), 705–717. doi:10.1037//0003 -066X.57.9.705.

Affinity diagram. (2017). Retrieved from realtimeboard.com/examples/affinity -diagram/.

Doyle, A. C., & Paget, S. (1975). *The complete adventures and memoirs of Sherlock Holmes: a facsimile of the original Strand magazine stories, 1891-1893* (1st ed). New York: C. N. Potter: distributed by Crown.

IIBA Business Analysis Competency Model (2016). Retrieved from www.iiba .org/Careers/Business-Analysis-Competency-Model.aspx.

Kahneman, D. (2013). *Thinking, fast and slow.* New York: Farrar, Straus and Giroux.

Locke, E. A., & Latham, G. P. (2002). Building a Practically Useful Theory of Goal Setting and Task Motivation. *American Psychologist, 57,* 705–717.

Nuzzo, R. (2015). How scientists fool themselves and how they can stop. *Nature—a Weekly Journal of Science, 526,* 182–185.

Power, B. (2017). How Harley-Davidson used artificial intelligence to increase New York sales leads by 2,930%. *Harvard Business Review*. Retrieved from Harvard Business Review website: hbr.org/2017/05/how-harley-davidson -used-predictive-analytics-to-increase-new-york-sales-leads-by-2930.

Wadman, M. (2017). Ninety-nine percent of ailing NFL player brains show hallmarks of neurodegenerative disease, autopsy finds. *Science*. Retrieved from www.sciencemag.org/news/2017/07/ninety-nine-percent-ailing-nfl -player-brains-show-hallmarks-neurodegenerative-disease.

CHAPTER 7

Data
Sensemaking

The real voyage of discovery consists not in seeking new lands but seeing with new eyes.

Marcel Proust

PROCESS OVERVIEW

A well-formed question is the foundation for all analytics. The previous chapter on problem framing explained the need for articulating a good question and conveying a clear problem statement.

Data Exploration

During problem framing, preliminary **data exploration** is typically performed in support of data gathering in order to do the following:

- Determine how big the problem is.
- Support your root-cause analysis and hypothesis generation activities.
- Position the business case value for doing the project in the first place.

You don't always know whether a project will be approved, so digging too deep during problem framing isn't always warranted. Further, you may have considered a number of hypotheses—some of which could not be tested with a formal study (i.e., project or product). Once your problem is captured, your question clearly articulated, your hypotheses generated, and your study design conceptualized, you are ready to assess which data assets will be most useful for your work.

 TIP

Be careful of the temptation to stop your analytic efforts with a reasonable hypothesis in hand. There is a big difference between hypothesis generation and hypothesis testing. While your theory may be viable, you need to test it before claiming victory! You need to know … not just think you know.

It is worth noting at this point that people often approach the process of data discovery differently. In some cases, you might follow a prescribed path of problem framing that helps you develop a hypothesis, and then go into exploration. However, additional work may be needed to properly develop your theories. Both approaches are fair and in common use.

Case Study: Pitfalls of Untested Theories

Read more about the potential pitfalls of not testing your theories. See this article on how to avoid the pitfalls of data analysis (Bar-Joseph, 2013).

Note that in both traditional hypothesis testing and data-driven analysis (Figure 7.1), hypothesis testing still occurs, but it may happen after **data sensemaking** or after hypothesis generation.

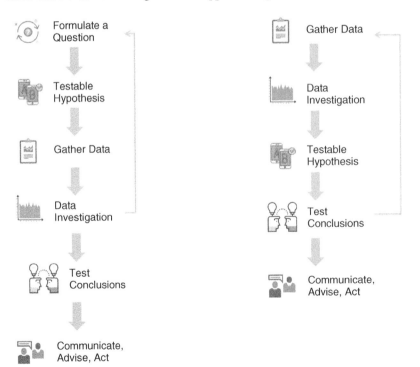

Figure 7.1 Hypothesis-based versus data-driven analysis

In Chapter 8, we will explore these two approaches in more depth, but remember that they both generally relate back to the scientific method. Key assumptions of these processes include the following:

- Knowledge is gained through empirical observation and measurement (study design).

- While we can never truly know, we can certainly demonstrate that our theories are potentially true (rejecting the null hypothesis).

- While we can never prove something with absolute certainty, empirical methods help us continue to refine what we know to be true (accepting the alternative hypothesis).

- What we know today may be proven wrong in the future; we make decisions every day with a degree of uncertainty.

> *If we wait for 100% of the data, we will lose our advantage on the battlefield because the enemy will have already moved on and we will not be agile. If we make decisions with too little data, it can also be disastrous. So I look for about 70% of the data necessary to make a decision. But by focusing on the problem, we can collect the right data quicker.*
>
> —General Colin Powell, responding to a question
> at a conference, about how much data was needed
> before making a decision (Ellens, 2016)

Why Do Sensemaking?

> *Only those data analysts who are given time to explore and analyze data thoughtfully and thoroughly are consistently successful.*
>
> Stephen Few, Perceptual Edge Newsletter (Few, 2015)

We perform data sensemaking to understand. We are trying to make sense of the world by exposing our theories to the realities of our data. In essence, we use data along with our perceptions, intuition and experience—guided by the rigor of the Analytics Lifecycle, as Stephen Few suggests.

The next chapter will discuss hypothesis testing, but before we can employ the tools of data science (statistics, mathematics, computer science) and determine the validity and significance of our findings, we first need to assemble data, explore it, determine its relevance, and discover patterns of utility.

PROCESS AREAS

Our discussion of data sensemaking and understanding is focused on the following key processes:

- Data identification and prioritization
- Data collection and preparation
- Data profiling and characterization
- Visual exploration

In order to support a data-driven, fact-based problem-solving approach with analytics, we will need to accurately define the problem in its simplest terms. By doing this, we can frame the problem as a question that can be answered with data.

Once we understand the problem, we use data sensemaking to begin to more fully explore the theories outlined in the previous best practice. This is where we begin our data exploration in earnest, by linking the problem and the processes that we worked to understand with the reality of the data we see as a result of those business processes (Figure 7.2).

Data Identification and Prioritization

One of the traps that I see data scientists often fall into is thinking they need some specific data—spending countless hours going after it and transforming it into something that can be used, only to find out that it had marginal value.

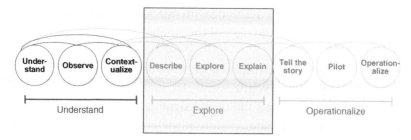

Figure 7.2 Data sensemaking focuses on describing, exploring, and explaining

 TIP

It is during the data exploration and understanding process that we reconcile the difference between the data we can get versus data that we want.

To avoid this trap, ask yourself, "If I had the data, what could I do?" In fact, I often recommend that people mock up the data they think they need and then test its utility. Randomly generated or handcrafted tables can go a long way in helping you visualize what is really needed.

Learn More

To learn 10 different techniques for simulating data in SAS, see Rick Wicklin's article "Ten Tips for Simulating Data with SAS" (Wicklin, 2015).

In this process, you must first articulate the data needed to help solve the problem. Second, you need to confirm that the data truly reflects the realities of the business (trace back to the operational workflows). This is necessary so that you can make certain that what you think has happened jives with what really happened and what you see in the data. Finally, it is important to verify the veracity of the data to prevent issues with interpretability, believability, and trust in your findings.

In organizations with a mature data pipeline, this is less critical, as the provenance of data and assumptions around governance should be built into the quality processes that feed your data exploration and data sensemaking processes.

But how do you know what data you need?

The choice of data will ultimately depend on the methods employed in your analysis. However, at this stage, remember that you are still trying to make sense of the data through exploration. The goal here is to understand the variables of interest (their distributions) and their associations (relationships) with other variables.

One technique that is useful in deciding what data you need is to "walk the halls" to see the process in action. Observe how people work, what software or systems they use, and shadow them as they work. You might do some of this in problem framing, but if not, this is the next best opportunity to see how people work and the digital footprint left behind. Ask lots of questions, observe, and test assumptions about what people say happens and what ends up in the persistent data.

Toolkit

Capture the process steps and the digital footprint in a journey map like the one available in the tools and templates.

At some point, you may realize that you can't get the data you need to test your theory—it's not available, or it's proprietary. So you have a decision to make—to revise your hypothesis or collect your own data. You may decide to collect data in other ways:

- Do posthumous coding of paper or other electronic data for information that currently does not exist in the right form.

- Use machine learning algorithms to classify data that is otherwise too unwieldy to deal with.

- Employ text mining against narratives, recordings, unstructured notes/fields, or other textual data to extract meaningful summaries that can be used in your analysis.

- Conduct surveys, focus groups, or interviews, and codify the data using a structured taxonomy useful for your data exploration.

Remember, you are trying to understand at this point, not test your theories, so there is no one right answer. The goal is to narrow down the things that you don't yet know, including your "known unknowns" and "unknown unknowns"—or as is commonly called, *unconscious ignorance*. Note: The concept is attributed to Noel Burch at Gordon International Training (Adams).

Finally, if you simply cannot know something, then all may not be lost. You can always consider Monte Carlo simulations or other types of decision analysis. Using these techniques, you can explore scenarios without necessarily having raw data. You essentially simulate possible outcomes using known probabilities, incidence, prevalence, and so on. and then use decision analysis tools to calculate outcomes.

Figure 7.3 shows a Markov microsimulation that I built to support health policy decision making.

Learn More

For a good summary of potential techniques to use when you don't have a good source of data, see "Deciding How to Decide" (Courtney, Lovallo, & Clarke, 2013).

Summary and Exercise

In sum, the data identification and prioritization process is critical to ensuring that you don't waste time going after data that might not prove useful. In the following exercise, consider an analytics effort that you are currently going through and answer the questions about the data sources you would like to use for your analysis.

 ACTIVITY EXERCISE

For your problem statement, answer the following questions:

What data do I think I need?

How will this be useful to my exploration of the phenomenon?

What assumptions must be true for this to work?

On a scale of 1 to 10, how important is getting this data to my success?

How feasible is getting this data?

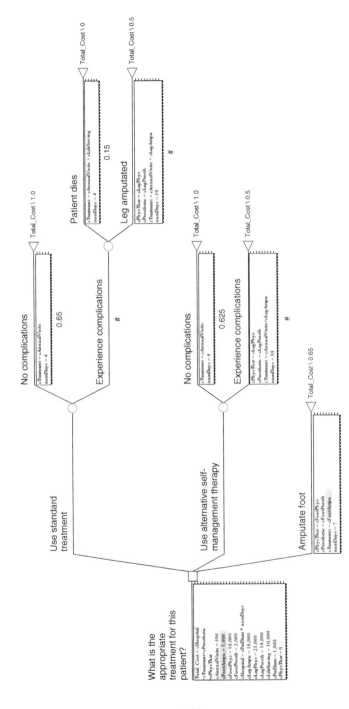

Figure 7.3 Example of Markov microsimulation for the comparison of various treatment strategies

Data Collection and Preparation

Acquiring data means putting your design for a measurement system (study design) into action. As outlined in the previous chapter, you can utilize qualitative and quantitative methods, research (e.g., experiments), sampling, or observational research (data already captured for other purposes, such as for operational processes).

In most organizations, data will be acquired from persistent data stores that exist for the express purpose of decision support and analysis. Having a mature data pipeline will accelerate the Analytics Lifecycle significantly since you won't need to spend time on these activities (Figure 7.4).

Your focus will be data that is already stored in systems such as corporate data warehouses, data marts, or data lakes, but realize that data collection can involve a number of methods, such as gathering information through visual observation, interviews, testing, and surveys. It is important to consider novel data that may need to be integrated at this point.

It is likely that not all of the data that could be useful for a specific problem will either be contained within your existing data stores or be structured exactly the way that you require. In this case, you will need to prepare and transform the data so that it is fit for use for a given problem. Successful organizations have employed an analytics sandbox environment for this specific purpose. The **sandbox** (Figure 7.5)

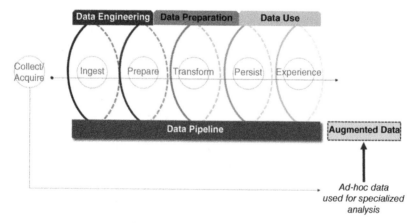

Figure 7.4 In analytics, we often augment analytics with data that lives outside of the traditional data pipeline.

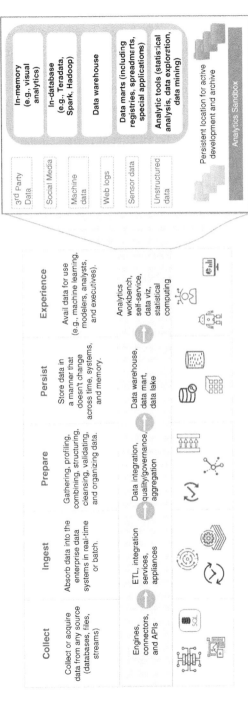

Figure 7.5 The analytics sandbox

195

is a place where you can acquire, transform, and store data for special projects or products, in a resource that meets the increased demands of a computationally intense environment required by the data scientist.

In this process area, you can use data management tools to extract, transform, and otherwise prepare data for analytics. These are often referred to as **data integration** tools that will vary, depending on the source of the data being ingested. For preparation, you can use everything from SQL or more complex data management or text categorization solutions. Several options for smaller datasets are available in desktop visualization packages that have limited data management capabilities.

A useful tool for helping you to plan your data transformation strategy is called **source-to-target mapping.** While most modern data integration solutions help support this process through metadata mapping, I have provided a spreadsheet tool that can be used to guide your logic. Note that for more complicated data transformation efforts, you may need a complete data conversion plan. This typically falls back to the stewards of the data pipeline rather than the analyst.

Toolkit

The source to target mapping spreadsheet can be used to help guide your decisions about what transformations must happen as you pull in data from a multitude of sources.

Hopefully, you will find that most of your data exists in a corporate data repository and is in the form needed for your data exploration. Beyond the physical activities of collection and transformation, you also need to make sure that you are doing your part to ensure data privacy and protection.

Structuring Data for Exploration

A common question is, "How should I structure my data for analysis and exploration?"

Unfortunately, there is no one perfect answer; it depends on several factors, including what tool you will use for data exploration, what questions you want to ask of the data, and what inferences you wish to make.

Most often, you will want as much detail in the data and at the lowest level possible (individual records), as it is much easier to summarize than it is to disaggregate. Some data exploration tools may require you to pre-summarize or structure the data differently. Similarly, you may need to sample the data, depending on the size and scale of the underlying data.

There are several potential data structures, and each have their own benefits and drawbacks based on the types of analysis that can be performed on this type of data structure. The process of structuring data for analysis is referred to as data modeling, which is a critical competency for those who want to be data scientists or data analysts. In my consulting work, I find that many people are not adequately prepared for this activity.

At this point you may need to think through how you want to structure the data. Data stored in long, skinny tables may be appropriate for time-series or event data such as web log data or laboratory values for patients whereas other types of data may be stored in wide tables. Consider what questions you have and whether we are seeking to understand:

- Differences between groups
- Associations between variables
- Predictions of future events
- Distribution of a single sample
- Time series, etc.

Summary and Exercise

Using your own business problem and the data sources that you identified, map out your data conversion strategy using the toolkit template provided in this section. While this may seem tedious, it will pay dividends if you can understand the transformations that need to occur before coding begins.

Data Profiling and Characterization

Part of the data sensemaking best practice is to actually explore the data. The decisions made in exploring, interpreting, and explaining data speaks to the true art of analysis. **Data profiling** is perhaps the most fun part of analytics—playing with data!

But a plan of attack is needed. It is often useful to both new analysts as well as experienced data scientists to have a set of questions when beginning to explore the data. As you will recall, during the process of data identification and prioritization, we did just that. It's time to pull those questions back out and use that to remind yourselves why you thought the data was a good idea in the first place. Data sensemaking gives you the space to do exactly that.

Data exploration and understanding methods are used to do the following:

- Summarize data (gestalt).
- Unearth patterns (and "weirdness").
- Develop theories that might address the problem.

Similarly, exploration (or exploratory data analysis) can be useful to do the following:

- Describe a single variable (center, spread, shape, outliers).
- Check data (for errors or other problems).
- Check assumptions (used in statistical analyses).
- Do forensic analysis (to unearth relationships).

In this process, we discuss the role of descriptive statistics as a tool for data understanding.

TIP

Comparisons, associations, and differences can be visualized, but descriptive statistics alone will provide no information about the certainty of our conclusions.

Profiling Data

One of the first things I like to do when exploring a new dataset is to get to know its personality, sometimes called the *culture* or *gestalt* of a dataset. What does it look like? Is it tall and lanky, short and chubby? Similarly, when we talk about a dataset, we might say that it is "left-brained" (i.e., full of big numbers or precise with lots of numbers to the right of the decimal). The data might be more logical, analytical, and objective. However, a dataset that is "right-brained" might have unstructured data like categorical values, long narratives, or open-ended responses to survey questions. Just as we say about "right-brained" people, we might consider this to be more intuitive, thoughtful, and subjective. Often, this data is left on the cutting room floor in our analytic process, but as tools for working with unstructured data become commonplace, we see increasing interest in these types of data.

 TIP

Understanding the structure of the data helps us get acquainted with it before we dig into the details.

Another part of assessing the personality of a data set involves assessing its quality. I view **data quality** through two lenses:

- *Technical quality*—the data fails the basic tests for valid values or has missing data. Specifically, we look for:
  - *Invalid data*—Are there incorrect values or overloaded fields?
  - *Missing data*—Is there an absence of content or of valid content?
- *Business quality*—often more critical and much harder to evaluate; some things to consider to determine data quality from a business perspective include:
  - *Relevance*—Is it meaningful?
  - *Accuracy*—Is the information accurate, or are errors introduced by "fat fingers" or laziness (duplicate records)?
  - *Consistency*—Do we see different business rules being applied?
  - *Timeliness*—Can we access it in the time frame that is useful?
  - *Comparable*—Can we compare values from different sources?
  - *Completeness*—Does the data tell the whole story?

In profiling data, you are assessing the utility of the data for addressing your business problem. To do that, you need to understand what is in the data. Profiling also entails assessing both business and technical quality. Specifically, look for the following:

- Missing values (nulls)
- Duplicate data
- Pattern detection (such as the pattern in a ten-digit phone number with hyphens)
- Invalid or out of range values (including univariate outliers such as a 118 year old middle school student)
- Multivariate outliers (using techniques like cluster analysis and distance measurements)

As data profiling for quality is beyond the scope of this topic, you may want to refer to other relevant resources. For example, see Svolba's book published by SAS on *Data Quality for Analytics* (Svolba, 2012).

Exercise in Data Quality

Data quality issues are all around us, but sometimes it is hard to truly understand the importance of data quality in analytics. In this exercise, you will perform some data quality analysis on the sample data that is provided (see the toolkit), then summarize what you find. In terms of data quality, the things you might typically look for include:

- *Accuracy*—Can you determine from the dataset whether the data was recorded correctly? Are there anomalies or nonsensical values? Examples might include a "pregnant male" or values that are out of the expected range.
- *Data glitches*—Do you see any typos, multiple formats representing the same data, missing/default values?
- *Completeness*—Can you determine whether all relevant data was recorded? What else would have been useful to tell the complete story that you are trying to convey?
- *Uniqueness*—Are there duplicate values?
- *Timeliness*—Do any measures of time present challenges or illustrate significant gaps in time? For example, lab results that don't seem to relate to an encounter?

■ *Consistency*—Do you see issues with the data not making sense in some way, such as a pregnant male?

Toolkit @
www.analyticslifecycletoolkit.com

Visit the companion website for a link to the data quality exercise referenced here.

Upon reflection, what was most challenging about this exercise? Was it finding a tool that could help you perform the analysis easily? Perhaps your biggest challenge was in understanding where the data came from or what the fields mean.

One of the competencies that every analyst must have is a solid understanding of the workflow that created the data. It would be nearly impossible to address most of the business quality questions without understanding the business context and workflows.

Characterizing the Data—Exploring a Single Variable

Once you have a feel for the "personality" of a dataset, it's time to understand just what's in the data. To do this, start with exploring one variable at a time, and later, the relationships between variables.

When you look at one variable at a time, you are essentially "characterizing" the data; that is, you are understanding how the values are distributed for that variable in order to assess its value and overall utility in solving the problem. For those grimacing at the slight reminder of statistical distributions, yes, we are talking about that distribution. But fear not, this is not a boring lesson on probability distributions!

TIP

Distribution of a variable means:

■ What values the variable takes, and
■ How often the variable takes those values.

Distributions are used in descriptive statistics to understand the type of variable under examination: categorical versus quantitative (Figure 7.6). The type of variable is one of the factors that determine

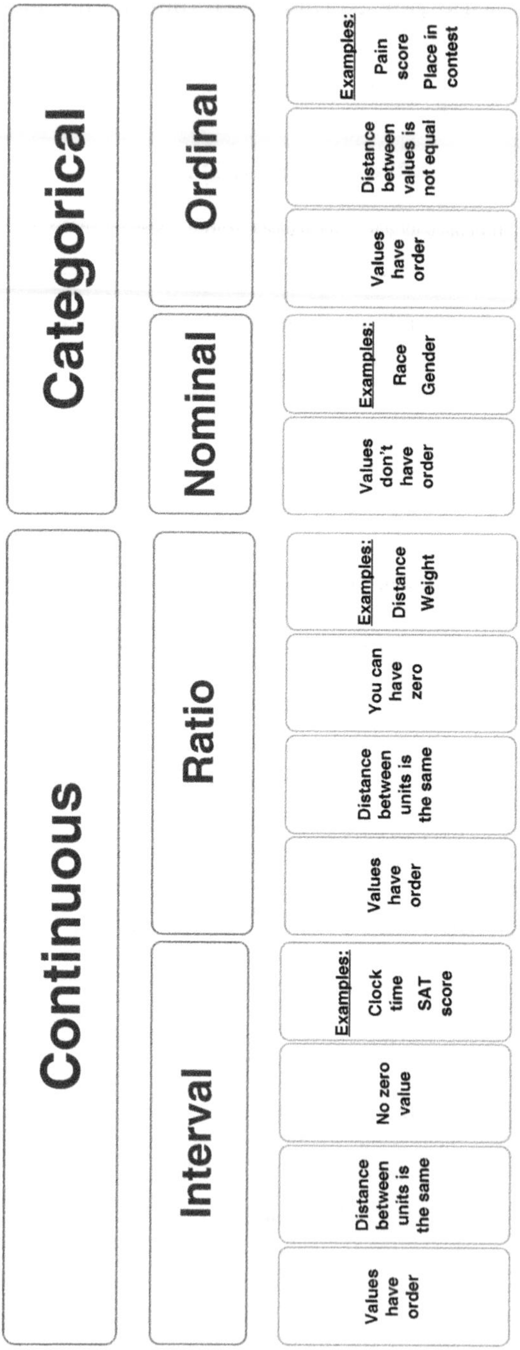

Figure 7.6 Types of variables

what tests you can use later to determine whether the relationships, associations or differences are significant. For now, think of distributions as how the variable looks. *Note: I prefer the term variable, but you can use column, attribute, or feature.*

When making comparisons, talking about differences or associations, and inferring something about those differences, you must be confident that the difference/ relationship is meaningful. You will often see this referred to as statistical significance. The type of variable directly relates to the choices of descriptive and inferential statistical methods that can be used.

There is not a single best method to determine the distribution of a variable, and this is the art of data exploration. Categorical variables have the fewest choices since statistical summaries are limited on categorical data. These are typically character data but can be expressed as a number; for example, you may have gender coded as 0, 1, 2, etc. But that numeric coding does not mean you can treat the data as an actual number. To calculate an average from these data, for example, would be meaningless.

There are two types of categorical variables:

1. *Nominal*—There is no natural ordering among the categories such as gender, eye color, political party, or ethnicity.

2. *Ordinal*—There is a natural order among the categories but the distance between values is undeterminable. Examples might include ranking scales (low, medium, high), letter grades (A to F), or placement in a contest (first, second, third).

When examining the distribution of a categorical variable, you can use a frequency distribution if you want a numeric summary of the distribution for both nominal and ordinal. Note that ordinal variables may be stored as numbers but cannot be used in traditional mathematical or statistical summaries. However, you can calculate median and percentiles for ordinal numeric data, but not for nominal.

If you wish to summarize the distribution of a categorical variable visually, you can use a bar chart, pie chart, or pictogram.

There are two types of continuous variables:

- *Interval*—the values have order and the distance between units is the same, but there is not a zero value. Examples include SAT scores or miles per hour (MPH)—the difference between 100 MPH and 90 MPH is the same difference as between 70 MPH and 60 MPH.

- *Ratio*—A ratio has all the properties of an interval variable, and also has a clear definition of 0.0; examples are variables like height, weight, or temperature in Kelvin.

Unlike categorical variables, continuous variables have a wider range of options for summarizing distribution. You can use statistical summaries such as these:

- Frequency distribution
- Median and percentiles
- Mean, standard deviation, standard error of the mean

However, you cannot calculate a ratio or coefficient of variation for interval data.

Visually, you can create a number of types of graphs, including box-plot, histogram, stemplot, and the dotplot.

In the mind map shown in Figure 7.7, we demonstrate the types of analysis used based on your intentions.

Finally, when examining a single quantitative variable, you should consider the features of its distribution, as shown in Figure 7.8.

Table 7.1 summarizes the meaning of the terms in Figure 7.8.

Characterizing the Data—Two or More Variables at a Time

When posing a question, we usually consider more than one variable. In exploratory data analysis, we often refer to the roles they play in the relationship. For example, if I want to understand whether incidence of heart disease differs by gender, then gender is the **explanatory variable** and heart disease is the **response variable**.

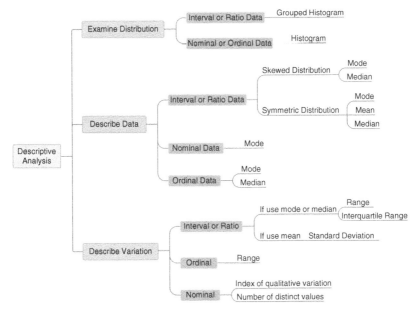

Figure 7.7   Descriptive analysis options

Distributions of Quantitative Variables

We should consider the following features of the Distribution for One
Quantitative Variable:

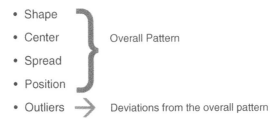

- Shape
- Center   } Overall Pattern
- Spread
- Position
- Outliers → Deviations from the overall pattern

Figure 7.8   Distribution of quantitative variables

Table 7.1 Measures important while examining the distributions of quantitative variables

Term	Definition	Example
Shape	Refers to the symmetry/skewness of the distribution and the peakedness, or the number of peaks (modes) the distribution has. Center of the distribution is often used to represent a typical value.	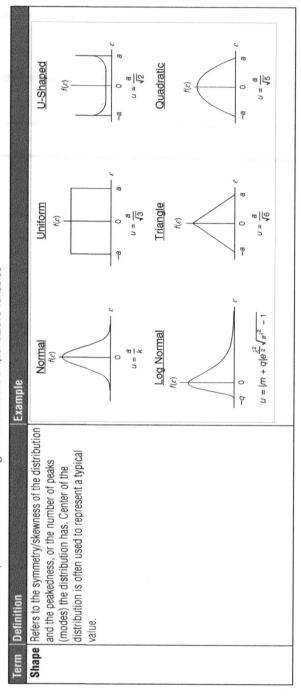

| Spread | The three most common numerical measures for the spread of a distribution include:

■ The range of the data is an intuitive measure of variability. The range is exactly the distance between the smallest data point (min) and the largest one (max).

■ Inter-quartile range (IQR) measures the variability of a distribution by giving us the range covered by the *middle* 50% of the data.

■ The standard deviation gives the average (or typical distance) between a data point and the mean.

From looking at the histogram, you can approximate the smallest observation (min), and the largest observation (max), and thus approximate the range. | 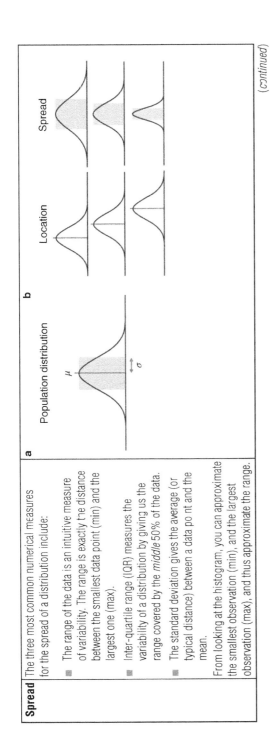 |

Table 7.1 *(continued)*

Term	Definition	Example
Position	Measures of position also allow us to compare values from different distributions. ■ *Percentiles*—The *P*-th percentile can be interpreted as a location in the data for which approximately *P*% of the other values in the distribution fall below the *P*-th percentile and (100 − *P*)% fall above the *P*-th percentile. ■ *Five-number summary*—The combination of the five numbers (min, Q1, Median, Q3, Max) provides a quick numerical description of both the center and spread of a distribution. ■ *Standardized scores (Z-scores)*—The standardized scores tell us how many standard deviations the raw score for that individual deviates from the mean and in what direction.	
Outliers	Outliers are observations that fall outside the overall pattern.	

208

TIP

When we seek to understand a relationship between two variables we tend to classify them into:

- Response variable—the outcome or dependent variable
- Explanatory variable—the variable that claims to explain, predict, or affect the response (independent variable, predictor variable, or covariate)

Just as shown above, the type of variable matters in the methods you can use to explore the relationship. There are four basic types of comparisons that can be made, depending on whether the response variable is categorical or continuous, and whether the explanatory variable is categorical or continuous.

Each of the four scenarios will determine what methods can be used to understand the relationship.

- C → C
  - Sample question: Summarize the data for two categorical variables into a 2 × 2 summary table.
- C → Q
  - Sample question: Compare the distributions of a continuous variable for two more groups.
- Q → C
  - Sample question: Compare the distribution of a continuous variable across the values of a categorical variable.
- Q → Q
  - Sample question: Compare the distributions of two quantitative variables

Note: We will explore this concept further in Chapter 8.

TIP

When confronted with a research question that involves exploring the relationship between two variables, the first and most crucial step is to determine which of the four cases represents the data structure of the problem.

During the data sensemaking process, characterization of the relationships between two variables is an important part of the discovery process as this helps you understand and appreciate the potential interactions that occur between data elements. At this point, you are looking for associations. Depending on whether your response (dependent) variable is categorical or continuous, you can also use statistical tests to determine the strength of the relationship. When trying to assess an association between a categorical explanatory (independent) variable and a categorical response (dependent) variable, you can use Chi-square or Fisher's exact tests. When assessing the association between two continuous variables, you can use correlation or regression.

Exercise on Exploring Data

The process of exploring data can be challenging at first. However, one technique that has proven useful time and time again is to ask people to find a story worthy enough to share. This exercise is derived from the work of Rahul Bhargava from Data Therapy based on one of his projects at the MIT Media Lab's Center for Civic Media (Finding a Story in Data, n.d.).

Consider the following types of stories that you can use to guide your data exploration process:

- *Interaction stories*—Interesting patterns may emerge when you look for the connections in things—under what conditions things hold true.

- *Comparison stories*—Find interesting patterns in the data based on the differences or similarities in things.

- *Change stories*—Discover changes over time that are interesting.

- *Personal stories*—Make a personal connection to the data that people can relate to.

- *Factoid stories*—Find one thing interesting about the data such as extreme values.

Using the toolkit, find your story by using a data set of your choosing. If you don't have one, the reference guide has some suggestions.

Toolkit @
www.analyticslifecycletoolkit.com

Download a copy of "Finding Your Data Story" reference guide and exercises.

Visual Exploration

Much of the activity in the data sensemaking best practices area will take advantage of tools that can be used to visualize a distribution of a single variable or explore relationships between two or more variables. I resist the temptation to define visual exploration as a separate process from data profiling and characterization, since visual methods are used heavily throughout. However, visual exploration is listed as a separate process to avoid criticism and to call attention to the fact that data sensemaking can be aided significantly by visualization tools.

 VISUAL DATA DISCOVERY

Visual data discovery is defined as the process of data profiling aided by interactive, highly agile visualization. We use visual data discovery to explore rather than to explain.

It is important to say that **visual data discovery** (also referred to as visual analytics) is a critical toolset in the Analytics Lifecycle. Visual methods are used to do the following:

- Perform visual data discovery of unknown data.
- Identify relationships in the data.
- Create visualizations that help express the context and insight of the data.

Chapter 9 includes an in-depth discussion of data visualization in support of storytelling and results explanation.

MAINTAINING AN ANALYTICS JOURNAL

Take time now to jot down your observations in your analysis notebook. If you have not started a notebook yet, this is the perfect time. Science has a long tradition of keeping a record of what happened. Much like early explorers and space travelers kept a log, start keeping your own.

Notebook examples to consider include:

- Rutter: en.wikipedia.org/wiki/Rutter_(nautical)
- Captains Log: apiratesportal.com/2012/10/14/the-captains-log/
- Engineering design notebook: www.sciencebuddies.org/science -fair-projects/engineering-design-process/engineering-design -notebook
- Learning portfolio: eportfolioreview.wordpress.com/eportfolio -list/
- Inventor's notebook: en.wikipedia.org/wiki/Inventor%27s_note book
- Laboratory notebook: en.wikipedia.org/wiki/Lab_notebook

In the analytics space, there are even tools that can help you capture your analytic journey while you explore data. Examples include Jupyter Notebook ("Jupyter Home Page,") and JMP Journal (Derby, 2013).

Consider the benefits of capturing your analytics experiences:

- Develop a living portfolio of your work—useful as you look back to see what you have learned or accomplished.
- Provide evidence of the robustness of your processes.
- Demonstrate that you have done your due diligence (and prevent accusations of research misconduct).
- Aid others in understanding (and potentially following) your process should the need arise.

TIP

An analytics notebook is a record of both physical processes as well as mental activities.

For the purposes of capturing the analytics process, the types of things that you should consider documenting in your notebook include:

- Data acquisition and transformation
    - Source of data
    - Data definitions
    - Data handling and transformation steps
    - Business rules and calculations
- Process
    - What you did
    - When you did it (including timelines for requesting and receiving data)
    - Why you did it
- Methods
    - Quantitative methods or algorithms
    - Statistical analyses
    - Assumptions
- Intangibles
    - Feedback or direction provided by others
    - Observations of results (expected and unexpected)
    - Interpretations and conclusions
    - Next steps

CHAPTER SUMMARY

The best practice area of data sensemaking includes a number of processes that help us identify and prioritize data, acquire and transform the data, and understand its content. This chapter outlined these processes in a way that perhaps was novel and not a recasting of prior work in statistics or visualization. Often times, statistics can be daunting. Lest we get too complicated and you start running for the hills with all of this talk about statistics, let's pause and summarize what we have learned so far:

- Profiling a dataset helps you understand its personality and whether this data is going to be useful for us in solving your problem.

- The type of variable determines what methods you can use to profile the data; for example, you cannot calculate measures such as mean or standard deviation on a categorical variable.

- The distribution of a categorical variable is summarized using a visual display such as a pie chart or bar chart, along with numerical measures such as frequency table of category counts and percentages.

- For the distribution of a quantitative variable we describe the overall pattern of the data (shape, center, spread), and any deviations from the pattern (outliers).

- Outliers are data points that fall outside the overall pattern of the distribution and need further research before continuing the analysis.

- When describing the shape of a distribution, one should consider the symmetry/skew of the distribution and the peakedness (modality), which refers to the number of peaks in the distribution.

By profiling and characterizing data, you can assess their suitability for helping to provide clarity in solving a problem or understanding a phenomenon. The activities included in the data sensemaking best practice area typically include:

- Inspecting data to understand what we have and how it is organized

- Evaluating the current quality of the data and identify possible issues

- Determining the overall utility of the data for addressing the problem
- Assessing other data that may be useful when combined

Questions that you should be asking yourself at this point include:

- What have I learned?
- Does this help me understand the phenomenon better than before?
- Do my theories about what might be impacting, influencing, or causing my problem have more clarity?

Toolkit @ www.analyticslifecycletoolkit.com

Access articles, best practices, and a sample template for maintaining your analysis notebook

---

TOOLKIT SUMMARY

Best Practice Area:	Data Sensemaking
Purpose:	*What is the intent of this best practice area?* The purpose of data sensemaking is to more fully understand the conditions under which the problem happens and to explore potential theories using data.
Key Competencies:	Knowledge, skills, abilities, and disposition
What do we need to be good at?	▪ Data discovery ▪ Analytics methods ▪ Visual exploration ▪ Theory generation ▪ Data manipulation and management ▪ Outlier detection ▪ Data summarization ▪ Evaluating tradeoffs ▪ Critical thinking

(continued)

Inputs	Processes	Outputs
■ Enterprise data access ■ Tertiary data sources ■ Problem framing outputs (e.g., problem statement)	■ Data identification and prioritization ■ Data collection and preparation ■ Data profiling and characterization ■ Visual exploration	■ Prioritized list of data assets ■ Assessment of data ■ Preliminary analysis (including summary presentations) ■ Analytics journal
Key Questions:	What should we know as a result of this best practice? ■ Based on our understanding of the problem, what data is most useful to support its resolution? ■ How confident do we feel that the data can support a solution? ■ What do we see as potential solutions? ■ How do we plan to test our theories? ■ Which analytic methods are going to be useful?	

REFERENCES

Adams, L. (2015). Learning a new skill is easier said than done. Retrieved from www.gordontraining.com/free-workplace-articles/learning-a-new-skill-is-easier-said-than-done/#.

Bar-Joseph, U. (2013). Big data = big trouble: How to avoid 5 data analysis pitfalls. *Search Engine Watch*. Retrieved from searchenginewatch.com/sew/how-to/2289574/big-data-big-trouble-how-to-avoid-5-data-analysis-pitfalls.

Courtney, H., Lovallo, D., & Clarke, C. (2013). Deciding how to decide. *Harvard Business Review* (November).

Derby, N. (2013). The JMP Journal: an analyst's best friend. Retrieved from www.mwsug.org/proceedings/2013/JM/MWSUG-2013-JM03.pdf.

Ellens, R. (2016). Data and decision making. Retrieved from www.gpstrategies .com/blog/data-decision-making.

Few, S. (2015). Data sensemaking requires time and attention. Retrieved from www.perceptualedge.com/blog/?p=2052.

Finding a story in data (n.d.). Retrieved from https://datatherapy.org/activities/ activity-finding-a-story-in-data/.

Jupyter Home Page. Retrieved from jupyter.org.

Svolba, G. (2012). *Data quality for analytics using SAS*. Cary, NC: SAS Institute.

Wicklin, R. (2015). Ten tips for simulating data with SAS. Paper presented at the SAS Global Forum, Dallas, TX. Retrieved from support.sas.com/ resources/papers/proceedings15/SAS1387-2015.pdf.

CHAPTER 8

Analytics Model Development

We may say most aptly that the Analytical Engine weaves algebraic patterns just as the Jacquard loom weaves flowers and leaves.

Ada Lovelace, English Mathematician (1815–1852)

PROCESS OVERVIEW

The purpose for describing analytics model development is not to recast the whole of quantitative science including statistical methods, machine learning algorithms, artificial intelligence, text analytics, operations research, or other mathematical endeavors. There is little doubt that analytics methods will continue to change at an increasing pace, making a comprehensive review of the analytical methods nearly impossible at any point in time. Furthermore, there are dozens if not hundreds of books on each of the analytics methods described here. Instead, the focus will be on the overarching **best practices** used in analysis, and on the people and process aspects of analytics model development.

The goal is to provide a framework for how to consider these techniques so that they are accessible and understandable by a wider audience of data champions, and to demystify them so that others may participate more fully in the development, testing, and use of analytics models.

Typically, treatments of analytics methods tend to focus on the tactics of the method and the hype of machine learning, which can cause confusion. For example, I was approached recently by a client about helping with a "predictive modeling" problem. After some discussion, it was clear that this was not a prediction problem at all, but, rather, a need to understand a phenomenon so that we could understand—at least directionally—where we needed to look. That is, they wanted to understand what is causing the issue—it was really a **sensemaking** problem.

It's easy to confuse the **analysis** method with the problem type. Therefore, it is critical to craft your problem statement in a clear and

219

concise manner so that you have a shared understanding of the problem you're dealing with and classify it accordingly.

A graphic commonly used by technology vendors and authors depicts the **analytics maturity** of an organization. While there are variations of this graphic, the essence is the same—analytics maturity is assumed to be a function of:

- The type of analytics used—descriptive, diagnostic, forensic, predictive, prescriptive, and cognitive
- The temporal focus—past, present, or future
- The technologies used—reports, queries, alerts, statistical analysis, forecasting, prediction, optimization
- The competitive advantage (or value) and degree of intelligence

 TIP

The use of specific analytics methods should not be the measure of maturity. Instead, maturity should be measured by the speed with which an organization can solve complex problems and the ability to integrate analytics findings into everyday processes.

These overly simplistic models seem to imply that only sophisticated organizations that plan to use analytics for a strategic purpose can get there, first by building out lower-end capabilities such as self-service reporting, and confuse techniques (e.g., machine learning) with temporal perspective (hindsight versus foresight.) In fact, in one depiction of this, the author had the concepts of data governance and end user adoption as "foundational" to analytics maturity. This is both unrealistic and challenging for even the most sophisticated organizations.

My personal belief is that some of these depictions serve marketing purposes and oversimplify the analytics landscape and contribute to executive confusion. I've seen organizations that never fully adopt business intelligence or deploy self-service capabilities well, but have done great work in developing machine learning **algorithms** that solve real-world problems.

Instead, I propose a view of analytics maturity that considers five vectors of maturity as expressed in Figure 8.1. We need to work hard

Figure 8.1 Vectors of analytics maturity

to develop capabilities across all five dimensions and build capabilities, as we are able, in each.

1. *Strategic alignment*—The degree to which analytics is aligned to the organization's strategy.

2. *Information management*—Data governance and how institutional knowledge is managed across the organization.

3. *Advanced analytics*—Creation, socialization, and operationalization of analytics insights.

4. *Data privacy and security*—Tactics for governing access and dissemination of data and its derived intelligence.

5. *Data management*—Deploying the roadmap around data strategy, including its storage and expectations for quality.

We need to strive to improve our analytics capabilities on all fronts. Analytics capability maturity relies on a strong foundation of data and a culture of curiosity and innovation.

Table 8.1 outlines a number of symptoms related to deficiencies found in each of the five vectors of analytics maturity.

Table 8.1 Major issues in achieving analytics maturity

Category	Common Issues
Strategic Alignment	■ We don't have the resources to meet the analytics demands of the business.
	■ Our culture doesn't promote sharing.
	■ Change management is often overlooked or under-resourced.
	■ Our leadership does not understand the value of analytics.
	■ Some groups get all the attention/resources and others are underserved; a "haves" and "have-nots" situation.
	■ We don't have a formal mechanism for talent development in our analytics staff.
	■ We need a good process for managing and measuring decisions and their impact on strategy.
Data Management	■ Our data is inconsistent, depending on who you talk to or where you go to get it.
	■ By the time the points of data are available, they are useless.
	■ We might have the data, but we can't get to it.
	■ It takes too long to get a new data source added to the enterprise data warehouse (EDW).
	■ We don't have a holistic view of the patient/customer/member, but rather, we have data silos based on our internal systems.
	■ There is an overreliance on Excel for data management.
	■ We don't have visibility into when new data sources will be integrated into the EDW.
Information Management	■ I didn't know we had that data.
	■ How can I be sure that this data is accurate?
	■ We don't have a standard set of terms/business rules/definitions for data elements. Which definition should I use for my report?
	■ I can't find the person responsible for ensuring that this data is accurate/complete/corrected.
	■ Individuals perform ad-hoc data quality efforts as needed and manually fix identified data issues; data issues are identified based on their usability for a specific business task.
	■ Too much time is spent doing "mundane" tasks rather than meaningful analysis.
	■ We lack confidence in our analytics results; if two different people were asked to perform the same analysis, we would likely get two different answers.

Table 8.1 *(Continued)*

Category	Common Issues
Advanced Analytics	▪ We don't have the skills internally.
	▪ We don't have a process to determine whether our models are working.
	▪ We don't have a process for ensuring that we learn from the work that our teams are doing.
	▪ There is no accountability for ensuring that action is taken and results are measured.
	▪ We have lots of dashboards but have no way of actually measuring the impact of action.
	▪ While we have canned dashboards and reports, it is not easy to develop and share new visualizations for insights.
Data Privacy and Security	▪ We are constantly finding protected data "lying around" on thumb drives, network directories, laptops, SharePoint, Excel.
	▪ We cannot share data internally because the policies are too restrictive.
	▪ We have no standard/consistent way of scrubbing, anonymizing, de-identifying our data.
	▪ Datasets that contain private information are not encrypted.
	▪ We do not have a mechanism to measure or monitor the risks of internal and external analytics processes.

Analytics Models Defined

It is useful to talk about what we mean by **analytics model development**. In this context, it means to translate a real-world phenomenon into mathematical relationships by examining the information that has been collected in ways that reveal relationships, patterns, and trends.

A model should help us explain a system and study the effects of different components, and to make predictions about behavior ("Definition: Analytical Modeling," 2017).

For example, if we want to understand the relationship between the amount of time that students spend studying for a test and their grades, we might use simple regression. In the plot shown in Figure 8.2, a simple linear model "fits" the data.

The model helps us translate what we see in our sample into a formula useful for describing the relationship as well as for prediction.

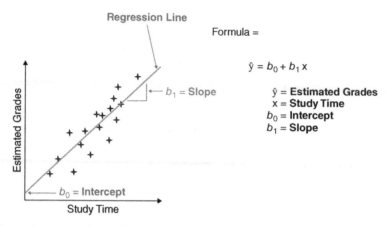

Figure 8.2 Regression model for predicting grades based on study time

In Figure 8.2, the line that goes through the observations is the regression line. Essentially, this line represents the optimal fit, and the resulting formula can be used to predict the grade if we know how much time a student spends studying.

Using the mathematical relationship from a regression model can help us make predictions about grades, depending on how long a student prepares for the test (Figure 8.3).

Using the regression plot, we can predict that a student who studies between seven and eight hours should get a grade of about 90 percent. It should be noted that regression is just one of a wide variety of modeling methods, but they all share a common goal—to specify a mathematical relationship that describes a response variable in terms of other variables.

Model Development

The process of deciding how to best characterize relationships into a model is referred to as **model development**. The most commonly used (and cited) methodology for model development is the Cross Industry Standard Process for Data Mining, commonly known by its acronym CRISP-DM (Figure 8.4) ("Cross Industry Standard Process for Data Mining," n.d.).

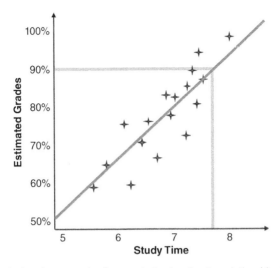

Figure 8.3 Plotting the regression line can help visualize the relationships between two variables

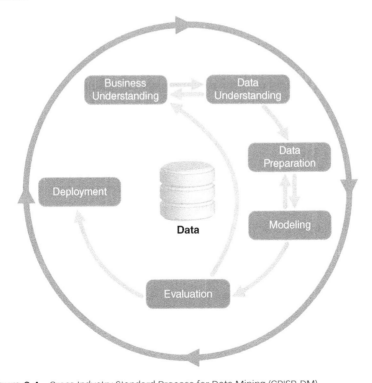

Figure 8.4 Cross Industry Standard Process for Data Mining (CRISP-DM)

There are, of course, variants of analytics model development processes, methodologies, and frameworks, including:

- IBM Analytics Solutions Unified Method for Data Mining/ Predictive Analytics (ASUM-DM) (Haffar, 2015)
- Microsoft Team Data Science Process (TDSP) ("Using the Team Data Science Process with Azure Machine Learning," n.d.)
- SAS SEMMA Model (Sample, Explore, Modify, Model, and Assess) ("SEMMA," n.d.)
- KDD Process (Fayyad, Piatetsky-Shapiro, Smyth, & Uthurusamy, 1996)

Ana Azevedo and M. F. Santos compared several of these methodologies in a paper (Azevedo & Santos, n.d.), but many of them were built well before the machine learning era of analytics and before the more agile approaches to development, except for the recent additions by IBM and Microsoft.

While there is no absolute prescription for the process of model development, it can be useful to reflect on two often competing but valid perspectives that inform the model development process and support a model which best suits the organizational culture.

The two cultures of analytics were first described in 2001 when Leo Breiman wrote a seminal paper titled "Statistical Modeling: The Two Cultures" (Breiman, 2001), where he described two cultures:

1. The data modeling culture assumes that the data are generated by a given stochastic data model and they seek to understand the relationship "inside the black box."

2. The algorithmic modeling culture uses algorithmic models and treats the data mechanism as unknown and therefore considers the inside of the box complex and unknown.

The ideologies of these two perspectives are reflected in Figure 8.5.

Breiman estimated at that time that 98 percent of all statisticians fit into culture 1 and that culture 2 represented only a small part of the traditional statistics community—perhaps what we consider data scientists today. Note that Breiman preferred the latter, arguing that statisticians rely too heavily on data modeling (formal and deductive),

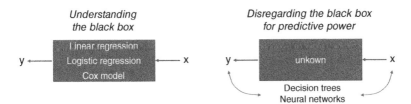

Figure 8.5 Statistical modeling cultures: Data modeling culture vs. algorithmic modeling culture

and that machine learning techniques are making progress by relying instead on the predictive accuracy of models. The argument was essentially that **statistics** emphasizes inference, whereas **machine learning** emphasizes prediction.

Learn More

Examine the fight between statistics and machine learning at Brendan O'Connor's blog (O'Connor, 2009).

After a decade and a half, we still see that culture conflict play out in today's organizations. Recently, I heard a senior director lamenting over the fact that she doesn't need a statistician to develop her predictive model but, rather, a "data sciencey" type who doesn't need to have clean data or to validate all of the assumptions—she just wanted someone who could solve the problem.

Galit Shmueli characterized these cultures a bit differently when she described the difference between explanatory modeling versus predictive modeling (Shmueli, 2010). Specifically, she noted that statistical models used in a number of disciplines (e.g., economics, psychology) are used for causal explanation and therefore inherently possess predictive power. This is contrasted with fields such as bioinformatics and natural language processing, where the focus lies with empirical prediction and less focus on causal explanation.

We often see these two approaches play out in practice as either hypothesis-driven analytics or discovery-driven analytics.

Hypothesis-Driven Analytics

Hypothesis-driven analytics is common in environments where objective research findings are regulated and often scrutinized (e.g., clinical trials, health-care research). These organizations follow a predefined framework that reflects its aims, objectives, and interests. Often criticized for its lack of curiosity or inventiveness, the hypothesis-driven method focuses on addressing specific questions that are raised a priori.

 TIP

Hypothesis-driven analytics uses a hypothesis to guide analysis and testing using deductive reasoning.

Consider the example of drug trials. In these studies, various interventions or dosages are varied with the intent of asking the specific question about a certain drug's efficacy or safety. The researcher captures the data by recruiting subjects with strict inclusion and exclusion criteria, and tests under conditions that are highly controlled (and perhaps artificial). The experiment is intentionally focused on removing conditions that might affect outcomes, like comorbidities, polypharmacy, and factors such as age in an attempt to say with certainty that the effect was caused by the intervention. This approach allows the researcher to focus on particular answers and abandon the rest.

The downside of hypothesis-driven analytics in business settings is that we often don't know where the problem lies or how to fix it without first exploring the data—with or without the use of advanced analytics tools. Further, the data points are rarely structured as precisely as that which is preferred by the traditional statistician.

Discovery-Driven Analytics

Discovery-driven (or data-driven) **analytics** is an approach that is exploratory in nature and encourages discovery over confirmation. We mentioned this in the previous chapter in the discussion of sensemaking. In trying to make sense of the world, we use traditional methods of statistics and data visualization to explore, which enables us to consider the possibility that we may not understand what might be hidden in the data. Exploratory analysis allows for the creation of new impressions that help shape our understanding in different and unexpected ways.

 TIP

- Hypothesis-driven analysis begins a proposition (theory), which then seeks to validate the truthfulness of the proposition.
- Discovery-driven analysis seeks to finds patterns, associations, and relationships among the data in order to uncover facts that were previously unknown.

Utilizing Multiple Approaches

Both exploratory and hypothesis-driven analysis have their challenges. In the case of exploratory analysis, we look for a potential relationship (or association, predictor, etc.) based on conducting many tiny experiments with the data. These experiments can take the form of visual analysis, statistical testing, or data mining. Often referred to as "fishing expeditions," they can often bear fruit, especially with automated discovery methods such as data mining or machine learning. Unfortunately, this approach can lead to false positives (type I errors).

An example of this was demonstrated over 20 years ago, in a 1997 Business Week commentary by Peter Coy titled "He Who Mines Data May Strike Fool's Gold" (Coy, 1997). The article described a case of data mining gone awry and the fact that patterns will occur by chance. In describing the pitfalls of data mining, Coy cited an example from David J. Leinweber, PhD, who "sifted through a United Nations CD-ROM and discovered that historically, the single best predictor of the Standard & Poor's 500-stock index was butter production in Bangladesh." The lesson to learn according to Coy is that a "formula that happens to fit the data of the past won't necessarily have any predictive value." See also the March 1998 *Money* magazine article "What's the Stock Market Got to Do with the Production of Butter in Bangladesh?"

We can gird ourselves against the potential pitfalls of exploratory analysis by using methods to help control for multiple comparisons, with techniques that include:

- Expected false discovery rate (FDR)
- Family-wise error rate
- False coverage rate (FCR)
- Experiment-wise error rate
- Closed testing procedures
- Bonferroni corrections

Learn More

To learn more about multiple comparison problems, see the article "Multiple Comparisons Problem" ("Multiple Comparisons Problem," n.d.)

I believe that we should always follow exploratory analysis with appropriate hypothesis-driven approaches. That is, after discovery, test the relationships for generalizability and robustness of the phenomenon under different circumstances. In fact, many of the methodologies such as CRISP-DM and TDSP explicitly call out processes of testing or conducting "experiments."

While exploratory analysis can suggest a potential relationship or association that can help us generate potential hypotheses (hypothesis-generating analysis), we need to follow this up with hypothesis-driven experimentation where we define the expected relationship a priori.

TIP

Resist the temptation to stop your analysis when you find something interesting in the data. Test your newly formed theory under different conditions.

As shown in Chapter 1, inductive reasoning is useful in observing and understanding what can be seen in the data, but this needs to be followed with deductive reasoning to be sure that we haven't simply seen what we wanted to or observed a special or unique set of conditions. Hypothesis-driven analytics is used to support the validation of a relationship and its generalizability.

However, all is not perfect with hypothesis-driven analysis, either. In fact, Karl Popper (Popper & Miller, 1983) argued for a distinction between confirmation and falsification. He suggests that "confirmation involves obtaining evidence to confirm the correctness of one's hypothesis," whereas falsification involves attempting to falsify hypotheses by experimental tests.

Consider the use of negative tests in your experimentation so as to not fall into the trap of seeking confirmation of what you want to believe rather than truly understanding the conditions under which a phenomenon may be true. Researchers have found that people are often loath to abandon their own initial hypothesis because of confirmation bias (Cowley & Byrne, 2005).

Learn More

A positive test is when numbers produced are an instance of your hypothesis. A negative test is when numbers produced do not conform to your hypothesis. Read more at Explorable ("Confirmation bias. . .and the Wason Rule discovery test," n.d.)

Why Do This?

Ultimately, the reason that we use advanced methods in analytics—statistics, data mining, machine learning, operations research, time-series analysis, text analytics, voice, and image recognition—is to know something. Beyond guess, gut, and theories, we want to know in more certain terms, with greater confidence, that there might be an association, a cause and effect relationship, a true difference, giving us strength of conviction that we can use our findings to understand, prevent, alter, predict, or optimize.

TIP

Be careful to not confuse causal explanation and empirical prediction.

Traditional statistical methods can show you whether there was actually a change in the outcome or dependent variable(s) you had theorized to be true. Using the term *significance* shows that the connections between or among various factors may influence the results of your evaluation and can imply or show the reasons that your work was effective or ineffective. Be careful, however, not to rely solely on *p*-values as your proof.

Analysis results can provide credible evidence to show your boss or key stakeholders that something was important, or that you've uncovered and are fixing, the elements that are barriers to success. However, no amount of *p*-hacking (Charpentier, 2015), JARKing (Nuzzo, 2015), or HARKing (Kerr, 1998) can convince others of the merits of a theory that doesn't have business relevance.

 TIP

The goal of problem solving goes beyond problem identification to supporting a change in behavior.

Analytical methods are more than just "proving" significance; they can include unearthing new things, detecting information in the data that would have otherwise gone unknown, or automatically processing what would be too costly or time-consuming.

PROCESS AREAS

In the CRISP-DM model, the first step in modeling is "Select Modeling Technique." Unfortunately, with so many choices of analytics models, that task can be daunting.

I continue to lament the fact that most people describe analytics processes by the methods used rather than the purpose they serve. For example, in machine learning most people describe the methods based on the level of supervision or human verification. Statistics has a long tradition of heuristics for deciding which technique to use based on a variety of factors such as type of data, type of question, distribution qualities, and so on. Several flowcharts, decision trees, books, websites, and guides exist summarizing these options for statistics, but often fall short of expanding the choices to include advanced analytics techniques.

We address this by focusing on four **best practices** based on the most common types of analysis. These four processes include:

- Making comparisons
- Measuring associations
- Making predictions
- Detecting patterns

Analytics is used to aid human cognition, intuition, judgment, and sensemaking, and to find meaning in data. The process descriptions below identify what is involved in each of the four areas. Ultimately, the problem statement should inform which process should be considered. Don't get caught up in the techniques; rather, focus on how to best understand and solve the problem. Not every problem is a predictive modeling problem, nor is it a machine learning problem.

 TIP

Often the simplest method that aids understanding, interpretation, and a plan of action is the best solution.

MAKING COMPARISONS

One of the most common activities in analytics is making comparisons and evaluating differences. Business questions often arise about how various things compare to one another. We often make comparisons between people, organizations, places, products, methods, and time. For example, we might want to compare:

- *People*—The performance of different sales representatives for a given year against their quota
- *Organizations*—The costs of common procedures in different health systems, or the credit ratings of a bank's largest customers (to determine credit risk)
- *Places*—The cost of living between two cities or geographies

- *Products*—The effectiveness of different drugs for the treatment of a given disease
- *Methods*—Different health policies for a given patient population, or different versions of an advertisement or web page layout (this type of comparison is referred to as A/B Testing ("Google AdWords," 2017)
- *Time*—The performance of a financial portfolio over time against a benchmark (this is also part of time-series analysis)

We will first review the process for making comparisons of a single variable. In the next section, we will discuss measuring associations between two or more variables.

Analytical Models for Making Comparisons

When making comparisons, we often utilize common statistical evaluation tools, including F-test, T-test, and regression analysis. Typically, we evaluate differences by looking at averages, variances, proportions, and slope, and then make inferences about what we see in the sample data back to the population. Statistical inference is when we infer something about the population based on what is measured in the sample.

The inference is actually about the population proportion when the variable of interest is categorical, and about the population mean when the variable of interest is **quantitative**.

TIP

Statistical inference differs based on type of variable:

- Population proportion (when the variable of interest is categorical)
- Population mean (when the variable of interest is quantitative)

For a single variable, inference for a single categorical or quantitative variable can be performed through:

- Point estimation
- Confidence intervals
- Hypothesis testing

Point Estimation

A **point estimation** is essentially a best guess of a specific unknown number (or parameter). This estimate of an unknown parameter is made from sample data, and inferences can be made about what that means for an entire population. For example, banks are required to estimate the amount of loss expected in a worst-case scenario as part of their risk management processes. The estimate is the worst loss expected in a financial portfolio to be suffered over a given period of time with a given probability (in risk management, this is known as value-at-risk, or VaR).

The risk management officer in this case is simply performing a point estimation. For example, a company might estimate its VaR over 10 days to be $100 million with a confidence interval of 95 percent. This would mean that there is a one-in-20 (5 percent) chance of a loss larger than $100 million in the next 10 days.

Other examples of point estimations include proportions or averages, such as to estimate the prevalence of a disease in a population or a deviation found during the manufacturing of a new BMW. A typical report might look like these:

- Based on sample results, we estimate that p, the proportion of all US adults who have type 2 diabetes, is 0.093.
- The average gap width on the driver's side headliner from a sample of cars is 0.01 mm.

Interval Estimation

Point estimates are often more useful when accompanied by a range or interval, often referred to as a confidence interval. In **interval estimation**, we estimate an unknown parameter using an interval of values that is likely to contain the true value of that parameter, along with a statement of our level of confidence that this interval indeed captures the true value of the parameter.

An interval is a range of values for a statistic. For example, you might think that the mean of a data set falls somewhere between 10 and 100. This, of course, differs from a point estimate shown above, which is an exact value, like 46.

An example of an interval estimation from health care can be seen in the Framingham Heart Study ("Framingham Heart Study," 2017).

In one cohort of the study 1,219 participants were being treated for hypertension and 2,313 were not on treatment. If treatment is the "success," then $x = 1219$ and $n = 3532.1$.

The point estimation is an estimate that the proportion of the population on treatment for hypertension would be 34.5 percent. The 95 percent confidence interval is (0.329, 0.361). Thus, we are 95 percent confident that the true proportion of persons on antihypertensive medication is between 32.9 percent and 36.1 percent.

Hypothesis Testing

When making comparisons, it is often useful to truly know whether the differences are important or significant. Without going into detail here, note that just because something is "statistically significant" doesn't mean that it is important or valid in the real world.

Learn More

To learn more about the concept of statistical significance see the article "What Does Statistically Meaningful Mean" at measuringu.com/statistically-significant/.

It is useful, however, to understand whether something is likely to occur by chance. Hypothesis testing begins with a claim about the population (the null hypothesis), and we check whether the data obtained from the sample provides evidence *against* this claim.

As shown, we can test the differences between proportions or means through hypothesis testing. For further explanation, see the following examples.

Hypothesis Testing: Proportions

A recent study estimated that 28 percent of all patients in the United States are pre-diabetic. We suspect that this is actually higher in our hospital. To confirm this, we choose a random sample of 400 patients, and find that 125 of them are pre-diabetic.

Stating the two claims:

- Claim 1: The proportion of pre-diabetic patients is 0.28.
- Claim 2: The proportion of pre-diabetic patients is different from 0.28.

Claim 1 basically says, "Nothing special goes on at our hospital; the proportion of pre-diabetic patients is no different from the proportion in the entire country." This claim is challenged by the head of Population Health Department, who suspects that the proportion of pre-diabetic patients is higher in our population.

Learn More

Take a look at a video from JMP Software on Hypothesis Tests and Confidence Intervals for Proportions (JMP, 2014a).

Hypothesis Testing: Confidence Intervals

A normal resting heart rate for adults ranges from 60 to 100 beats a minute. An exercise performance company conducted a study in their performance lab and found the range to be 49 to 65. The marketing director believes that this proves that we can safely state that her program is shown to lower resting heart rate.

Stating the two claims:

- Claim 1: At the 95 percent confidence interval, we believe that resting heart rates for our patients is not different than the population interval of 60 to 100 bpm.
- Claim 2: At the 95 percent confidence interval, we believe that resting heart rates for our patients is significantly lower than the population interval of 60 to 100 bpm.

Claim 1 basically says, "Darn, we can't make the claim that our patient results are different than the population." This claim is challenged by the head of marketing, who wants to say that our patient heart rates are much lower than the average.

Hypothesis Testing: Means

According to a study conducted in the United Kingdom (R & RR, 2015), people diagnosed with type 2 diabetes (T2DM) in the 1970s and 1980s had a median BMI (body mass index) of only 28 kg/m2. In a recent review of our T2DM patients, we found that the median BMI was 29.5. We want to determine if this is significantly different.

Stating the two claims:

- ▪ Claim 1: The average BMI for our patients is not different from the comparison study of 28 kg/m2.
- ▪ Claim 2: The average BMI for our patients is different than the comparison study of 28 kg/m2.

Note that in this case, we ignore the directionality. That is, we only care if there is a difference in a two-tailed test, rather than a one-tailed test, which would say, "The average BMI for our patients in this study is *greater* that the comparison study of 28 kg/m2."

Claim 1 basically says, "No worries; our patients are not different from the comparison study." This claim is challenged that our patients really do have a larger BMI.

Learn More

To learn more about Hypothesis Testing for Means, take a look at a video from JMP software on using the one sample t-test and confidence intervals (JMP, 2014b).

As shown, a number of approaches can be used in making comparisons. The use of a decision tree such as this one in Figure 8.6 from Stats with Cats Blog (Kufs, 2010) can be a useful tool as you consider which statistical test might be appropriate given the type of comparison being made.

While this book is not intended to replace the knowledge gained from studying statistics, it does provide an overview of the processes used in making comparisons. At the end of this chapter, we will identify resources for those interested in learning more about statistics, hypothesis testing, and making inferences.

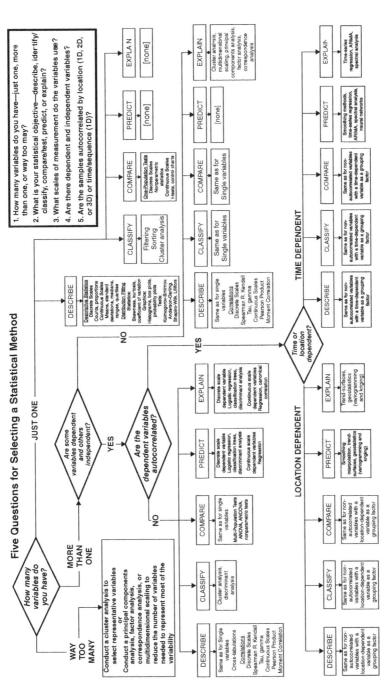

Figure 8.6 Five questions for selecting a statistical model

Source: Stats with Cats

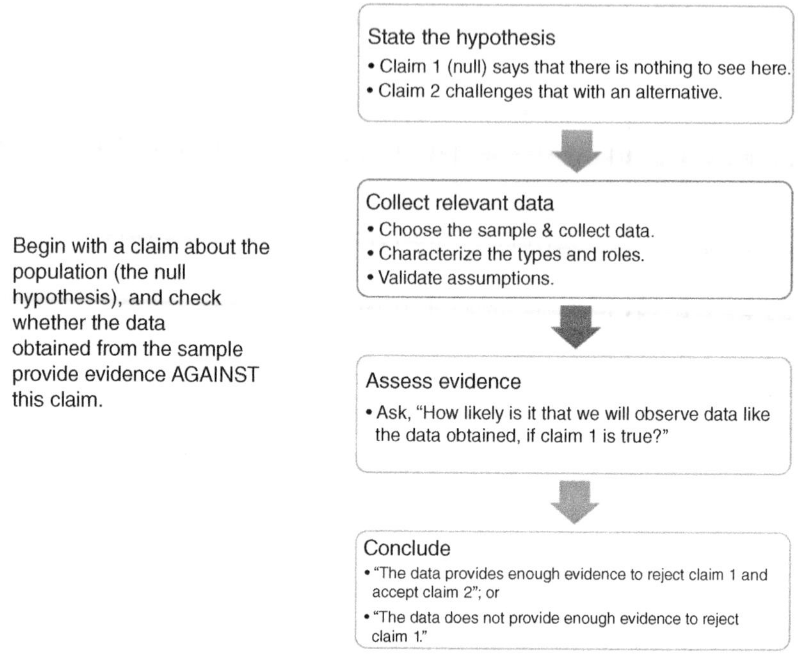

Begin with a claim about the population (the null hypothesis), and check whether the data obtained from the sample provide evidence AGAINST this claim.

State the hypothesis
• Claim 1 (null) says that there is nothing to see here.
• Claim 2 challenges that with an alternative.

Collect relevant data
• Choose the sample & collect data.
• Characterize the types and roles.
• Validate assumptions.

Assess evidence
• Ask, "How likely is it that we will observe data like the data obtained, if claim 1 is true?"

Conclude
• "The data provides enough evidence to reject claim 1 and accept claim 2"; or
• "The data does not provide enough evidence to reject claim 1."

Figure 8.7 Steps used in the evaluation of a hypothesis

More important is that we outline the overall process used in evaluating a hypothesis (Figure 8.7).

Hypothesis testing is different from hypothesis generation seen in the previous chapter in that we aren't looking for potential causes but, rather, we are testing to see if our theory is true, or at least has a low probability of occurring by chance alone.

Step 1. State the hypothesis.

Start by outlining the claim in the form of a hypothesis. This should directly relate back to the problem statement that was developed earlier. Craft your hypothesis using both a null hypothesis (claim that says that there is nothing to see here—e.g., there is no difference) and an alternative hypothesis that challenges the null hypothesis with an alternative explanation.

Step 2. Collect relevant data.

Depending on your study design you may need to collect, sample, or create data appropriate to your objectives. Data collection and preparation were discussed in detail in Chapter 7, so it won't be repeated here. In general, however, this step includes:

- Choosing the sample and collecting data
- Characterizing the types and roles
- Validating assumptions

Step 3. Assess evidence.

This is the meat and potatoes of statistical testing when you ask, "How likely is it that we will observe data like the data we obtained, if our claim is true?" Using the example that looked at hypothesis testing when comparing means, you need to assess the evidence from your comparison test. You have two choices:

- Claim 1: The average BMI for our patients is not different from the comparison study of 28 kg/m2.
- Claim 2: The average BMI for our patients is different (or greater) than the comparison study of 28 kg/m2.

To evaluate these differences, you can use statistical testing. In this case, you are testing the difference between two population means and utilizing a two-sample Z test to determine if two population means are equal or unequal.

Step 4. Conclude.

In the final step of hypothesis testing, you are making a conclusion about your findings. "Does the data provide enough evidence to reject claim 1 and accept claim 2?"; or "The data do not provide enough evidence to reject claim 1."

It is important to understand the question you are asking here. Note these potential options: as you assess the validity of this claim, which do you believe is the correct interpretation of the question being asked?

1. How likely is it that in our patients, the median BMI is as high as 29.5?
2. How likely is it that the true population median is 28?
3. How likely is it that the true population median is greater than 28?

4. How likely is it that in our patients, the median BMI is as great as 29.5 if the true population mean is 28 percent?

If you answered #4, great job! In hypothesis testing, in order to assess the evidence, you need to find out how likely it is to get data like those observed, assuming that claim 1 is true. Note that you can infer something only about the population, but your claim was a sample of patients from a single health system, and therefore, the inference can be made only about the health-care system's population of patients.

MEASURING ASSOCIATIONS

As noted in the previous section, hypothesis testing can be used when making comparisons for a single variable such as average BMI. When you want to say something about the relationships between two or more variables, you are making inferences about relationships or associations between two variables in a population, based on an observed relationship between the variables in a sample.

In statistics, measures of association are used to identify variables that are related to or associated with one another. If the variables are quantitative, techniques such as correlation or regression are often used. If the variables are categorical, other measures of association, such as the Chi-square, can be utilized.

 TIP

Dependence or association does not mean cause and effect; it simply notices that a relationship exists but makes no assertion about the form of the relationship (e.g., causal).

It is useful to visualize the relationships found in data. For example, to compare and contrast distributions of quantitative data, a scatter plot might be used, as shown in Figure 8.8.

Similarly, you can produce a correlation matrix heat map, as shown in Figure 8.9.

The correlation matrix heat map shows the association using color gradients to signify the direction and strength of the association. Similarly, scatter plot matrices (Figure 8.10) can display the relationships between several variables in a single view.

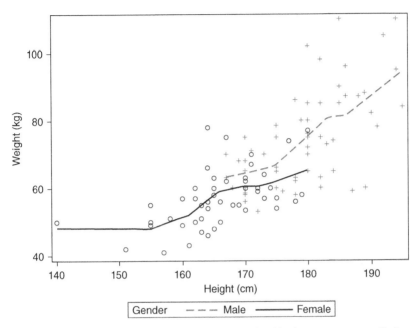

Figure 8.8 Example scatter plot to visualize the relationships between two quantitative variables

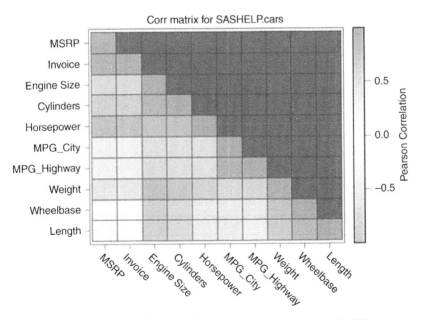

Figure 8.9 Example of correlation matrix heat map showing the strength of the relationships between variables (Hemedinger, 2013)

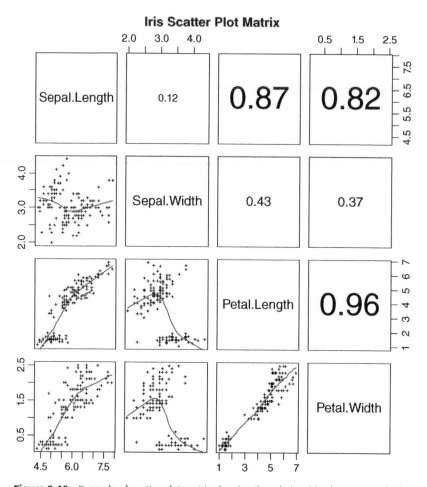

Figure 8.10 Example of scatter plot matrix showing the relationships between variables

 TIP

When measuring an association, frame it as a question that can be evaluated, such as: "Does a relationship exists between the variables X and Y in a population of interest?"

As we saw in Chapter 7, when posing a question, consider the role that variables play:

- *Response variable*—The outcome or dependent variable; and

- *Explanatory variable*—The variable that claims to explain, predict, or affect the response (independent variable, predictor variable or covariate).

The independent (explanatory) variable is referred to as X and the dependent (response) variable as Y.

As shown above, the hypothesis test comes in the form of:

- Ho: There is no relationship between X and Y.
- Ha: There is a relationship between X and Y.

Alternatively, to indicate the direction of the relationship, you would use a one-tailed test of significance. The way the above hypothesis is written indicates that you don't know (or care) about directionality, and thus will use a two-tailed test.

Learn More

Review one-tailed versus two-tailed tests of significance at UCLA's Institute for Digital Research and Education ("What are the differences between one-tailed and two-tailed tests?," n.d.).

Statistical Testing for Associations

To test for association between two variables, use the 2×2 matrix in Figure 8.11 to determine what type of question is being asked.

In Figure 8.11, categorical variables are classes or categories of values (despite whether they may be coded as numeric such as 1 for yes and 0 for no.) Quantitative variables in this context are those that can

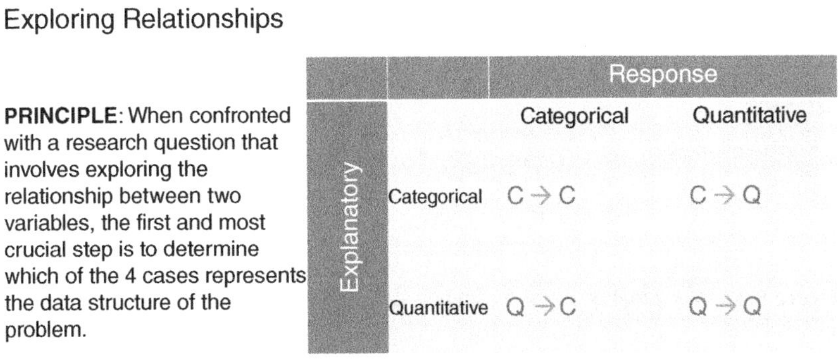

Exploring Relationships

PRINCIPLE: When confronted with a research question that involves exploring the relationship between two variables, the first and most crucial step is to determine which of the 4 cases represents the data structure of the problem.

		Response	
		Categorical	Quantitative
Explanatory	Categorical	C → C	C → Q
	Quantitative	Q → C	Q → Q

Figure 8.11 2 × 2 matrix to help classify the type of question being asked

be treated as numbers (e.g., continuous). The letter C is intended to mean categorical and the letter Q refers to quantitative.

The first step in measuring an association is to determine what is the response variable and what is the explanatory variable. Next, for each of the variables, assess which type of variable you have. Finally, use the table in Figure 8.12 to determine the typical form of hypothesis testing that can be made.

Note in the table that tests are typically used for two types of associations:

▪ Categorical to categorical variables

▪ Quantitative to quantitative variables

These are the four most common types of association tests:

1. *Pearson's correlation coefficient (r or rho)*—This is used for quantifying the association between two variables measured on an interval/ratio scale, e.g., height versus weight.

2. *Spearman rank-order correlation coefficient (Spearman rho)*— Designed to measure the strength of a monotonic (in a constant direction) association between two variables measured on an ordinal or ranked scale, e.g., Likert-scale survey or rank ordered list.

3. *Chi-square test (contingency table)*—Measures the significance of the association rather than the strength of the association;

Tests of Differences and Association

		Response (dependent)	
		Categorical	Quantitative
Explanatory (independent)	Categorical	Chi-square test* Fisher's exact test* McNemar test **	Two independent samples t-test ** Wilcoxon-Mann-Whitney test ** One-way ANOVA ** Kruskal Wallis ** Paired t-test ** Wilcoxon Signed Rank Test ** One-way repeated measures ANOVA ** Friedman test ** 2-way/ n-way/Factorial ANOVA **
	Quantitative	Simple logistic regression Multiple logistic regression Discriminant analysis	Correlation* Non-parametric correlation*

* Association

** Difference between two groups

Figure 8.12 2 × 2 matrix outlining common statistical tests for differences and associations

it is used to examine the association between categorical variables.

4. *Relative risk and odds ratio*—The ratio is used for categorical data and measures the strength of an association by considering the number of items or incidence of an event as compared with another group, e.g., a baseline group.

While outside of the scope of this book, most statistical software will allow you to test associations between variables using a variety of test statistics, including:

- Kendall (tau)
- Partial correlations
- Lambda
- Somer's D
- Cramer's V
- Conditional gamma

Other Tests for Measuring Associations

While the tests described above are most common for measures of association, there are a number of other analytics approaches:

- *Linear regression and multiple regression*—Utilizes correlation coefficients to plot a line illustrating the linear relationship of two variables X and Y. Multiple regression is the same as simple linear regression except that in the case of multiple regression we attempt to predict Y from two or more independent X variables (versus just one in linear regression). Note that regression will be explored in greater detail in the next section the discussion of prediction.

- *Discriminant analysis*—Like multiple regression, except that the dependent variable consists of a categorical dependent variable (grouping variable) rather than a continuous range of values; one or more continuous or binary independent variables (called predictor variables) are used.

- *Factor analysis*—Useful with a large number of correlated variables; you want to create "factors" that might explain the relationships by some unobserved factor. It is a means of grouping data into clusters or factors when you have variables that are moderately to highly correlated with each other.

Several advanced techniques are also used to visualize and measure associations, such as multidimensional scaling (D. & Arabie, 1997) (Kruskal & Wish, 1978), path analysis (Loehlin, 1992), association rule learning ("Association Rule Learning,"), affinity analysis ("Affinity Analysis,"), high dimensionality analysis (Strehl & Ghosh, 2003), and taxonomic search techniques (Waller & Meekl, 1998).

MAKING PREDICTIONS

Prediction refers to the development of analytics models that can predict (e.g., forecast, guess, or estimate) the value of one variable given the values of other variables. Most often, predictive models are used to anticipate a given value based on other factors.

As Galit Shmueli posits in his *Statistical Science* article "To Explain or to Predict?" explaining and predicting are different (Shmueli, 2010).

Examples of predictive analytics include:

- Predicting high risk and high cost patients (Bates, Saria, Ohno-Machado, Shah, & Escobar, 2014)
- Forecasting civil unrest in Latin America (Ramakrishnan)
- Identifying which customers will likely churn (used in retention/attrition models) (Neslin, Gupta, Kamakura, Lu, & Mason, 2006)
- Anticipating which ads mobile gaming users are likely respond to (Ramark, 2015)
- Predicting the emergence of Alzheimer's disease in trial subjects (Cirigliano, 2013)

Prediction is the area of analytics where traditional statistics and more advanced analytical methods including data mining, forecasting, multivariate models, and machine learning begin to overlap. In traditional statistics, a number of tests are used in prediction models, as shown in the 2 × 2 matrix in Figure 8.13.

As data mining techniques have evolved, we have seen the introduction of additional approaches that include decision trees, neural

Statistical Tests for Prediction

		Response (dependent)	
		Categorical	Quantitative
Explanatory (independent)	Categorical	Repeated measures logistic regression Factorial logistic regression	Ordered logistic regression
	Quantitative	Simple logistic regression Multiple logistic regression Discriminant analysis	Simple linear regression Multiple regression

Figure 8.13 2-x-2 matrix of common statistical tests for prediction

networks, and *ensemble* models that have helped us utilize the results of several models to improve predictive ability. Similarly, both naive Bayes and Bayesian networks can be used to support prediction tasks.

> *Ensemble modeling is the process of running two or more related but different analytical models and then synthesizing the results into a single score or spread in order to improve the accuracy of predictive analytics and data mining applications.*
>
> searchbusinessanalytics.techtarget.com/definition/Ensemble-modeling

Case Study: Spaghetti Plots: Note all Models are not Created Equal

At the time of the writing of this book in the fall of 2017, we had three major hurricanes hit the United States. One of the most well-known forms of prediction in everyday use is in forecasting weather, and in this case, specifically the projected path of a hurricane. The projected paths are often displayed as a series of lines referred to as a *spaghetti plot*.

One of the exciting things about this for me is that it gives an everyday example with which to explain the concept of ensemble models. That is, I encourage the use of multiple models to understand how features and weightings of various models impact a risk score, for example. This is often preferred over a single point estimation.

The challenge in using these plots is the unbridled (and often untrained) use. It is important to realize that not all models are created equally, and some suggest that spaghetti

(Continued)

(Continued)

plots should never be used, as they oversimplify the concept and assume equal weighting among models.

To learn more about the downsides of spaghetti plots, read more from Ars Technica (Berger, 2017).

In moving from statistics and data mining to machine learning, additional methods can be found that can help predict an unknown value from known data. In general, machine learning considers two subclasses of prediction models:

- Regression
- Pattern classification

As noted earlier in this chapter, regression models are based on the analysis of relationships (associations) between variables, and the relationship is used to illustrate a trend that can help in making predictions about a continuous variable.

In machine learning, a number of supervised methods are used for regression:

- Trees (random forests, GBM)
- Linear/GLMS
- Linear smoothing (LOESS)
- Ensemble
- Neural networks

In contrast to regression models, the focus of pattern classification is to assign discrete class labels to particular observations as outcomes of a prediction. In the example above: A pattern classification task in the student grades examples could be the prediction of a letter grade or whether the student eventually matriculates.

Supervised machine learning techniques to support pattern classification predictions include:

- Support vector machines
- Discriminant analysis

▪ Naive Bayes

▪ Nearest neighbor (instance-based)

Detecting Patterns

Pattern detection or recognition represents a broad class of problems in analytics. Nearly synonymous with machine learning, pattern recognition is the science of making inferences or "identification of implicit objects, types or relationships from data." ("Rochester Institute of Technology Computer Science," 2017). In other words, it is the act of recognizing hidden information or anomalies. In machine learning, think of pattern recognition as assigning labels to objects (Kuncheva, 2004).

Examples of pattern detection might be as simple as determining the identity of a person (image recognition), an event based on a picture (event recognition), the content of spoken words (voice recognition), or language in text (language detection). In data discovery, when we find a pattern that jumps out at us through visual or statistical techniques, we celebrate that "Aha!" moment.

A great example of this is depicted in Sam Savage's book *The Flaw of Averages* (Savage, 2009), where he shows raw data with very little informational value (a negligible correlation) until it is graphically depicted in just the right way (Figure 8.14).

As organizations grapple with larger and larger amounts of data, it becomes necessary to consider how to utilize computer-aided methods to find patterns hidden in the vast mass of organizational data. Traditional techniques often rely on brute force methods such as exploratory data analysis and traditional statistical analysis/model building, but access to more and more data along with increased computing power allows for greater access to platforms for analysis. As computers become faster and are able to handle larger amounts of data, it seems appropriate now to turn to artificial intelligence (such as machine learning) to support the pursuit of finding patterns in data.

To detect patterns in data, we can utilize visual data discovery techniques or automated approaches that utilize statistics, probability theory, computational geometry, machine learning, signal processing,

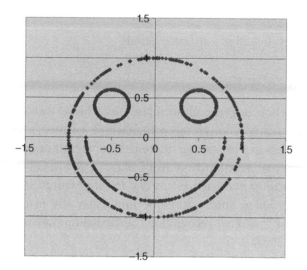

Figure 8.14   Scatter plot revealing patterns in the data
Source: Sam Savage, The Flaw of Averages

and other computer algorithms. Generally, there are two approaches for pattern recognition in common use:

- Classification
- Discrimination

Classification Models

Classification models are used to identify things that go together. They are used in both the model-building process to build the variables used in the model (i.e., feature engineering) as well as in the model itself (model selection). As we see in Figure 8.15, classification can be used to support either hypothesis or data-driven analytics and includes both supervised and unsupervised methods.

Feature Engineering

In practical terms, **feature selection** is the process of identifying a subset of relevant features (explanatory variables, predictors) for use in model construction. In traditional model building, the researcher (statistician) would examine the data to determine which variables

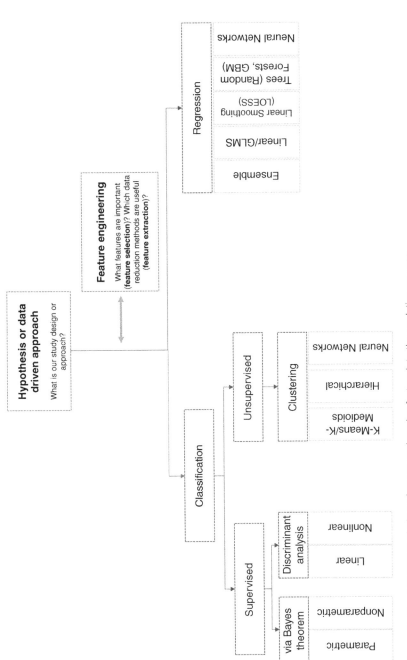

Figure 8.15 A depiction of where feature engineering factors into the analytics process

were interesting and novel in their ability to predict an outcome. By using feature selection techniques, models can be built more quickly, reducing the likelihood of overfitting the models.

Learn More

The answer to, "How much data do I really need?" is a function of the variety of possible attributes needed based on the method you choose. To read more about how to answer this question, take a look at this article (Deshpande, 2015).

Feature extraction, on the other hand, begins with a set of variables and assists in creating derived variables that otherwise would be labor-intensive to do manually. For example, you may find that deriving a new variable that combines age and gender in just the right way helps in understanding the data better than if the features had been left untransformed (see dimensionality reduction).

 TIP

Feature selection is used to determine a subset of initial features or variables. Feature extraction supports the creation of features by transforming the original variables.

Feature Selection

It is important to identify the features that are useful as a tool for assigning objects to one or more predefined groups or categories. However, the real value lies in the power to solve real-world problems. Common examples of classification problems include:

- Classifying spam email (classifying the header or content as spam) (Guzella & Caminhas, 2009)
- Identifying malignant cells (in applied health-care settings or biomedical research) (Leggett et al., 2016)
- Language identification (determining the language and/or meaning of a given text) ("Language Identification," 2017)
- Anomaly detection (K. Das, 2009) (see also multivariate outliers)
- Document classification (Sebastiani, 2002)

Classification techniques can be used to describe a phenomenon such as classifying the features that are useful in defining group membership (c.g., descriptive analysis), or they can be used for prediction and forecasting tasks, diagnosis, and pattern recognition.

Generally, a classification technique follows three approaches: statistical, machine learning, and neural network. Some examples of classification methods include:

- Naive Bayes classifier
- Artificial neural networks classifier
- Support vector machines/ensemble classifiers
- k nearest neighbor
- *knn* classifier
- Decision trees/classification trees
- Cluster analysis (e.g., statistical cluster analysis, K means, spectral clustering GMM)
- Classification and regression tree (CART)

Discrimination Models

Discrimination is used to find a combination of features (attributes or variables) that distinguish or separate two or more classes of objects or events. Discrimination is a special type of classification that identifies not what goes together (what things cluster) but, rather, what distinguishes something.

Examples of discrimination include:

- *Facial recognition*—to determine whether an image is a known person (Geitgey, 2016)
- *Financial solvency*—to distinguish firms that have entered bankruptcy (Tam & Kiang, 1992)
- *Events, landmarks, logos detection*—to determine Easter egg hunt versus other types of children's activities (M. Das & Loui, 2014)

Analytics methods can be used for discrimination for both linear and nonlinear data. Examples include:

- Linear discriminant analysis (LDA)
- Singular value decomposition

- Generalized discriminant analysis (GDA)
- Principal component analysis (PCA)
- Graph-based kernel PCA
- Factor analysis
- Discriminant correspondence analysis
- Multivariate discriminant analysis (MDA)

Other Classification Models

It is worth noting that while the most common types of classification models include those described above (classification and discrimination), other types of models can be used, such as logistic regression to model the probability of an object being in a particular class or regression algorithms used in predicting real-valued labels. Similarly, classification can be performed using unsupervised text-mining methods (Kalyanarangan, 2017).

Pattern Detection Processes

The generalized process for analyzing data to determine whether a pattern exists can be summarized in Figure 8.16.

As shown in Figure 8.16, adapted from Ludmila I. Kuncheva's "Combining Pattern Classifiers Methods and Algorithms" (Kuncheva, 2004), several methods can be used in pattern recognition. However, the general process consists of the following activities (beyond those described in the prior chapters):

1. *Clarification of the problem*—Once again, it is important to remember the business problem and to ensure that the approach is best suited to the type of question being asked of the data.

2. *Data collection*—Simply, acquire and structure the data appropriate to the type of analysis being considered.

3. *Data exploration*—Use data exploration and sensemaking to evaluate the data for accuracy, completeness, and reflection of the underlying process. This is also the step that begins to consider which variables are candidates for use in the model.

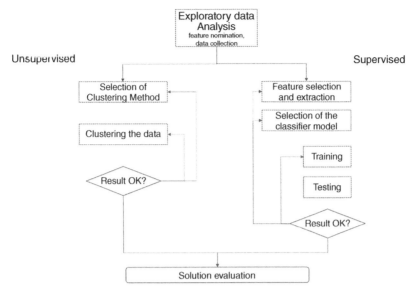

Figure 8.16 Pattern detection process flow for supervised and unsupervised model development

4. *Feature engineering*—Conduct feature engineering with subset of the features appropriate for the analysis, and feature reduction to derive variables of interest.

5. *Pattern classification or clustering*—Using unsupervised methods, apply various models as part of the exploratory data analysis process. Alternatively, use supervised classification as a way of preprocessing the data.

6. *Evaluation and interpretation*—Using what has been learned about the data, the model, and the results obtained, always apply the learnings back to the business problem. This will often involve applying the trained classifier to an independent test data set.

CHAPTER SUMMARY

Analytics Model Development is the **best practice** area concerned with the "analysis" of data to extract a meaningful mathematical model used to represent the real world.

Many process models exist for the data scientist that touch on what we mean by "modeling" but often fall short of helping us know what is meant by "select modeling technique." In fact, in the CRISP-DM methodology, the treatment of the former is limited to a single paragraph in the original guide (Chapman et al., 2000) and expanded only slightly in subsequent versions (IBM, 2011).

Instead of treating model development as generalized activities used in selecting and building a model, we focused on four primary processes based on the problem type of each analysis. These processes include making comparisons, measuring associations, making predictions, and detecting patterns.

It is always important to remember your problem as you go through these processes, lest you stray from your intended outcome. As you go through the process of model development, keep these simple ideas in mind:

- The simplest model that can be easily explained is often the best model.

- Even if the techniques are complicated, be sure to carefully consider your problem and the workflows that will be impacted by your analysis.

- Techniques that obscure the details (read: insert magic here) often raise more questions. It is best practice to compare a variety of methods to see the balance between predictive power and interpretability.

- Be careful to not overfit your model; using realistic data and generalizing it to other samples can help test the reliability of a model.

- When dealing with data, there is always some degree of uncertainty. Develop relationships with those on the front lines where the data is generated to ensure that it truly reflects on the reality of the business.

 TIP

Document what you hope to obtain by doing the analysis to keep your problem in front of you.

As a final word on model development, use design-thinking techniques to imagine what it's going to be like to use or receive information from your analysis. Will it be helpful? Will it be understandable? Will it be actionable?

PROBLEM SUMMARY AND EXERCISES

Analytics model development techniques continue to evolve, but it is useful to consider what you are asking of the data, how much data will be used in your analysis efforts, and what data you have to work with.

Table 8.2 summarizes the four general types of problems, along with some sample questions that you might be asked to help guide your model development.

Table 8.2 Model development best process areas, common questions, and common methods

Best Practice Processes	Representative Business Questions	Example Methods
Making comparisons	▪ Do males and females differ with respect to BMI? ▪ Is there a difference between two web pages in terms of which one yields higher click-throughs?	▪ T-test ▪ ANOVA/ANCOVA ▪ McNemar test ▪ Wilcoxon-Mann-Whitney test ▪ Kruskal Wallis ▪ Wilcoxon signed rank test ▪ Friedman test ▪ 2-way/*n*-way/Factorial ANOVA
Measuring associations	▪ Is there a relationship between smoking and obesity? ▪ Is there an association between time spent on a website and purchasing behavior? ▪ Is there a relationship between exercise and depression? ▪ Is there an association between what items people tend to buy most often together?	▪ Chi-square ▪ Simple linear regression ▪ Relative risk and odds ratio ▪ Pearson's (R) product-moment correlation coefficient ▪ Spearman (rho) rank correlations ▪ Fisher's exact test ▪ A priori association rules

(continued)

Table 8.2 *(Continued)*

Best Practice Processes	Representative Business Questions	Example Methods
Making predictions	▦ How well can we predict a patient's BMI from the minutes they spend exercising or other psychosocial factors? ▦ Which example of handwriting is most like the suspect? ▦ Which documents are written in French? ▦ What is the predicted median home price for a given zip code? ▦ What is the probability that someone will default on their home loan?	▦ Multiple regression ▦ Logistic regression ▦ Trees (random forests, GBM) ▦ Linear smoothing (LOESS) ▦ Ensemble ▦ Time-series analysis ▦ Neural networks ▦ Linear discriminant analysis ▦ Support vector machines ▦ Discriminant analysis ▦ Naive Bayes ▦ Nearest neighbor (instance-based) ▦ Density estimation
Detecting patterns	▦ What clusters are useful in determining the types of customers we see? ▦ Which medical images are likely indicative of a diseased lung?	▦ Cluster analysis (e.g., statistical cluster analysis, K means, spectral clustering GMM) ▦ Ensembles of decision trees (aka "random forests") ▦ Fisher's linear discriminant analysis (LDA) ▦ Naive Bayes classifier ▦ Artificial neural networks classifier ▦ Support vector machines/ Ensemble classifiers ▦ *k* nearest neighbor ▦ *knn* classifier ▦ Classification and regression tree (CART)

Toolkit @
www.analyticslifecycletoolkit.com

Using the model development template item found at www.analyticslifecycletoolkit.com, complete the exercise for this chapter where you use a business question to decide which type of analysis is most appropriate, given the business question and types of data available.

TOOLKIT SUMMARY

Best Practice Area:	Analytics Model Development	
Purpose:	*What is the intent of this best practice area?* The purpose of analytics model development is to design and develop a mathematical model that can be used to help us to explain a system, study its component parts, and make predictions or optimize some phenomenon.	
Key Competencies:	*Knowledge, skills, abilities, and disposition*	
What do we need to be good at?	▪ Analytical thinking ▪ Statistical analysis ▪ Hypothesis testing ▪ Results evaluation and comparison	▪ Mathematical modeling ▪ Visual analysis ▪ Technical fluency ▪ Analytical methods ▪ Data management
Inputs	**Processes**	**Outputs**
Enterprise data Other data as required Outputs from data sensemaking Problem statement	▪ Making comparisons ▪ Measuring associations ▪ Making predictions ▪ Detecting patterns	▪ Updates to analytics journal ▪ Analytics model ▪ Model comparison results
Key Questions:	*What should we know as a result of this best practice?* ▪ What assumptions must be true for the model to be truly reflective of the real world? ▪ What are the implications of this model?	

Key Questions:	▪ How can this be translated into an operational model?
	▪ What biases or blind spots did we not consider?
	▪ What assumptions would make this model fail?
	▪ What alternative explanations were considered?

REFERENCES

AdWords A/B Testing with Experiments Posted June 23rd, 2017 by Kirti & filed under AdWords Experiments. Retrieved from http://www.karooya.com/blog/adwords-ab-testing/.

Affinity Analysis. Retrieved from en.wikipedia.org/wiki/Affinity_analysis.

Association Rule Learning. Retrieved from https://en.wikipedia.org/wiki/Association_rule_learning.

Azevedo, A., & Santos, M. F. *KDD, SEMMA and CRISP-DM: a parallel overview.* Bitstream. Retrieved from recipp.ipp.pt/bitstream/10400.22/136/3/KDD-CRISP-SEMMA.pdf.

Bates, D. W., Saria, S., Ohno-Machado, L., Shah, A., & Escobar, G. (2014). Big data in health care: using analytics to identify and manage high-risk and high-cost patients. *Health Affairs, 33*(7), 1123–1131. doi:10.1377/hlthaff.2014.0041.

Berger, E. (2017). Please, please stop sharing spaghetti plots of hurricane models. Retrieved from arstechnica.com/science/2017/09/please-please-stop-sharing-spaghetti-plots-of-hurricane-models/.

Breiman, L. (2001). Statistical modeling: The two cultures. *Statistical Science, 16*(3), 199–231.

Carroll, J. D., & Arabie, P. (1997). *Multidimension scaling.* San Diego: Academic Press.

Chapman, P., Clinton, J., Kerber, R., Khabaza, T., Reinartz, T., Shearer, C., & Wirth, R. (2000). CRISP-DM 1.0: Step-by-step data mining guide. Retrieved from www.the-modeling-agency.com/crisp-dm.pdf.

Charpentier, A. (2015). P-Hacking, or cheating on a P-value. Retrieved from freakonometrics.hypotheses.org/19817.

Cirigliano, J. (2013). It's only logical. *DDN News*. Retrieved from www.ddn-news.com/index.php?newsarticle=7135.

Confirmation bias…and the Wason rule discovery test. Retrieved from explorable.com/confirmation-bias.

Cowley, M., & Byrne, R. M. J. (2005). When falsification is the only path to truth. Paper presented at the Cognitive Science Society 27th Annual Conference, Mahweh, NJ. www.psych.unito.it/csc/cogsci05/frame/poster/2/f299-cowley.pdf.

Coy, P. (1997). He who mines data may strike fool's gold. *BusinessWeek*.

Cross Industry Standard Process for Data Mining. Retrieved from en.wikipedia.org/wiki/Cross_Industry_Standard_Process_for_Data_Mining.

Das, K. (2009). Detecting patterns of anomalies. Carnegie Mellon University, Pittsburgh, PA. Retrieved from reports-archive.adm.cs.cmu.edu/anon/ml2009/CMU-ML-09-101.pdf (ML-09-101).

Das, Madirakshi; Loui, Alexander C. Detecting recurring events in consumer image collections 2014 Patent version # 458634662 B2 Patent classification: 382/225, 707/737, 382/305 Application #:US 12/862,806 International Patent classificaiton: G06K9/62 URL: http://www.google.com.pg/patents/US8634662.

Definition: Analytical Modeling. (2017). *OpenEI*. Retrieved from openei.org/wiki/Definition:Analytical_Modeling.

Deshpande, B. (2015). 4 rules of thumb for machine learning on big data. Retrieved from www.simafore.com/blog/3-key-considerations-for-machine-learning-on-big-data.

Fayyad, U. M., Piatetsky-Shapiro, G., Smyth, P., & Uthurusamy, R. (1996). Advances in knowledge discovery and data mining. In: Framingham Heart Study. (2017). Retrieved from www.framinghamheartstudy.org/.

Geitgey, A. (2016). Machine learning is fun! Part 4: Modern face recognition with deep learning. Retrieved from medium.com/@ageitgey/machine-learning-is-fun-part-4-modern-face-recognition-with-deep-learning-c3cffc121d78.

Guzella, T. S., & Caminhas, W. M. (2009). A review of machine learning approaches to spam filtering. *Expert Systems with Applications, 36*(7), 10206–10222. doi: dx.doi.org/10.1016/j.eswa.2009.02.037.

Haffar, J. (2015). Have you seen ASUM-DM? Retrieved from developer.ibm.com/predictiveanalytics/2015/10/16/have-you-seen-asum-dm/.

Hemedinger, C. (2013). How to build a correlations matrix heat map with SAS. Retrieved from blogs.sas.com/content/sasdummy/2013/06/12/correlations-matrix-heatmap-with-sas/.

IBM. (2011). *IBM SPSS Modeler CRISP-DM Guide*. Retrieved from inseaddataanalytics.github.io/INSEADAnalytics/CRISP_DM.pdf.

JMP (Producer). (2014a). Hypothesis tests and CIs for proportions. Retrieved from www.youtube.com/watch?v=esnKgkClV1U&feature=youtu.be.

JMP (Producer). (2014b). One sample t-test and confidence intervals. Retrieved from www.youtube.com/watch?v=UoUeyFph5vI&feature =youtu.be.

Kalyanarangan, V. (2017). Text clustering: Get quick insights from unstructured data 1. Retrieved from machinelearningblogs.com/2017/01/26/text -clustering-get-quick-insights-from-unstructured-data/.

Kerr, N. L. (1998). HARKing: Hypothesizing after the results are known. *Personality and Social Psychology Review*.

Kruskal, J. B., & Wish, M. (1978). *Multidimensional scaling*. Beverly Hills, CA: Sage Publications.

Kufs, C. (2010). Statistical selection techniques. *Stats with cats blog*. Retrieved from statswithcats.files.wordpress.com/2010/08/selection-methods-8-21 -2010.png.

Kuncheva, L. I. (2004). *Combining pattern classifiers: methods and algorithms*. Hoboken, N.J.: Wiley-Interscience.

Language Identification. (2017). Retrieved from en.wikipedia.org/wiki/ Language_identification.

Leggett, S. E., Sim, J. Y., Rubins, J. E., Neronha, Z. J., Williams, E. K., & Wong, I. Y. (2016). Morphological single cell profiling of the epithelial– mesenchymal transition. *Integrative Biology 11*.

Loehlin, J. C. (1992). *Latent variable models: an introduction to factor, path, and structural analysis* (2nd ed.). Hillsdale, NJ: Lawrence Erlbaum Associates.

Multiple Comparisons Problem. Wikipedia. Retrieved from en.wikipedia.org/ wiki/Multiple_comparisons_problem.

Neslin, S. A., Gupta, S., Kamakura, W., Lu, J., & Mason, C. H. (2006). Defection detection: Measuring and understanding the predictive accuracy of customer churn models. *Journal of Marketing Research, 43*(2), 204–211.

Nuzzo, R. (2015). How scientists fool themselves—and how they can stop. *Nature, 526*, 182–185.

O'Connor, B. (2009). Statistics vs. machine learning, fight! Retrieved from brenocon.com/blog/2008/12/statistics-vs-machine-learning-fight/.

Popper, K., & Miller, D. (1983). A proof of the impossibility of inductive probability. *Nature, 302*, 687–688.

Ramakrishnan, N. *'Beating the News' with EMBERS: Forecasting civil unrest using open source indicators*. Virginia Tech. Retrieved from people.cs.vt.edu/ naren/papers/kddindg1572-ramakrishnan.pdf.

Ramark, M. (2015). Three ways predictive analytics will change mobile games—Part 1. Retrieved from dev-gamerefinery.pantheonsite.io/3-ways -predictive-analytics-will-change-mobile-games-part-i/.

Rochester Institute of Technology Computer Science. (2017). Retrieved from www.cs.rit.edu/.

Savage, S. L. (2009). *The flaw of averages: Why we underestimate risk in the face of uncertainty.* Hoboken, NJ: John Wiley & Sons.

Sebastiani, F. (2002). Machine learning in automated text categorization. *ACM Computing Surveys, 34*(1), 1–47.

SEMMA. Retrieved from en.wikipedia.org/wiki/SEMMA.

Shmueli, G. (2010). To explain or to predict? *Statistical Science, 25*(3), 289–310. doi:10.1214/10-STS330.

Strehl, A., & Ghosh, J. (2003). Relationship-based clustering and visualization for high-dimensional data mining. *Journal on Computing, 15*(2), 208–230.

Tam, K. Y., & Kiang, M. Y. (1992). Managerial applications of neural networks: The case of bank failure predictions. *Management Science, 38*(7), 926–947.

Taylor, R., & Holman, R. R. (2015). Normal weight individuals who develop Type 2 diabetes: The personal fat threshold. *US National Library of Medicine.* Retrieved from www.ncbi.nlm.nih.gov/pubmed/25515001.

Using the team data science process with azure machine learning. Retrieved from azure.microsoft.com/en-us/documentation/learning-paths/data -science-process/.

Waller, N. G., & Meekl, P. E. (1998). *Multivariate taxometric procedures: Distinguishing types from continua.* Thousand Oaks, CA: Sage.

What are the differences between one-tailed and two-tailed tests? Retrieved from stats.idre.ucla.edu/other/mult-pkg/faq/general/faq-what-are-the -differences-between-one-tailed-and-two-tailed-tests/.

CHAPTER 9

Results Activation

Numbers have an important story to tell. They rely on you to give them a clear and convincing voice.

Stephen Few, Author & Visualization Guru

PROCESS OVERVIEW

The concept of **results activation** sounds far less exciting than **storytelling** or **analytics evangelism** but it is important to encapsulate the notion that results, no matter how interesting, do not solve problems by their mere existence. The Analytics Lifecycle is wrought with **barriers to successful adoption**, but none worse, perhaps, than an interesting result without a purpose or a plan of action.

 TIP

An interesting finding without action is the death knell for analytics.

Later, I will address some of the barriers that organizations find during the transition from prototype to production. But for now, the discussion of this results activation best practice area will outline the processes that support moving a finding from "prototype" to testing and to operationalization.

Relating the Analytics Lifecycle to design thinking, results activation can be viewed as the "testing and implementation" phase (Figure 9.1).

We begin by testing analytics findings first by socializing them with the people who matter. The stakeholders of analytic results include those who translate the mathematics into everyday workflows, as well as those whose problem sparked the cause during problem framing. Analytic models are often automated alerts, business rules for decision making, or work instructions that guide operational processes. An analytic model may guide call-center interactions, or for a disease management company to work behind the scenes to prioritize high-risk patients who need proactive interventions.

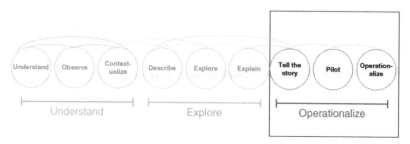

Figure 9.1 Results activation in the context of design thinking

Why Do This?

Just as with other forms of organizational change, strong, proactive leadership is needed in managing analytics results and its implications throughout the business. You cannot assume that people will just accept the results, especially if the results are counterintuitive or require people to change their normal behaviors.

 TIP

When we talk about organizations changing, we are really talking about the creation of a mindset that helps individuals make a personal transition in the context of technology and processes wrapped inside an organizational culture.

It is often said that a future state is achieved only when people do their jobs differently and make their own transition from their current state to future state. Change management is not about forcing change, but rather helping people prepare for the change (awareness), understanding the rationale and impact (knowledge), helping them with the tools that allow for skills development (adoption), and also anchoring those skills and integrating them into their work and behaviors (commitment).

The discussion on the problem framing best practice focused on the change imperative. That is, it included the development of a problem statement and associated questions to help create a shared understanding of the problem. In results activation, everyone is reminded of the issue and why it is important to solve. This serves as a rallying point for the desired future state and paves the way for change.

In the sensemaking best practice area, root-cause analysis was performed and we tried to make sense of the factors that could impact the problem. This was an essential path to understanding and explaining the features that turn out to be important in describing the relationships seen in the data.

The analytics model development best practice area hones in on the model that best represents the relationships between elements (or features) that can be used to solve or mitigate the problem.

Work in the results activation best practice area is done to:

- remind everyone of the future state goal (solving the problem)
- validate the interpretation of the data and its interdependencies
- evaluate the proposed solution
- assess the feasibility of the solution, and
- determine the impact of the solution on people, processes and systems

But perhaps most importantly, this best practice area serves to communicate the "story" in ways that are efficient, insightful, and one that helps to create a shared view and alignment on actions. I find that most executives often lack the mathematical and analytical skills required to understand how algorithms work or why the data says what it does, so it is up to us to use our skills to connect the analytics insights with the people who can leverage them in pursuit of change.

As John Pyhtila, the former head of analytics at Cigna (now Chief Analytics Officer at Partners Health System) suggests (Woodie, 2015, Seven Powerful Analytic Lessons from the CAO Summit), we need to get better at telling the story. "Telling a cohesive and accurate business analytics story requires somebody with a specific skillset. Having the right talent that's consultative in nature to understand that underlying question, and then work with the analytics COEs [centers of excellence] to structure the response."

Process Areas

In the results activation best practice area, the discussion of **results interpretation, program evaluation,** and **actioning** analytics is focused on the following key processes:

- Solution evaluation
- Operationalization
- Presentation and storytelling

Note that the discussion begins with solution evaluation and operationalization, but this doesn't necessarily mean that storytelling won't be interleaved throughout each of these areas. This chapter looks at these sections in more detail.

SOLUTION EVALUATION

In Chapter 6, one of the process areas that helped support the prioritization of the problem was outlined in a process known as "Business Case Prioritization." In the current context, solution evaluation is a check on whether the solution truly satisfies the promises made earlier in the Analytics Lifecycle. That is, does the solution solve the problem, and do the analytics results provide a clear path for action?

The questions to be asked in this process are:

- Is the proposed solution feasible?
- What is the impact to the business?
- What data and technology are required?
- Does it meet the needs, i.e., solve the underlying problem?

The analytics model development process involves the following steps:

1. Model review and validation
2. Evaluation of results
3. Impact assessment

Step 1. Model Review and Validation

As part of the analytics model development effort, the data scientist will validate the model using techniques most appropriate for the type of analysis. For example, in a prediction model, care is taken so as to not over-fit the model by separating out the training data from the test and validation data (EliteDataScience, 2017, Overfitting in Machine Learning). While not always practical due to sample size issues and other constraints, it is necessary for the model development process to be internally validated.

By using a well-crafted study design, you can confidently say that the test design is suitable to demonstrate that your model is a good representation of the underlying business process. A number of criteria help demonstrate overall model performance, including the concordance (or c) statistic for discriminative ability (or area under the receiver operating characteristic (ROC) curve), net reclassification improvement (NRI) and reclassification tables, integrated discrimination improvement (IDI), and goodness-of-fit statistics for calibration, fit statistics, and error rates. See for example, (Steyerberg et al., 2010), (J. Ibrahim, Chen, & Sinha, 2001), (Microsoft, 2017), and (Kiranmai & Pamodaram, 2014).

Best practice is to conduct a thorough review of the methods used, assumptions made, and even participation in code reviews and/or presentations to friendly peers to ensure that mistakes were not made or implications overlooked. The unintended consequences of a misstep at this point can erode confidence in the model building process and the analytics data product.

 TIP

By demonstrating the robustness of your analytics processes, you engender confidence in your results.

Step 2. Evaluation of Results

Beyond the validation of the model itself, it is also necessary to consider if there are issues that may be important in the business context that were not previously considered. If you were sufficiently engaged with your stakeholders during the previous activities, you can often avoid this mistake. This step is an important reminder to purposefully evaluate the results.

As part of the evaluation process, it is important to look at the results in the context in which they were intended to operate. You may have, for example, developed the model on data that was pulled weeks or months ago. By using current data combined with a deep understanding of the current state of the business, you can apply your results to see if the issue still persists and whether the model adequately addresses the issue. Model development often occurs outside of the normal business context and new information is gained during that timeframe that could have aided the process. It is time to apply this new information and consider other results, interventions, or assessments that were used or considered.

Results interpretation is a key component in the best practice of results activation. It is critical to exercise critical thinking skills to ensure that what is seen in the data and the resulting mathematical model competently addresses the problem as outlined in the problem statement.

One of the metrics that matter most during this step is whether the results are accurate and the model generalizable.

TIP

The goal of this step is to thoroughly evaluate analytics findings and their relevance to the business.

Step 3. Impact Assessment

Once you have evaluated the findings, you must turn to evaluating the impact and real world implications of the model. **Impact assessment** seeks to uncover potential implications in a number of areas that include:

- *Process impacts*—Workflow or process changes, operational performance impacts, measurement and management systems.

- *Technology impacts*—Tools, technology, software, systems, infrastructure, or data.

- *Organizational impacts*—Capabilities required.
- *People impacts*—Culture, skills/expertise, roles and responsibilities, workload, and incentives.

During problem framing, data sensemaking, and analytics model development, you should have been inventorying these impacts and working proactively to mitigate them as part of your solution. However, it is at this point where detailed interviews and an accurate assessment of the proposed solution should be conducted. Topics for these discussions should include the drivers of change (both to confirm with and to remind all stakeholders), how people will be affected, and what will be required to successfully implement the change.

 TIP

Critical to ensuring that analytics are actionable is an accurate assessment of the impact, breadth, depth, and criticality of change and its impacts.

It is useful to consider alternatives explanations at this point in the process. Understanding options can help create "quick wins" if more involved solutions require longer-term efforts. Look for behavior, process, and technology changes that are relatively easy to implement, and use these to build momentum quickly.

At the end of this phase, a decision on the use of the analytics model results should be reached.

Toolkit @ www.analyticslifecycletoolkit.com

Download a sample questionnaire that will guide you through the evaluation questions.

OPERATIONALIZATION

Operationalization defines how to translate an analytics model into practice. Generally speaking, this includes deciding how to implement the solution along with updates to work instructions, policies, and procedures, as well as a plan for monitoring the model's performance.

Robin Way, the chief executive officer of the Corios Group, an analytics consultancy, outlined the following key findings in a red paper on **model deployment** (Way, 2017):

Key Findings

1. Many companies are not realizing the full economic potential of their analytics model assets due to lack of adoption, largely the result of failing to deploy them properly.

2. Businesses need a common language for understanding and implementing analytics models that they can share with constituencies in information technology and the customer-facing field.

To mitigate the risk of not realizing the full value of analytics, organizations should follow these critical steps:

1. Deployment planning
2. Definition of key metrics
3. Program evaluation

Step 1. Deployment Planning

This step considers the evaluation of results and determines the most appropriate strategy for deployment. That is, plan the activities that are needed to go from the analytics laboratory to the real world.

In the impact assessment above, all of the impacts are considered in order to design the solution that will most benefit the organization. More often than not, I see organizations that plan around the technology but neglect the people and process side of the analytics solution. The capabilities needed for a successful implementation of an analytics solution require alignment between the strategy and the tactics—including how people will work and how they will be incentivized.

The areas that need careful planning include those described above as "impacts." One useful strategy that I have found in my own consulting work is to conduct pilots in order to bridge the gap between the known and the unknown. That is, pilots help translate what we think we know into reality.

Activities that should be considered during operationalization include:

- *Pilot strategy*—How to socialize and validate the model as delivered and to truly appreciate the impact on the business.

- *Technology transfer*—Moving from the analytics sandbox, using test data (and test structures) to a production system; this includes understanding how production systems need to operationalize the code and whether the model code will need to be rewritten into a production capable package (e.g., Java, C, or PMML).

- *Business processes*—What will need to be updated as the business uses the model. Consider the processes that need to be refined, developed, and documented, and explore the development of individual skills required to support the model in practice.

- *Capability development*—Capabilities developed in a lab are not automatic in the business; it is critical to plan for the activities needed to develop them. Examples might include how to operationalize the data feeds used in model construction or how best to provide alerts in operational systems.

- *Performance testing*—While a consideration of most software projects, analytics projects often skip this critical step of seeing how well the analytics models run under real-world circumstances (production hardware, full data sources).

**Toolkit @
www.analyticslifecycletooklit.com**

Download a sample deployment project plan.

Step 2. Definition of Key Metrics

In addition to planning for a successful deployment of an analytics model, it is also important to dust off your business case and activate your measurement strategy for your program. Remember, analytics data projects can come in a number of flavors depending on size, scope, and complexity. (Note that Chapter 5 referred to these as requests, projects, and products.)

Putting your measurement strategy to work is an essential part of knowing whether your strategy is successful. Not only does it help reinforce the business case for the original effort, but it also serves to solidify the role of analytics in creating value for the organization as a long-term proposition.

Be careful when creating a measurement strategy, as metrics have a way of driving behaviors. Some useful measures of a model's performance can include:

- *Number of decisions made in non-autonomous systems*—Human judgment is usually augmented by the model's recommendation. This metric looks at how often human beings forgo the judgment of the model and make other decisions.

- *Error rate*—Identifies how accurately the model "gets it right." In classification models, consider using percent correct classification, confusion matrices, specificity and sensitivity, lift, gain, ROC, and area under the curve (AUC). For estimation models, you can use R^2, average error, mean squared error (MSE), median error, average absolute error, and median absolute error. Any assessment of a model should be based specifically on what is appropriate to the test.

- *Business value*—Perhaps the most critical measure; it determines if the model helped create business value by raising, reducing, or eliminating something based on the model results. For example, did the model reduce the number of fraudulent activities, raise patient satisfaction, create new business opportunities or eliminate waste.

- *Speed and agility*—Some of the long-term sustainability measures of an analytics function are how quickly new models can be developed and operationalized. A related measure considers how soon the model decays, or determines the effective lifespan of an analytics model before retuning or replacement has to occur.

Step 3. Program Evaluation

Beyond the tactical measures of performance for a model, it is also useful to conduct lessons learned and an overall evaluation of the analytics program. While it is critical to capture the knowledge before, during, and after model development, it is just as important to consider conducting performance reviews on each of the analytics data products that the team develops.

During these reviews, ask the following questions:

- What were the bright spots?
- What issues were encountered?
- What are the areas of opportunity/improvement?
- What did we learn?
- Where were the pitfalls, rabbit holes, or misleading approaches found?
- What are some best practices or hints that can be used in selecting techniques in similar situations?

As a best practice, remember to update the project notebook and gather input from all stakeholders—both inside and outside the analytics team.

**Toolkit @
www.analyticslifecycletooklit.com**

Download a sample lessons learned questionnaire.

PRESENTATION AND STORYTELLING

Stories can move, mobilize, and motivate people toward change and action.

Ideo, on the power of storytelling

Of all the resources available within a data-driven organization, executive attention is likely to be in the shortest supply. Most executives rarely have a background in analyzing data and are more likely to get new information regarding analytics and change management from the *New York Times* or *Harvard Business Review* than from scholarly journals. As a result, the **presentation** strategy for analytics results must change from a didactic format to one that tells a compelling story about a business problem, using visuals that help create an image in the mind's eye.

TIP

The reality is, data means little without the ability to convey it.

To that end, those who develop great stories understand how people learn, think, and consume information. Whether building a business case to open a new clinic, presenting research findings, or evaluating business outcomes, you are crafting a story that is defined by the methods that you use to convey the narrative.

The sad fact is that while there are numerous courses, videos, and workshops on storytelling, as well as countless resources on giving effective presentations, few of them tackle the real challenge of telling a compelling story using data. I liken this to learning how to be funny. I can *want* to be funny. I can *study* the art of humor. I can *take classes*. I can even *participate* in workshops on stand-up comedy. The same is true for the art of storytelling with data—it must be developed, and that requires *practice, coaching,* and *feedback.*

> *... acquisition of skills requires a regular environment, an adequate opportunity to practice, and rapid and unequivocal feedback about the correctness of thoughts and actions.*
>
> —Daniel Kahneman, *Thinking, Fast and Slow* (Kahneman, 2013)

Data Storytelling Resources

Here are some of my favorite works categorized by the way I think about storytelling. Later, some recommended practices for storytelling with data will be outlined.

Motivation, Perception, Biases, Thinking, and Learning

- Daniel Kahneman (and Amos Tversky)
  - *Thinking, Fast and Slow* (Kahneman, 2013)
  - *Judgment Under Uncertainty: Heuristics and Biases* (Amos Tversky & Kahneman, 1974), (Kahneman, Slovic, & Tversky, 1982)
  - *Choices, Values, and Frames* (A. Tversky & Kahneman, 1981) (Kahneman, Tversky, & J. Gregory Dees Memorial Collection., 2000)
- John Rauser
  - *How Humans See Data* (Rauser, 2016)
  - *Statistics Without the Agonizing Pain* (Rauser, 2014)
  - *Investigating Anomalies* (Rauser, 2012)
  - *Look at Your Data* (Rauser, 2011)
- William S. Cleveland and Robert McGill
  - *The Elements of Graphing Data* (W. S. Cleveland, 1985)
  - *Graphical Perception and Graphical Methods for Analyzing Scientific Data* (W. Cleveland & McGill, 1985)

Inventory of Visualization Techniques

- *Periodic Table of Visualization Methods* (literacy.org)
- *The Data Visualization Catalogue* ("Data visualization catalogue," n.d.)
- *Duke University Data Visualization Lab—Data Viz Types* (Zoss, 2017)
- *A Tour Through the Visualization Zoo* (Heer, Bostock, & Ogievetsky, n.d.)

Presentation Best Practices

- Nancy Duarte
  - *slide:ology: The Art and Science of Creating Great Presentations* (Duarte, 2008)
  - *Resonate: Present Visual Stories that Transform Audiences* (Duarte, 2010)

- *HBR Guide to Persuasive Presentations* (HBR Guide Series) (Harvard Business Review Guides) (Duarte, 2012)

- *Illuminate: Ignite Change Through Speeches, Stories, Ceremonies, and Symbols* (Duarte & Sanchez, 2016)

- Dave McKinsey

  - *Strategic Storytelling: How to Create Persuasive Business Presentations* (McKinsey, 2014)

- Garr Reynolds

  - *Presentation Zen: Simple Ideas on Presentation Design and Delivery* (Reynolds, 2011)

Data Visualization Techniques and Considerations

- Scott Berinato

  - *Good Charts: The HBR Guide to Making Smarter, More Persuasive Data Visualizations* (Berinato, 2016)

- Alberto Cairo

  - *The Functional Art: An Introduction to Information Graphics and Visualization* (Cairo, 2012)

  - *The Truthful Art: Data, Charts, and Maps for Communication* (Cairo, 2016)

- Stephen Few

  - *Signal: Understanding What Matters in a World of Noise* (Few, 2015)

  - *Information Dashboard Design: Displaying Data for At-a-glance Monitoring* (1st ed.) (Few, 2006)

  - *Now You See It: Simple Visualization Techniques for Quantitative Analysis* (Few, 2009)

  - *Show Me the Numbers: Designing Tables and Graphs to Enlighten* (2nd ed.) (Few, 2012)

- Andy Kirk

  - *Data Visualisation: A Handbook for Data Driven Design* (Kirk, 2016)

- Edward Tufte

  - *The Visual Display of Quantitative Information* (Tufte, 2001)

  - *Envisioning Information* (Tufte, 1990)

- *Beautiful Evidence* (Tufte, 2006)
- *Visual Explanations: Images and Quantities, Evidence and Narrative* (Tufte, 1997)
- Colin Ware
  - *Visual Thinking for Design* (Ware, 2008)
  - *Information Visualization, Perception for Design* (Ware, 2004)
- Nathan Yau
  - *Data Points: Visualization That Means Something* (Yau, 2013)

Storytelling

- Giorgia Lupi
  - *Dear Data* (Lupi, Posavec, & Popova, 2016)
- Cole Nussbaumer Knaflic
  - *Storytelling with Data: A Data Visualization Guide for Business Professionals* (Knaflic, n.d.)
- Videos/Courses
  - Khan Academy—*Pixar's Perspective on Storytelling* (Academy, 2017)
  - TED Talk—*Clues to a Great Story* (Stanton, 2012)
  - Ideo University—*Storytelling for Influence* ("Storytelling for Influence," 2017)

Best Practices for Storytelling with Data

A large part of creating shared alignment is through storytelling, and one of the tools in the storytelling toolkit is data visualization. As John Rauser (Rauser, 2016) says, "the act of creating a visualization is fundamentally an act of communication."

The goal of visualization is to make new ideas appear in the heads of other people.

John Rauser, How Humans See Data

In terms of best practices, the following steps can be useful in helping you develop the ability to convey a story successfully. Note that many of these have been derived from feedback from my students, courses that I have taken, and the many experts I have seen, read, or followed over the years. My best practices for storytelling with data include the following.

Understanding Your Audience

In practical terms, understanding your audience is all about empathy. What does your audience care about? This will likely change depending on who they are. Consider the different perspectives that each of these professionals might have—executives, lawyers, engineers, data geeks, operational types, physicians, or statisticians. First and foremost, the critical part of telling stories with data is to understand and empathize with those responsible for enacting your recommendations. Specifically, empathy is framed through a lens that seeks to understand:

- What are their motivations?
- What biases do they have?
- What do they care about?
- How they are incentivized?
- What motivates them to action (or inaction?)
- Do they support your success (or failure?)
- What keeps them awake at night?
- How data literate are they?
- How risk tolerant/averse are they?

Understanding your audience's perspective will help you design the right message. To understand more about empathy, learn more about **design thinking** (Dam & Siang, 2017), as empathy is central to the design thinking process and has influenced organizations to rethink their entire strategy for how products are developed (Elmansy) and services delivered (Sutton & Hoyt, 2016).

> *Empathy is the centerpiece of a human-centered design process. The Empathize mode is the work you do to understand people, within the context of your design challenge. It is your effort to understand the way they do things and*

*why, their physical and emotional needs, how they think
about the world, and what is meaningful to them.*

Hasso Plattnew, Stanford Institute of Design

In analytics, we empathize to observe, engage, and listen. We
observe how business processes work, we understand how data is
created, transmitted, and transformed. We learn about the role of
data in decisions and appreciate the processes used. We engage users
through discussions, interviews, and through informal conversations.
Empathy is all about understanding the people that have to contribute
to, validate, and consume our analytics products. Furthermore, as you
will see in Chapter 11, we use these same processes to design how
analytics services are delivered.

 TIP

A critical part in understanding your audience is to know where they are today.

Designing Your Story Blueprint

Once you understand where your audience is with respect to your message, it is important to frame the design of your story around the message. For example, are you looking to update an executive on the status
of your project, convey important data useful in their decision-making
progress, or hoping to spark action?

If, for example, everyone is aligned on what should happen, then
the transformation from where they are to where you would like
them to be (influencing change) is small and the story can reflect this
objective. In this case, you may want to focus on a quick summary or
update rather than a persuasive presentation. This is referred to as the
Approach-Findings-Implications Framework and used for informative
presentations as described below.

 TIP

Understanding the goal of the story is critical, as stories are often about transforming
someone's understanding, perception, or opinion.

As Dave McKinsey points out in his book *Strategic Storytelling: How to Create Persuasive Business Presentations* (McKinsey, 2014), if the audience transformation is wide, you may want to use the Situation-Opportunity-Resolution Framework, which he explains is a subtle variation on the Situation-Complication-Resolution Framework (SCR).

Several design patterns can be used to frame your presentation:

- *Pyramid Principle or Situation-Complication-Question-Answer (SCQA)*—Barbara Minto evolved the approach used in the nineteenth-century German playwright Gustav Freytag's dramatic story arc into the SCQA approach as a way to frame introductions to business communications. See Barbara Minto's approach in Chapter 2, where she advocates inductive logic for most problem-solving exercises, stressing the importance of considering mutually exclusive and collectively exhaustive (MECE) sets of ideas (Minto, 1996) (Hare, 2007).

- *Situation-Complication-Resolution Framework (SCR)*—SCR is used extensively in management consulting (such as McKinsey), this technique is rooted in the scientific method including hypothesis testing, inductive logic, and deductive logic. Common for presentations used in strategic storytelling, the steps start with describing the situation in a way that is easy to understand, then outlining why the situation is problematic, which leads to a solution or proposed set of solutions (Hansen, 2017).

- *Situation-Opportunity-Resolution Framework (SOR or S.Co.R.E. method)*—This is a subtle variation on SCR that comes in handy when you want decision makers to act in order to capture a set of benefits (Abela, 2011).

- *Situation, Background, Assessment, Recommendation (SBAR)*—SBAR is a technique used extensively in healthcare for performance improvement projects. It is well suited for use in analytics projects and provides a structured way of presenting analytics projects and standardizing communication, making it easy for participants to have common expectations related to what is to be communicated and how the communication is structured. This technique includes a concise statement of the problem, relevant background information, an analysis and consider-ations of options, and the action requested/recommended (Permanente, n.d.).

- *The Pilot-Results-Scale Framework*—This is simply another variation on SCR where the pilot (or small test) is the situation, the results of the pilot are the complication, and the recommendation to scale-up is, well, the recommendation (Smith & Harrison, 2009).

- *Matt Abrahams's "What? So what? Now what?"*—This is a generalized version of the SCR model. When using this structure, start with your central claim, then explain its significance, and conclude with a call to action (Abrahams, n.d.).

- *Bottom-line-up-front (BLUF)*—Used extensively in the US military, BLUF outlines the conclusions and recommendations at the beginning of the presentation, rather than the end, in order to facilitate rapid decision making ("BLUF," 2017).

- *Journalism's inverted pyramid*—Used in writing news copy, the inverted pyramid suggests that news be told in order of most interesting/important to least interesting/important (e.g., headlines first). It can be adapted to presentations but is not used as often as other techniques ("Inverted Pyramid (Journalism)," 2017).

In my consulting work, I use a framework designed to outline the important aspects of a data story:

- Content
  - Why: Why are we doing this presentation, and why should the audience care?
  - What: What are the key messages?
  - How: How will we tell the story?
  - What if? If this resonates, what will success look like?
- Audience
  - Who: Who are the key individuals or groups involved in this discussion?

- ▪ Learning and decision styles: What balance is needed between education and setting the scope for decisions? How does this vary for each of the decision makers and their key influencers?
- ▪ Story
  - ▪ Structure: What is the framework for the story?
  - ▪ Character: Who or what are the key characters? What are the factors that will allow the audience to empathize with the characters?
  - ▪ Sense of urgency: Why should the audience make a choice to support the change/recommendations now?
  - ▪ Delivery plan: What is the sequence of people, places, and events to tell the story for the audience? What is the "ask" in each telling to move to the next step?
- ▪ Tell
  - ▪ Design: What are the relevant formats for the visual content? Are there cultural, organizational, or personal expectations from the audience?
  - ▪ Test: What is the target level of comprehension and background information required from the audience? Who should be included in the testing of the story? Will it help to involve key members of the audience?

In Figure 9.2, I illustrate this method using a RealTimeBoard template.

**Toolkit @
www.analyticslifecycletooklit.com**

Access the storytelling plan template.

Framing the story in this manner makes it possible to capture the essence of the story and the context in which it should be told. It reflects the story's blueprint.

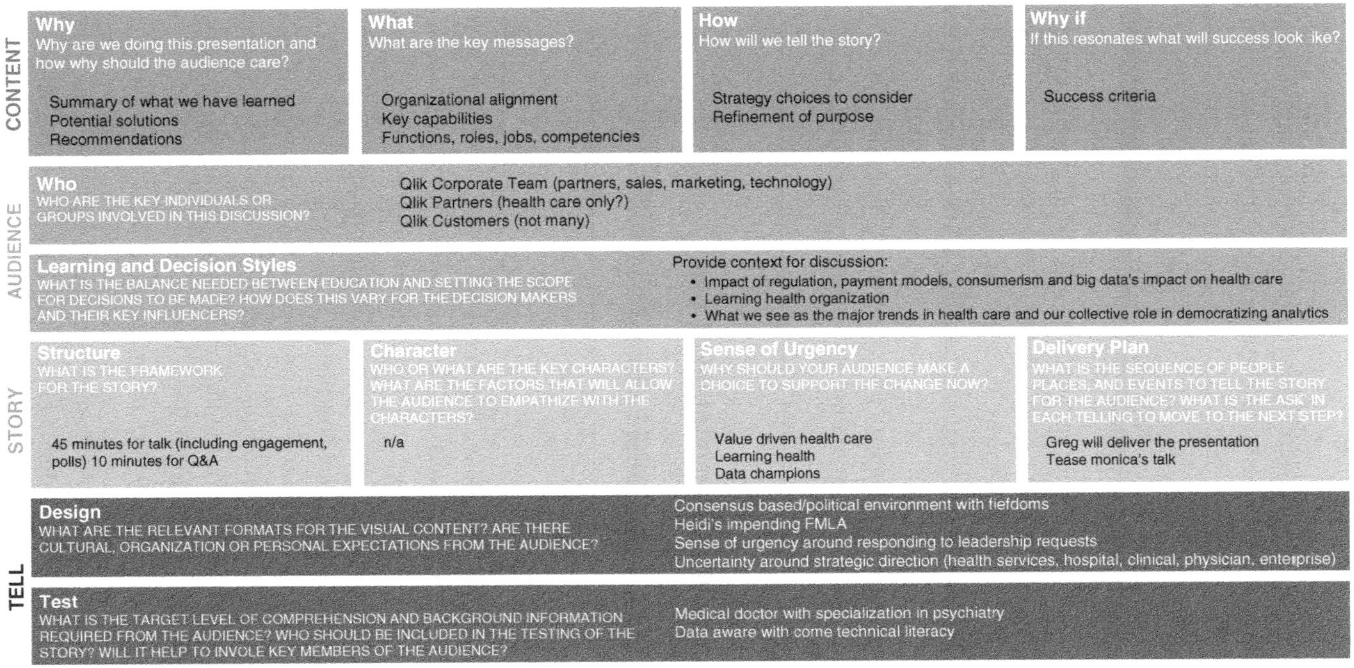

CONTENT

Why
Why are we doing this presentation and how why should the audience care?

Summary of what we have learned
Potential solutions
Recommendations

What
What are the key messages?

Organizational alignment
Key capabilities
Functions, roles, jobs, competencies

Why if
If this resonates what will success look like?

Success criteria

AUDIENCE

Who
WHO ARE THE KEY INDIVIDUALS OR GROUPS INVOLVED IN THIS DISCUSSION?

Qlik Corporate Team (partners, sales, marketing, technology)
Qlik Partners (health care only?)
Qlik Customers (not many)

How
How will we tell the story?

Strategy choices to consider
Refinement of purpose

STORY

Learning and Decision Styles
WHAT IS THE BALANCE NEEDED BETWEEN EDUCATION AND SETTING THE SCOPE FOR DECISIONS TO BE MADE? HOW DOES THIS VARY FOR THE DECISION MAKERS AND THEIR KEY INFLUENCERS?

Provide context for discussion:
- Impact of regulation, payment models, consumerism and big data's impact on health care
- Learning health organization
- What we see as the major trends in health care and our collective role in democratizing analytics

Character
WHO OR WHAT ARE THE KEY CHARACTERS? WHAT ARE THE FACTORS THAT WILL ALLOW THE AUDIENCE TO EMPATHIZE WITH THE CHARACTERS?

n/a

Sense of Urgency
WHY SHOULD YOUR AUDIENCE MAKE A CHOICE TO SUPPORT THE CHANGE NOW?

Value driven health care
Learning health
Data champions

Structure
WHAT IS THE FRAMEWORK FOR THE STORY?

45 minutes for talk (including engagement, polls) 10 minutes for Q&A

Delivery Plan
WHAT IS THE SEQUENCE OF PEOPLE, PLACES, AND EVENTS TO TELL THE STORY FOR THE AUDIENCE? WHAT IS THE ASK IN EACH TELLING TO MOVE TO THE NEXT STEP?

Greg will deliver the presentation
Tease monica's talk

TELL

Design
WHAT ARE THE RELEVANT FORMATS FOR THE VISUAL CONTENT? ARE THERE CULTURAL, ORGANIZATION OR PERSONAL EXPECTATIONS FROM THE AUDIENCE?

Consensus based/political environment with fiefdoms
Heidi's impending FMLA
Sense of urgency around responding to leadership requests
Uncertainty around strategic direction (health services, hospital, clinical, physician, enterprise)

Test
WHAT IS THE TARGET LEVEL OF COMPREHENSION AND BACKGROUND INFORMATION REQUIRED FROM THE AUDIENCE? WHO SHOULD BE INCLUDED IN THE TESTING OF THE STORY? WILL IT HELP TO INVOLVE KEY MEMBERS OF THE AUDIENCE?

Medical doctor with specialization in psychiatry
Data aware with some technical literacy

Figure 9.2 Planning for telling your data story

Transforming the Audience

While there is no one right way to translate your blueprint into a specific delivery mechanism, one useful technique that I learned from Joe Ross from *Ideas on Stage*, is called the audience transformation matrix.

In this process, you outline the key message and what you want your audience to know, believe, feel, and do as a result of your story. This is done based on three time periods: what people know (and believe, feel, and do) when you arrive (before the story begins), and what you want them to know (believe, feel, and do) afterwards. The gap that exists between what they already know and what you want them to know provides the content strategy for your story.

Figure 9.3 is an example of an audience transformation matrix that was developed for a presentation using RealTimeBoard.

**Toolkit @
www.analyticslifecycletooklit.com**

Access the templates shown in steps 1 to 3.

Telling Your Story

Beyond the planning stage, you must tell your story. This is where the countless videos, books, articles, and other resources on effective presentations, storytelling, and visual design principles come into play. The best practice resources noted earlier in this chapter can provide just the advice and council you need.

The medium that you use to tell your story matters. To get you started, some different mediums are outlined below for your consideration. Think about how a medium helps you convey your story, and don't be limited to traditional forms for data stories. After all, you want your story to resonate. Tactics to engage your audience include:

- *Experiences*—Albert Einstein was credited with saying, "The only source of knowledge is experience." In creating understanding and shared understanding, you can use experiences to help

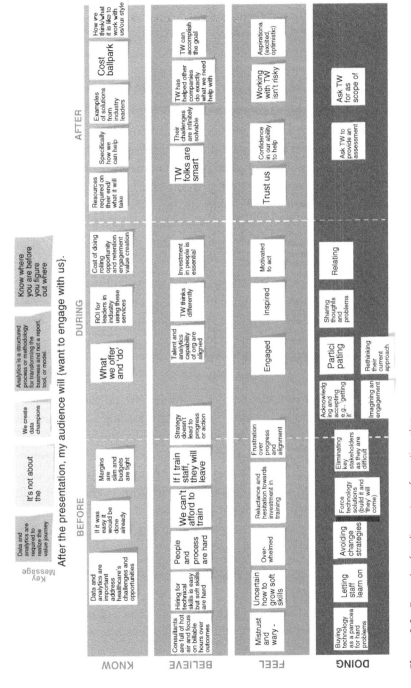

After the presentation, my audience will (want to engage with us).

Figure 9.3 Example of audience transformation plan

289

translate the impact of a problem (and your solution) by having people live the problem and see your solution in context. An example of data experiences is the Gemba Walk, also referred to as a process walk (O'Rourke, 2014), which is focused on the discovery of the issues through real-world activities. (Note that you can use this in concert with physical visualizations below.)

■ *Interactions*—By having your audience play with the data (using dashboards or visual analytics) before, during, or after your presentation, you can engage them in data sensemaking on their own. Remember, they didn't get a chance to work the entire Analytics Lifecycle. For research on factors that affect engagement with big data, see Kennedy, Hill, Allen, and Kirk (2016). Utilizing tools such as the Jupyter Notebook or a JMP Journal can be useful, as it allows for active data exploration with your audience.

■ *Videos and animations*—Often cited as the masters of storytelling, Pixar has shown us what it is like to engage audiences and make them feel (Starr, 2015). For data stories, there are great examples of telling data stories with videos and animations. For example, Hans Rosling popularized the use of animations in telling his story (Rosling, 2006).

■ *Physical visualizations*—Similar to animations, physical visualizations help bring your stories to life. Hans Rosling is an expert on physical visualizations and incorporates physical objects as part of his story ("The best Hans Rosling talks you've ever seen.") In fact, he popularized the concept of physical visualizations by using pebbles, toy construction kits, fruit juice, snowballs, and even toilet paper. Pierre Dragicevic and Yvonne Jansen maintain a list of physical visualizations to inspire us! (Dragicevic & Jansen)

The next time you are telling a story, consider an alternative to "death by PowerPoint."

Note, however, that you need to link the choice of medium back to understanding our audience as these techniques may not always be appropriate.

The University of Washington *Interactive Data Lab* has a unique perspective. In their work on "Narrative Visualization: Telling Stories with Data" (Segel & Heer, 2010), Edward Segel and Jeffrey Heer advise us to focus on what they call "reader-driven" storytelling. Here, they change the dynamic from having us, as data scientists, tell the story with data (referred to as "author-driven" storytelling) to one in which the reader is allowed to construct the relationships they find interesting and useful. The reader-driven narrative provides ways for the reader to play with data.

This modality is also evident in Alberto Cairo's work in infographics where he emphasizes the importance of engaging the reader in self-exploration and understanding. See, for example (Cairo, 2012).

 TIP

Data visualizations serve to complement the narrative and improve engagement.

Creating a Sense of Urgency and a Clear Pathway

Rudyard Kipling once wrote, "If history were taught in the form of stories, it would never be forgotten." For data stories, we don't want people to forget, we want them to remember and to take action. Analytics without action is pointless. If action is not the goal, then we should consider whether stopping earlier in the process (problem framing or sensemaking) would have been a better use of resources.

While not every presentation should be about persuasion, stories are often presented to both educate and align. As John Sviokla posits, "It can help create a shared view of a situation and align folks on needed actions" (Sviokla, 2009).

 TIP

By asking yourself at the outset, "So what?" you can help frame your story in a way that answers that essential question.

Be prepared to help the audience member answer that question for themselves, rather than having them guess, or worse, not finding an answer. One technique useful for all analytics professions is what Andrew M. Ibrahim, MD, MSc calls "the Visual Abstract" (Ibrahim, 2017). While applied to scientific findings published in the health-care literature, this technique forces us to consider the "Cliff Notes" version of our story and whether it is worth telling.

**Toolkit @
www.analyticslifecycletooklit.com**

Download the primer on How to Create a Visual Abstract.

Storytelling with data should create a sense of urgency and provoke action. The sense of urgency was built during the problem framing, and now is the time to link the impact of the problem to your solution.

CHAPTER SUMMARY

Most organizations recognize that being a successful, data-driven company requires skilled developers and analysts. Fewer grasp how to use data to tell a meaningful story that resonates both intellectually and emotionally with an audience.

Daniel Waisberg[1]

Results activation is the best practice area that takes data and analytics out of the lab and into the hearts, minds, and behaviors of human beings. As shown in this chapter, a number of processes are needed to serve as a critical bridge to realizing the full benefit of analytics.

The key processes discussed in this chapter include:

■ Solution evaluation

■ Operationalization

■ Presentation and storytelling

---

[1] www.thinkwithgoogle.com/marketing-resources/data-measurement/tell-meaningful-stories-with-data/.

This best practice area provides the critical linkage between the promises made (in the business case) to the value of change. In solution evaluation, we consider a number of questions designed to review the results and evaluate them for fit and feasibility. A key competency in this area is **critical thinking** as results are translated through the lens of interpretation, application, and impact.

In operationalization, we explored the processes used for the successful deployment of an analytics model to ensure that the full benefit is realized. Here, we discussed the critical step of planning for the deployment, defining the **critical success factors**, and discussed how best to assess analytics impact through program evaluation.

Finally, we outlined some recommendations for presenting analytics findings and discussed data storytelling. There are a number of tools in our proverbial toolbox that can help us tell meaningful stories. As data storytellers, we can learn from a diversity of talent outside our industries, including data journalists. NPR, for example, has outlined 13 steps to plan a newsroom project that have direct applicability on our data storytelling projects (Athas, 2016).

The NPR 13-step process for planning your story follows, along with my personal takeaways for data storytelling:

Step 1: Set aside time. Plan for your story to be told.

Step 2: Get the supplies you need. Equip yourself for success.

Step 3: Begin with a sticky note brainstorm. Collaboration helps people think creatively.

Step 4: Cluster. Conceptualize the content into groups.

Step 5: Rank the themes. Arrange content categories appropriate to your message.

Step 6: Prioritize and choose themes. Prioritize your topics.

Step 7: Define themes. Organize around your key message(s).

Step 8: Identify audiences. Understand that there may be multiple stakeholders.

Step 9: Plan how you'll reach audiences. Define the medium for your message.

Step 10: Outline story ideas. Convert your themes/key messages into stories that resonate.

Step 11: Write a mission statement. Get everyone on board.

Step 12: Set a date. Don't get caught in analysis paralysis.

Step 13: Repeat. The analytics imperative is never done. Continue to find challenges and solve them.

While you or I may disagree with the order of these steps or with specific items (in relation to analytics storytelling), they are thought provoking indeed.

EXERCISE

Perhaps one of the most critical best practice areas of the Analytics Lifecycle, results activation is often the most overlooked.

In this exercise, you will take a problem that you have been working on and complete the activities below. The templates can be found at www.anayticslifecycle.com:

- *Task 1. Complete the solution evaluation template*—This step asks you to consider the fit and function of the analytics model, how you intend to validate the model, and how you plan to evaluate the results. In addition, the questionnaire guides you through your assessment of the model's impact to the organization.

- *Task 2. Complete the operationalization template*—In this task, you will complete a high-level, agile project plan for how you intend to deploy the model. The critical success factors matrix guides you through the development of a measurement plan. The program evaluation template structures your documentation of the lessons learned from your project.

- *Task 3. Develop your data story*—Using the tools provided, document your audience through an empathy questionnaire and resultant **empathy map**, then go through the story-framing exercise, and finally, build your **audience transformation matrix**.

- *Task 4. Tell your story*—Select the most appropriate storytelling design pattern using the templates provided, decide on how you want to unfold your story, then tell it through the example modalities described.

▣ *Task 5. Document your experience*—Reflection is one of the most powerful tools in learning. You can use our analytics journal (see Chapter 7) to capture the details of the process in addition to documenting what you learned and how you felt about the experience. This is a powerful tool for learning and growth.

TOOLKIT SUMMARY

Best Practice Area:	Results Activation	
Purpose:	*What is the intent of this best practice area?* The purpose of results activation is to ensure that the analytics models can be implemented and have the intended effect in the organization.	
Key Competencies:	*Knowledge, skills, abilities, and disposition*	
What do we need to be good at?	▣ Data visualization ▣ Change management ▣ Storytelling ▣ Strategic presentations ▣ Leadership and influence ▣ Critical thinking ▣ Analytical thinking	▣ Understanding of the underlying business and operational context and processes ▣ Analytical model interpretation ▣ Impact assessment ▣ Measurement strategy
Inputs	**Processes**	**Outputs**
▣ Analytics model results ▣ Problem statement ▣ Business case and justification	▣ Solution evaluation ▣ Operationalization ▣ Presentation and storytelling	▣ Impact assessment ▣ Audience transformation matrix ▣ Stakeholder map ▣ Storyboard ▣ Analytics summary presentation

Key Questions:	*What should we know as a result of this best practice?* ▪ Is the proposed solution feasible? ▪ What is the impact to the business? ▪ What data and technology are required? ▪ Does it meet the needs, i.e., solve the underlying problem? ▪ What were the bright spots? ▪ What issues were encountered? ▪ What are the areas of opportunity/improvement? ▪ What did we learn? ▪ Where were the pitfalls, rabbit holes, or misleading approaches found? ▪ What are some best practices or hints that can be used in selecting techniques in similar situations? ▪ How are analytics results best communicated to key stakeholders?

REFERENCES

Abela, D. (2011). The S.Co.R.E. Method for creating a story. Retrieved from extremepresentation.typepad.com/blog/2011/02/the-score-method-for-creating-a-story.html.

Abrahams, M. Valuable Presentation structure = What? So what? Now what? Retrieved from www.nofreakingspeaking.com/valuable-presentation-structure-what-so-what-now-what/.

Academy, K. (2017). The art of storytelling. Retrieved from www.khanacademy.org/partner-content/pixar/storytelling.

Athas, E. (2016). Storytelling tips and best practices. *NPR Training*. Retrieved from training.npr.org/digital/plan-your-newsroom-project-in-13-steps-and-with-lots-of-sticky-notes/.

Berinato, S. (2016). Good charts: the HBR guide to making smarter, more persuasive data visualizations. Retrieved from https://services.hbsp.harvard. edu/services/proxy/content/70368940/70368942/a555650eca34574666 a91f558f21196c.

Boston, Massachusetts: Harvard Business Review Press. Retrieved from https:// datavizcatalogue.com/.

BLUF. (2017). Wikipedia. Retrieved from en.wikipedia.org/wiki/BLUF_ (communication).

Cairo, A. (2012). *The functional art: An introduction to information graphics and visualization.* Berkeley, CA: New Riders.

Cairo, A. (2016). *The truthful art: Data, charts, and maps for communication.* New York: Pearson.

Cleveland, W., & McGill, R. (1985). Graphical perception and graphical methods for analyzing scientific data. *Science, 229*(4716), 828–833.

Cleveland, W. S. (1985). *The elements of graphing data.* Monterey, CA: Wadsworth Advanced Books and Software.

Dam, R., & Siang, T. (2017). Design thinking: Getting started with empathy. Retrieved from www.interaction-design.org/literature/article/design -thinking-getting-started-with-empathy.

Dragicevic, P., & Jansen, Y. (Eds.) Data visualization catalogue. In List of physical visualizations and related artifacts. Retrieved from dataphys.org/list/.

Duarte, N. (2008). *Slide:ology: the art and science of creating great presentations* (1st ed.). Sebastopol, CA: O'Reilly Media.

Duarte, N. (2010). Reonate: Present visual stories that transform audiences. Retrieved from getitatduke.library.duke.edu/?sid=sersol&SS_jc=TC00004 27129&title=Resonate%3A%20Present%20Visual%20Stories%20That% 20Transform%20Audiences.

Duarte, N. (2012). *HBR guide to persuasive presentations.* Boston: Harvard Business Review Press.

Duarte, N., & Sanchez, P. (2016). *Illuminate: Ignite change through speeches, stories, ceremonies, and symbols.* New York: Portfolio/Penguin.

Elmansy, R. Design thinking case study: Innovation at Apple. Retrieved from www.designorate.com/design-thinking-case-study-innovation-at -apple/.

Few, S. (2006). *Information dashboard design: The effective visual communication of data* (1st ed.). Beijing; Cambridge, MA: O'Reilly.

Few, S. (2009). *Now you see it: Simple visualization techniques for quantitative analysis.* Oakland, CA: Analytics Press.

Few, S. (2012). *Show me the numbers: Designing tables and graphs to enlighten* (2nd ed.). Burlingame, CA: Analytics Press.

Few, S. (2015). *Signal: Understanding what matters in a world of noise.* Burlingame, CA: Analytics Press.

Hansen, J. (2017). The most persuasive sales presentation structure of all. Retrieved from ncmagroup.com/2017/05/03/the-most-persuasive-sales -presentation-structure-of-all/.

Hare, R. (2007). The Minto Pyramid Principle (SCQA). Retrieved from www .richardhare.com/2007/09/03/the-minto-pyramid-principle-scqa/.

Heer, J., Bostock, M., & Ogievetsky, V. A tour through the Visualization Zoo. Retrieved from homes.cs.washington.edu/~jheer/files/zoo/.

Ibrahim, A. M. (2017). A primer on how to create a VISUAL ABSTRACT. Retrieved from www.surgeryredesign.com/.

Ibrahim, J., Chen, M. H., & Sinha, D. (2001). Criterion-based methods for Bayesian model assessment. *Statistica Sinica, 11,* 419–443.

Inverted Pyramid (Journalism). (2017). Wikipedia. Retrieved from en.wiki pedia.org/wiki/Inverted_pyramid_(journalism).

Kahneman, D. (2013). *Thinking, fast and slow.* New York: Ferrar, Straus and Giroux.

Kahneman, D., Slovic, P., & Tversky, A. (1982). Judgment under uncertainty: Heuristics and biases. Cambridge; New York: Cambridge University Press.

Kahneman, D., Tversky, A., & J. Gregory. Dees Memorial Collection. (2000). *Choices, values, and frames.* New York; Cambridge, UK: Russell Sage Foundation; Cambridge University Press.

Kennedy, H., Hill, R. L., Allen, W., & Kirk, A. (2016). Engaging with (big) data visualization: Factors that affect engagement and resulting in a new definition of effectiveness. *First Monday, 21*(11).

Kiranmai, B., & Pamodaram, D. A. (2014). A review on evaluation measures for data mining tasks. *International Journal of Engineering and Computer Science, 3*(7), 7217–7220.

Kirk, A. (2016). *Data visualisation: A handbook for data driven design.* London: Sage.

Knaflic, C. N. (2015). *Storytelling with data: A data visualization guide for business professionals.* Hoboken, NJ: John WIley & Sons.

literacy.org, v. A Periodic table of visualization methods. Retrieved from www.visual-literacy.org/periodic_table/periodic_table.html.

Lupi, G., Posavec, S., & Popova, M. (2016). *Dear data: A friendship in 52 weeks of postcards.* Hudson, NY: Princeton Architectural Press.

McKinsey, D. (2014). Strategic storytelling: How to create persuasive business presentations. CreateSpace Independent Publishing Platform.

Microsoft. (2017). Testing and validation (data mining). Retrieved from docs.microsoft.com/en-us/sql/analysis-services/data-mining/testing-and -validation-data-mining.

Minto, B. (1996). *The Minto pyramid principle: Logic in writing, thinking, and problem solving* (New and expanded ed.). London: Minto International.

O'Rourke, T. (2014). 4 best practices to help ensure your process walk is successful. Retrieved from goleansixsigma.com/4-best-practices-to-help-ensure-your-process-walk-is-successful/.

Permanente, K. SBAR toolkit. Retrieved from www.ihi.org/resources/Pages/Tools/sbartoolkit.aspx.

Rauser, J. (Producer). (2011). Look at your data. Retrieved from www.youtube.com/watch?v=coNDCIMH8bk.

Rauser, J. (Producer). (2012). Investigating anomalies. Retrieved from www.youtube.com/watch?v=-3dw09N5_Aw.

Rauser, J. (Producer). (2014). Statistics without the agonizing pain. Retrieved from www.youtube.com/watch?v=5Dnw46eC-0o.

Rauser, J. (Producer). (2016). How humans see data. Retrieved from www.youtube.com/watch?v=fSgEeI2Xpdc&feature=youtu.be.

Reynolds, G. (2011). *Presentation zen: Simple ideas on presentation design and delivery* (2nd ed.) (Voices That Matter). Berkeley, CA: New Riders.

Rosling, H. (2006). Debunking myths about the Third World. Retrieved from www.gapminder.org/videos/hans-rosling-ted-2006-debunking-myths-about-the-third-world/.

Segel, E., & Heer, J. (2010). Narrative visualization: Telling stories with data. Retrieved from vis.stanford.edu/files/2010-Narrative-InfoVis.pdf.

Smith, L. J., & Harrison, M. B. (2009). Framework for conducting and planning pilot studies. *Ostomy Wound Management*. Retrieved from researchgate.net website: www.researchgate.net/publication/40805735_Framework_for_planning_and_conducting_pilot_studies.

Stanton, A. (Producer). (2012). The clues to a great story. *TED X*. Retrieved from www.ted.com/talks/andrew_stanton_the_clues_to_a_great_story.

Starr, B. (2015). 22 Rules to perfect storytelling from a Pixar storyboard artist. Retrieved from www.visualnews.com/2015/09/23/22-rules-to-perfect-storytelling-from-a-pixar-storyboard-artist/.

Steyerberg, E. W., Vickers, A. J., Cook, N. R., Gerds, T., Gonen, M., Obuchowski, N., Pencina, M. J., Kattan, M. W. (2010). Assessing the performance of prediction models: a framework for some traditional and novel measures. *Epidemiology (Cambridge, Mass.)*, 21(1), 128–138. doi:10.1097/EDE.0b013e3181c30fb2.

Storytelling for Influence. (2017). Ideo University. https://www.ideou.com.

Sutton, R. I., & Hoyt, D. (2016). Better service, faster: A design thinking case study. *Harvard Business Review*. Retrieved from hbr.org/2016/01/better-service-faster-a-design-thinking-case-study.

Sviokla, J. (2009). Swimming in data? Three benefits of visualization. *Harvard Business Review* (December 4).

The best Hans Rosling talks you've ever seen. Retrieved from www.ted.com/playlists/474/the_best_hans_rosling_talks_yo.

Tufte, E. R. (1990). *Envisioning information* (11th printing, Nov. 2006. ed.). Cheshire, CT: Graphics Press.

Tufte, E. R. (1997). *Visual explanations: Images and quantities, evidence and narrative*. Cheshire, CT: Graphics Press.

Tufte, E. R. (2001). The visual display of quantitative information (2nd ed.). Cheshire, CT: Graphics Press.

Tufte, E. R. (2006). *Beautiful evidence*. Cheshire, CT: Graphics Press.

Tversky, A., & Kahneman, D. (1974). Judgment under uncertainty: Heuristics and biases. *Science, 185*(4157).

Tversky, A., & Kahneman, D. (1981). The framing of decisions and the psychology of choice. *Science, 211*(4481), 453–458.

Ware, C. (2004). Information visualization: Perception for design (2nd ed.). San Francisco, CA: Morgan Kaufman.

Ware, C. (2008). *Visual thinking for design*. Burlington, MA; Amsterdam: Morgan Kaufmann; Elsevier Science & Technology.

Way, R. (2017). Model Deployment: The moment of truth. Corios Red Papers. Retrieved from coriosgroup.com/download/redpaper-deploy/.

Wikipedia. (2017). Overfitting. Wikipedia. Retrieved from en.wikipedia.org/wiki/Overfitting.

Yau, N. (2013). *Data points: Visualization that means something*. Indianapolis, IN: John Wiley & Sons.

Zoss, A. (2017) Data visualization: Visualization types. https://library.duke.edu/data/about.

CHAPTER **10**

Analytics Product Management

Success is not delivering a feature; success is learning how to solve the customer's problem.

—Eric Ries, *The Lean Startup*

PROCESS OVERVIEW

Product management as applied to analytics is a sparsely covered topic and, in my opinion, reflects on the evolving maturity of analytics as a whole. The idea is that analytics data products (including requests, projects, and products) need to be managed as a "product of data science." This concept was introduced in Chapter 5 when the five best practice areas were identified. The management of data products, processes, and teams is the focus of the analytics product management best practice.

In this chapter, the broad term **analytics data product** is used as a reference to all analytics deliverables—including ad-hoc requests and special projects. Throughout this book, an analytics data product is referred to as the deliverable of data science. Where appropriate, the term *services* is used when discussing how the analytics organization satisfies the needs of customers across the enterprise.

Product

Anything that can be offered to a market for attention, acquisition, use, or consumption that might satisfy a want or need (Kotler & Armstrong, 2010: 7).

Service

An activity or benefit that one party can offer to another that is essentially intangible and does not result in the ownership of anything (Kotler & Armstrong, 2010: 603) (Kotler, 1991).

Note, however, that many organizations treat analytics as "consulting engagements" rather than the analytics products. The danger of this is that consultants are often perceived of as stepping in for only a limited time period and then on to the next project. We need to ensure the long-term success of analytics products.

Regardless of where teams sit from an organizational design perspective, the best practice of analytics product management holds true for requests, projects, and products. That is, for the purposes of describing analytics product management, both **analytics products** and **analytics services** are considered as "products" in the discussion of this best practice area.

Jeremy Howard, president and chief scientist at Kaggle, and his co-authors touched on the concepts of data products in their eBook for O'Reilly, *Designing Great Data Products* (Howard, Loukides, & Zwemer, 2012). The book outlines a four-step method they called the "Drivetrain Approach," inspired by the emerging field of self-driving vehicles. In one of the steps, they illustrate the process as a model assembly line (Figure 10.1), depicting analytics models moving through a production assembly line for data products that transforms the raw data into an actionable outcome.

While this eBook and the associated metaphor are useful, they are overly simplistic, merely scratching the surface of the entirety of the analytics product management best practice area.

My personal view is that analytics product management includes those processes that help ensure that the Analytics Lifecycle functions smoothly and that both are efficient and effective. It broadly considers the processes needed to monitor the fidelity, health, and wealth of the analytics product lifecycle. (The difference between efficiency and effectiveness will be defined in Chapter 11.)

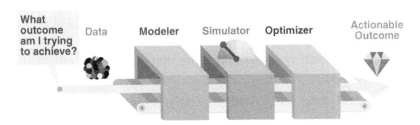

Figure 10.1 Model assembly approach illustrated
Source: Howard, Loukides, and Zwemmer (2012)

The application of product management principles for analytics is intended to address the increased scale, complexity, and cost of analytics product development, and includes the advances that have been made in quantitative methods and data visualization, as well as the advancement of platforms for in-memory and in-database analytics. Analytics product management facilitates more efficient approaches to analytics **product design**, lifecycle processes, oversight, and benefits realization, while continuing to ensure product reliability and durability of analytics results.

Why Do This?

Product management is an essential part of the Analytics Lifecycle and includes governance of many of the processes that are core to turning insights into action. Teams involved in product management range from quality managers who oversee quality processes to project managers who scope projects, maintain project plans, set team priorities, and even mentor teams in effectively using suitable processes.

The analytics product management function is concerned with the following key objectives:

- Implement systems to manage quality throughout all stages of the Analytics Lifecycle.
- Enforce processes that govern the disposition of all analytics team deliverables.
- Manage projects and the entire analytics portfolio.
- Manage the scope, cost, and schedules as deputized by analytics leadership.
- Identify the linkages and dependencies between data products, business policies, and real-world workflows.
- Ensure security and privacy protection for analytics results and their inputs.
- Identify risks across Analytics Lifecycle processes and data.
- Assess the impact of risks and mitigate it through risk controls.
- Manage communication across all stakeholder groups.

- Use quality management approach and increase visibility into analytics product development processes.
- Manage and maintain analytics models and ensure the integrity of analytics results across the portfolio.
- Manage analytics requests, projects, products, and quality processes using a risk-based approach.

PROCESS AREAS

Analytics product management is a multidisciplinary function that reaches across the organization to plan, design, deploy, measure, and improve analytics data products.

Traditionally, these responsibilities have fallen to lead analysts, data scientists, or statisticians who participate in most, if not all, project activities. In some organizations, specialists focus on core activities in the Analytics Lifecycle but leave the bigger picture issues to team leads or managers.

As analytics continues to mature, the need for comprehensive analytics product leadership has become increasingly important. The complexity of the lifecycle, evolving analytics methods, and increased demand make analytics product management an essential best practice for organizations.

The Analytics Product Manager

The role of product manager (or solution manager) is well known in other disciplines, including technology product design (Nelson & Metaxatos, 2016), games (Bay), interactions (Moggridge, 2007), movies (Theus, 2016), everyday products (Norman, 2002), and consumer brands (Kumar, Townsend, & Vorhies, 2014). An analytics product manager takes ownership over a complete line of analytics data products or a product line that represents one or more segments of an organization's analytics needs. We often see titles ranging from project manager to system owner, but the job of the analytics product manager is to lead all aspects of analytics data products for an analytics data product or product line, including strategy, **product roadmap** and prioritization, and feature definition.

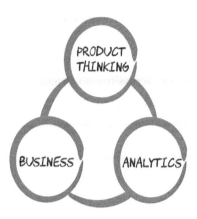

Figure 10.2 Well-rounded analytics product manager maintains balance in business, analytics, and product thinking.

Marty Cagan, the founder of Silicon Valley Product Group, describes the role of the product manager in his book *Inspired* (Cagan, 2008) as "to discover a product that is valuable, usable and feasible." In my view, analytics product management is the intersection between business, analytics, and **product thinking** (Figure 10.2). A well-rounded analytics product manager must be experienced in at least one of these three areas, serve as an evangelist for all three, and converse with experts in all three.

> *Business*—Analytics product management is about applying innovative techniques and quantitative methods to solving problems and in creating business value. A key requirement for the product manager is to be obsessed with finding, creating, and evangelizing that value. Managing and prioritizing the portfolio of analytics projects is a major part of this function.
>
> *Analytics*—While analytics product managers do not need to know how to build a model, they do need have both technical and analytics fluency. That is, they need to be able to sit down with a quant (data scientist), statistician, data modeler, or business analyst and understand how they participate in the Analytics Lifecycle. An untrained project manager will not suffice (nor survive). They need to not only understand the processes involved but also what to expect in terms of deliverables and quality processes, and what it takes to develop and deploy analytics data products.

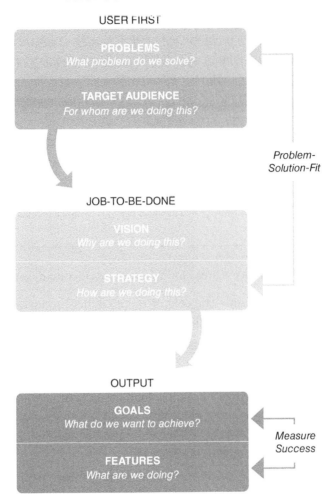

Figure 10.3 Product thinking explained
Source: Nikkel Blaase

Product thinking—Consumers of analytics products and services depend on solutions that meet their needs. Nikkel Blaase, product designer at XING, refers to this as a blend of traditional product management and UX design as "product thinking" (Blasse, 2015), as shown in Figure 10.3. Traditional product management is applied to create a much-needed linkage between the Analytics Lifecycle and the customer experience.

> *By defining the problems the product tackles, it answers the question, "Why do we build this product?" Defining the target audience: "Who has these problems?" and defining the solution: "How are we doing this?" will give enough guidance to create a new feature.*
>
> —Nikkel Blaase

 TIP

Analytics product management is a separate function that requires business acumen, a deep understanding of the technology and methods of analytics, and a product thinking mindset.

There are five process areas for analytics product management:

1. *Value management*—The role of the analytics product manager is to define the overall strategy for the product management function. This includes defining the right product management culture and the methods used to facilitate the product discovery, design, and delivery processes needed in the organization. Techniques are outlined to catalog analytics efforts, measure value, and ensure alignment between strategic priorities and analytics activities. This process will touch on product marketing and the importance of analytics evangelism.

2. *Analytics Lifecycle execution*—The product manager works closely with data scientists, business and technical analysts, and analytics teams to make sure features are delivered efficiently and effectively. This best practice area is concerned with how analytics organizations receive, triage, prioritize, develop, test, and deliver potential analytics data products.

3. *Quality processes*—Analytics product quality management includes quality control, quality improvement, and testing, validation, and verification approaches both for product (and service) quality as well as team processes. It also touches on

analytics product governance as well as assurance for product provenance.

4. *Stakeholder engagement and feedback*—Throughout the Analytics Lifecycle, customer feedback plays a key role in validating and improving proposed features for analytics products and services. This area includes the processes used to engage stakeholders, promote collaboration, and gather insights. The purpose is to understand how we are doing and to create awareness of new problems.

5. *Capability and talent development*—It is important to recognize the critical capabilities needed for the organization to be successful. This process area includes talent development strategies that align needed capabilities with team and individual competencies. A critical aspect of capability development is the capture of knowledge for continuous learning and growth, referred to as *knowledge management*.

The following sections outline each of these five processes in more detail.

Value Management

A critical role in analytics product management is managing the ongoing value proposition for the analytics function and its deliverables. While ensuring alignment to organizational strategy and objectives is the primary responsibility of analytics leadership, it is the product management function that is tasked with maintaining ongoing focus on value creation. This is done by investing in the right problems to solve and ensuring that Analytics Lifecycle processes are both effective and efficient.

Key components of the value management process include:

- Maintaining alignment with organizational strategy
- Leading the product management culture
- Defining quality for all analytics products
- Measuring and promoting value

Maintaining Alignment with Organizational Strategy

> *Quite simply, it's the product manager's job to articulate two simple things:*
>
> ■ *What game are we playing?*
> ■ *How do we keep score?*

—Adam Nash, Technology Executive & Angel Investor
(and former VP of Product Management
at LinkedIn) (Nash, 2012)

Chapter 2 outlined the importance of the linkage between the overall organization's mission, vision, values, and strategy to that of the analytics function in an organization. The relationship between strategy, organizational capabilities, resources, and management systems is the lifeline that tethers analytics to success—and in fact, creates success.

Analytics leadership, including analytics product management, must not only derive its strategy from that of the organization but also maintain line of sight with that strategy in order to ensure that ongoing activities are advancing the mission of the organization. Alignment of the analytics strategy to the organization provides clarity around which activities to pursue and, perhaps more importantly, which activities should not be pursued.

Without a clearly communicated corporate strategy, the analytics product team is often forced to focus on tactical roadmap activities and deliverables. The way that this is often translated in practice is that the loudest voice in the room gets served, while others get left behind. This usually results in organizations with the "haves" and the "have-nots."

Big Data in Human Resources: A World of Haves and Have-Nots

Josh Bersin, an expert in talent development, writes about how organizations are investing in big data and analytics tools to help make their HR departments more data-driven. He found that there is a huge chasm between the "haves" and the "have-nots."

A 2013 study found that only 4 percent of companies have achieved the capability to perform "predictive analytics" about their workforce. In HR, examples of how to use analytics include:

▪ Understanding the drivers of performance and retention

▪ Deciding who to hire

▪ Analyzing how pay correlates to performance

Bersin describes the gap between those deriving value from analytics as the "haves" as compared with the "have-nots" who lack the interest, skills, or ability to action analytics.

To read more, see the article "Big Data in Human Resources: A World of Haves and Have-Nots" in *Forbes* (Bersin, 2013).

Without a guiding strategy, the analytics team is often left to fend for itself. The lack of guidance can cause analytics teams to wander aimlessly, focus on the wrong things, or create misalignment between them and the strategic imperatives of the organization. This often plays out in analytics organizations that turn into "reporting machines," as one such client referred to itself. Reactive organizations suffer from responding to the urgent rather than prioritizing the important.

 TIP

The tyranny of the urgent cannot overshadow the important.

Actuation Consulting conducts ongoing research in the area of product management and marketing with the goal of continuously improving our understanding of why some product management teams excel while others struggle. In its report titled "Study of Product Team Performance" (Consulting, 2016), it highlighted the importance of having a corporate strategy that the product team can link to and align with, which remains a significant indicator of a product team's ability to achieve high performance.

Daniel Magestro, vice president of Research for the International Institute for Analytics (IIA), outlines six areas where the lack of alignment creates a loss of value (Magestro, 2016):

1. *Investments*—Investments in analytics talent and technology are not optimal for supporting business needs.

2. *Analytics project assumptions*—Assumptions are not in line with enterprise assumptions (e.g., return on capital).

3. *Sponsor/partner identification*—Analytics projects are not supported or connected to relevant business teams.

4. *Strategic planning assumptions*—Business strategy is not data-driven or fails to utilize prescriptive analytics.

5. *Resource allocation and opportunity cost*—Analytics staffs are not working on "right" projects, and higher value projects are missed.

6. *Executive/GM adoption*—Likelihood of implementation decreases without connection to strategic priority.

The difference between reactive analytics product development teams and their more effective counterparts may well lie in the latter's unrelenting focus on a forward-looking analytics product strategy that supports the attainment of the organization's business strategy.

Leading the Product Management Culture

The culture of product management reflects on the approach used for product design and delivery. This includes the lifecycle of data products and the processes used to support them. Product management follows a simple trajectory:

1. Opportunity identification
2. Design
3. Testing
4. Launch
5. Assessment

Organizations differ with respect to how they organize to get work done. Further, there may be historical reasons for adopting certain execution strategies. Consultants often hear expressions of frustrations from analytics leadership who lament the fact that if they had a clean slate, they would design their organizations and processes much differently. Since analytics product management is likely a new or evolving function for most analytics shops and all are striving to create value, one of the most important aspects of organizational design and team processes is to get the product management culture right.

Chapter 3 stressed the importance of establishing a culture of numeracy across the organization to support fact-based decisions. Establishing a product management culture refers to how analytics products get built and how customers experience both deliverables—the product as well as the service journey.

All too often, organizations (perhaps unintentionally) create a culture through the technology and processes that are used to engage with customers that run counter to the ideals of empathy and collaboration. For example, analytics teams that have a highly visible and transparent process for how requests are handled and how progress is made can dramatically influence the perception of such factors as equality or fairness as well as value.

On the other hand, organizations that adopt draconian processes to receive, triage, and prioritize analytics requests often suffer criticisms from external customers. Some real-life examples of typical comments include:

- "I have no idea how they (the analytics group) prioritizes the things they work on."
- "I've submitted my request, but am not sure when it will be done. In fact, I have no idea whether they even have it on their list to do!"
- "I heard from the business analyst once after submitting my request. They asked me a few questions and said they would get back to me if they needed anything else. That was two months ago."

The role of empathy was emphasized throughout this book. Service design must consider the customer experience during each and every aspect of the Analytics Lifecycle. There is, perhaps, no more important experience than the first impression. Customers want to be heard. This is the opportunity to make sure that they are.

The need to establish a culture of service is clear.

TIP

The culture of services can be seen in analytics teams that have an intrinsic desire to proactively address customer problems and "delight" them through the delivery of data products. Service and "doing the right thing" are valued over policy and organizational charts.

The way in which analytics products are managed can directly influence the perception of value. Organizations that adopt design-thinking strategies as a way to engage customers, to facilitate collaboration, to develop ideas and test them, are more likely to demonstrate value. This often requires a shift in mindset—to walk the fine line between fully developed, production quality products, and the minimally viable product (MVP) (see Figure 10.4) (Roed, n.d.).

The advantage of this mindset is that by the time the analytics product (or project) is ready to be distributed widely, it will already have been tested and evaluated.

On the other hand, analytics processes that utilize aging and rigid processes, such as the waterfall method, that all require prescriptive steps to be followed, will surely suffer criticisms; but customers will

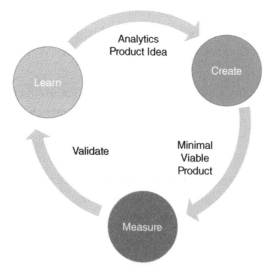

Figure 10.4 Create-measure-learn feedback loop is at the core to the lean startup model and essential to building an MVP for analytics.

also find alternatives to get what they need to get done quicker and with greater transparency.

Consider, for example, the case study below.

Changing Requirements Exercise

The consulting arm of an analytics function was tasked with developing a prediction model for one of the organization's largest service lines. They had scoped the work, gathered requirements, and were well under way with the development of the deliverables.

Midway through the effort, they found evidence to support the idea that some of the features originally defined in the model had a high degree of intercorrelation that did not add unique predictive value. Furthermore, some of their early theories about what would have an impact turned out to be false paths.

These false starts and revelations impacted not only the timeline but also ultimately the value of the project.

As a product manager, you are faced with a number of questions from management and from your team. How would you address these comments and questions?

- Why can't we just deliver what we promised and revisit the new "requirements" later? (assuming the perception is that requirements have really changed ...)
- Why didn't you find this earlier?
- How could this have been avoided?
- We have so many other projects, let's set this one to the side until they (the customer) figure out what they want!

  In addition, consider these questions:

- How does the product management culture influence how you deliver projects or products?
- What product management culture do you have in your organization?
- How can you bring analytics discovery and prototyping closer to the customer?

Defining Quality for All Analytics Products

Later in this chapter, the importance of quality processes will be outlined, but it is worth noting that in the context of value management, the role of product management is to define what it means to deliver a quality product or service.

In my consulting experience, I've not once heard anyone say, "We don't believe in quality." However, there is a distinct difference between believing in quality and ensuring a culture of quality, the difference being that many organizations often find themselves reacting to pressure to deliver on time and on budget and to reduce the tsunami of backlog. Expressions of this sentiment can be heard in statements like: "Quality is important and we recognize that we could do better, but we just have so much to do."

I understand the challenge of prioritizing and delivering on customer requests. I also believe that leadership has the responsibility to create a culture such that each and every person on the analytics team ought to feel empowered to "stop the line" if they see the need to review a defective or subpar deliverable. False starts and rabbit holes are inevitable, but individual empowerment begins with establishing a culture of quality and creating a safe place for people to raise concerns and to fail. We need to celebrate our failures almost as much as our wins. This is especially true in analytics where theory building and hypothesis testing are part of our experimentation DNA.

In addition, we need to give people the time and space to think. All too often, we are focused on the activities of analytics that we forget to focus on the "why." A quote from Stephen Few was mentioned in Chapter 7, but it is worth repeating here:

> *Only those data analysts who are given time to explore and analyze data thoughtfully and thoroughly are consistently successful.*
>
> —Stephen Few (Few, 2015)

Measuring and Promoting Value

I often talk about the importance of analytics evangelism as a way to express the importance of the value that we derive from analytics. In value management, we need to first measure and then promote the value.

One of the roles of analytics product management is to market the success of analytics across the enterprise. It not only builds morale within analytics teams but also improves relationships across the ecosystem of data consumers.

Guy Kawasaki was perhaps the best-known "evangelist." In his *Harvard Business Review* article, he said, "The idea is simple: derived from a Greek word that means, roughly, 'to proclaim good news,' evangelism is explaining to the world how your product or service can improve people's lives."

> *Evangelism isn't a job title, it's a way of life.*
> —Guy Kawasaki

In analytics, the benefits of having a strategy for evangelism can include:

- Builds morale within the analytics teams
- Improves relationships across the ecosystem of data consumers
- Highlights applications or use cases that may have gone unnoticed
- Reminds everyone involved of the mission and clarifies your purpose
- Demonstrates a culture of service and celebration
- Creates a transparent story
- Engages others in helping improve data quality and stewardship
- Allows organizations to connect the dots from activity back to value
- Builds C-suite support for analytics

A number of companies market their analytics successes internally. At Google, for example, Avinash Kaushik served as an "analytics evangelist," working with Google's marketing team on internal analytics, and with the Google analytics team to spread the analytics gospel to the masses.

Learn More

Listen to the podcast on "Selling the Value of Analytics" with Sayf Sharif (Sharif, 2017).

At Anne Arundel Medical Center, analytics product deployment takes on a celebratory tone. Staff at the medical center announce new analytics content by literally rolling out a mobile coffee cart to announce the success and celebrate the win. Texas Children's Health conducts pre- and post-ROI on all major analytics projects.

Analytics organizations that create transparency engender greater trust and openness between analytics teams and their customers. Cleveland Clinic, while not unique in this regard, offer customers a way to see into the progress of analytics deliverables. Furthermore, it tracks reports and dashboard usage to communicate their relevance across the business. Figure 10.5 highlights the current status of the projects so that customers don't have to guess. Cleveland Clinic communicates project status through an internal portal (Donovan, 2014). In this simple SharePoint dashboard (Figure 10.5), anyone can look at the status of a given project, the last time someone remarked on it, and who owns it.

There are some fantastic examples of organizations that have developed strong brand identities around their analytics product organizations. For example, Figure 10.6 from Seattle Children's

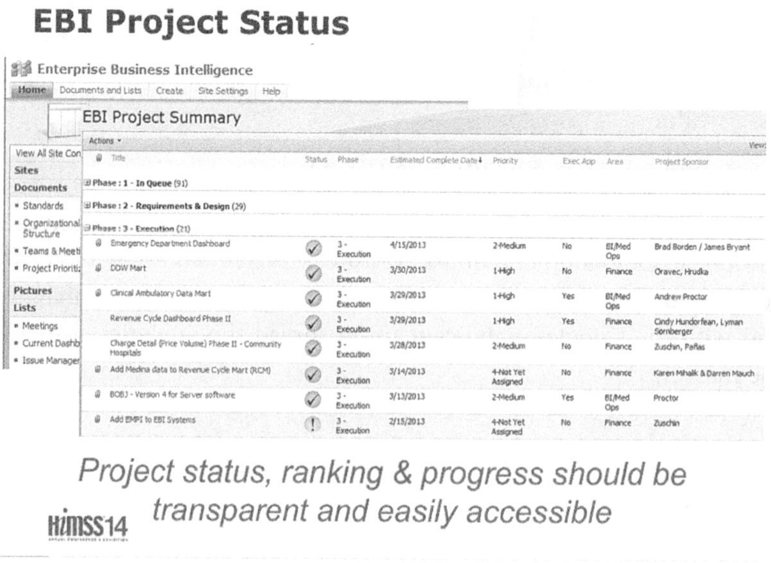

Figure 10.5   Visible progress is tracked and shared.

YOUR EXPERIENCE + DATA = BETTER HEALTHCARE

We translate complex, clinical data into better healthcare and healthcare delivery

Figure 10.6　Seattle Children's analytics home page

Hospital looks more like a commercial B2B website than an internal analytics website. There is a centralized data model for analytics and a strong brand identity aimed at providing data services consumers with a trusted, if not trendy, resource.

I've seen countless examples of organizations that have evolved from "throw-it-over-the-wall" reporting shops to truly engaged organizations. I find it refreshing when organizations develop a brand identity around their analytics services—a sense of pride—that engenders trust and socializes accomplishments (Figure 10.7).

This is especially true of highly centralized analytics organizations where distance from the day-to-day activities may negatively influence the connection to the business. One way we recommend that analytics groups deal with some of the cultural and communication challenges is to develop a strong brand presence with which to promote service adoption, engender trust, and share success stories.

> *The CDO Analytics team annually presented recommendations for three strategic approaches aimed at improving the hospital as a whole, as well as outlining specific opportunities for improving medical service lines.*
>
> — Dr. Greg Redding, Chief and Surgeon, Department of Pulmonology

Figure 10.7　Testimonial from satisfied customer at Seattle Children's

A word of caution with regard to the promotion of analytics success across the organization—make sure that you can measure value and not just anecdotes. It is essential to talk about the contribution of analytics to the organization, using terms like *return on investment (ROI)* or, even better, stories to convey value. At the end of the day, we need to speak to the impact and actionability of analytics.

This is not about the "promise of analytics," but rather, the reality of what it means to people, processes, and organizations. The way that you talk about value in your organization may be different, and there are both subjective and objective measures of value, as identified in Table 10.1.

In their report "Analytics in Action: Breakthroughs and Barriers on the Journey to ROI" (Accenture, 2013), Accenture reported the three most common reasons why analytics projects fail:

1. *Measuring the wrong metrics*—Companies are measuring the wrong things or have gaps in the way they are measuring (e.g., around the customer experience).

2. *Flawed insights*—Users are not identifying and validating cross functionally the correct insights and associated actions suggested.

3. *Faulty execution*—Companies fail to embed analytical insights in key decision processes across the enterprise so that analytics capabilities are linked to business outcomes.

NUCLEUS Research found in their research on analytics ROI that the average return on every analytics dollar invested was $10.66. The 2014 research project revealed that the return had increased to

Table 10.1 Objective and subjective measures for calculating return on investment

Subjective Measures	Objective Measures
▪ Customer satisfaction	▪ Financial ROI
▪ Trust and data integrity	▪ Cost savings
▪ Confidence in decision making	▪ Increased revenues
▪ Risk avoidance or mitigation	▪ Improved time to decision
▪ Greater insights/deeper understanding	▪ Reduced rework/improved productivity
▪ Employee morale	▪ Reduced turnover

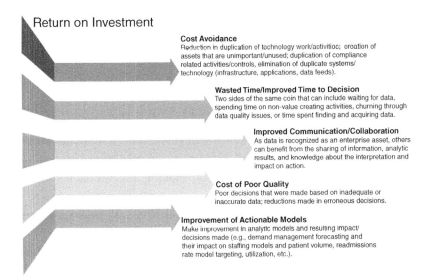

Figure 10.8   Measuring return on investment for analytics can come in many forms.

$13.01 for every analytics dollar invested (Research, 2012). When analytics are strategically aligned and deployed across organizations, they see a 968 percent average ROI.

In Figure 10.8, I summarize some of the ways in which you can think about return on investment.

Analytics Lifecycle Execution

While analytics organizations may take on any number of forms, including those described in the options detailed in Chapter 3, product management is ultimately responsible for the analytics data product and the processes that produce value. The analytics product manager defines the processes and standards that are used throughout the Analytics Lifecycle, evaluates current capabilities, and identifies impact and linkages between data products, user behavior, real-world workflow, and business policies.

Within the Analytics Lifecycle execution the focus is on the following key elements of product management:

- Product lifecycle management
- Product and portfolio management

While organizations may differ with respect to how they manage work, priorities and backlog, most have some process around how products mature from ideation to benefits realization.

Product Lifecycle Management

As previously discussed, the product lifecycle is a subset of the overall Analytics Lifecycle that facilitates the development of analytics products. The Analytics Lifecycle, however, sits in the larger context of how analytics support overall decision making and problem solving (Figure 10.9).

The key process steps found in **product lifecycle management** include:

1. Opportunity identification
2. Design
3. Testing
4. Launch
5. Assessment
6. Retirement

Like most of the processes that have been covered in this book, these steps are iterative. For example, you may find that during design, you identify additional opportunities. Similarly, during **testing,** you may have to go back to design. But here we will explore each step.

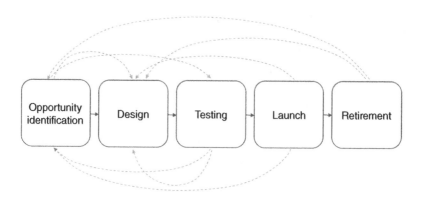

Figure 10.9 Analytics Lifecycle is iterative.

Opportunity Identification

In a world of analytics opportunity, what should you focus on?

Opportunities for new analytics or data products can come in many forms, including customer requests, executive inquiries, a crisis, or new venture discovery. As outlined in Chapter 5, opportunities may take on the form of a simple ad-hoc request, a special project, or a full-blown product.

In this step of the product management process, new suggestions, ideas, and feature requests are captured in the product backlog. Inspiration for the products often comes in the form of enhancements to or evolution from an existing product, or a new organizational challenge or crisis. Regardless, opportunities need to be captured, triaged, and prioritized. This is why it is critical to have a good system for capturing the details of these requests. In some of the other best practice areas, data scientists, analysts, and others will perform much of the actual work, but this is one of the areas where product management leadership plays a strong role.

In this step, it is also important to consider the product's impact. Earlier, we discussed the importance of understanding and documenting the impact of an analytics finding or product. In the early stages of evaluating opportunities, business priority and feasibility are assigned (Figure 10.10).

Figure 10.10 Analytics product prioritization matrix

In some form, business impact assessment responsibilities are shared by all members of an analytics team if there is true alignment between analytics effort and organizational goals. In my consulting work, I have seen prioritization schemes that range from a single "decider" that makes the determination of what gets done, to formal assessments that evaluate effort and impact ("high-medium-low") to triage teams that combine business and analytics teams in a collaborative exercise to evaluate value, feasibility, level of effort, fit, and abilities.

This process interrelates analytics process to business outcomes to ensure that analytics teams can be successful and continue to build capabilities. Activities in these sessions will often include:

- Discussion and negotiation of any data difficulties with project stakeholders
- Identification of both risks and impact
- Availability of skills and resources on all sides to tackle the problem
- Proactive identification of unintended consequences as well as business benefits
- Defined measures of success in doing the work

Once the opportunity is triaged and the priority classified, it may be decided that the opportunity to extract value is just not possible based on the value equation—the cost and effort to deliver. The open and honest conversation is critical in collaboration with both internal and external customers. In organizational design and a culture of service, you need to allow for the correct positioning of an analytics project in an objective manner and not let this be driven by politics or pandering.

For those projects or products that are prioritized, additional effort may be needed where requirements are unknown, where uncertainties exist, or where merely an additional elaboration of requirements is needed. Note that these processes played out in detail in Chapter 6 in the discussion of the problem framing best practice area.

In moving ideas and feature requests from the product backlog, they must be fleshed out in more detail in order to gain a better understanding of the impact and effort expected for each. Note that here I distinguish between triage and detailed analysis. The former includes a quick assessment of the impact and feasibility, whereas the latter requires a deep dive to uncover the unknowns.

TIP
The differences in scale, scope, impact, and complexity warrant the need for analytics processes to be right-sized accordingly.

Right-sizing the **requirements management** process should be done based on the potential impact and complexity of the analytics product. This is also referred to as a risk-based approach—that is, determining the risk of uncovering new information or getting something wrong either now or later in the project. For well-understood business processes with known and predictable data, the risk may be low so as to warrant moving forward without all of the details. Higher-risk situations where the level of uncertainty is significant and overall confidence in a true understanding is low, it is wise to proceed with caution.

Design
Once a product is prioritized, planning takes place to ensure that it can be successfully delivered. The demarcation between opportunity and commitment to move forward with a product is usually made through conscious decision, although sometimes projects get moved from backlog to in-progress as a result of resource availability or external pressures.

Much like software projects, analytics products need to be designed. These processes involve requirements iteration through the best practice areas including problem framing, data sensemaking, and model development. In **design thinking**, these are **empathy, definition, ideation,** and **prototype.**

It is during design that ideas are translated into something that the analytics team can implement. One of the terms used in innovation and design circles is the concept of minimum viable product (MVP). In the context of analytics, that simply means, "What is the minimally featured data product that we can build that will address the opportunity adequately for our customer?" In model development, the design thinking term *prototyping* is used to express this concept as a way to gain feedback, and to validate the idea and its impacts.

Eric Reis illustrated the concept of minimum viable product in his book *Lean Startup* (Ries, 2011).

> *As you consider building your own minimum viable product, let this simple rule suffice: remove any feature, process, or effort that does not contribute directly to the learning you seek.*

> —Eric Ries, *The Lean Startup*

Consider, for a moment, the relationship between usability and experience in analytics products and service delivery. An analytics product may come in the form of an answer, an automated alert, recommendation engine, or a hundred other mechanisms. By stopping at the utility of an analytics model, we fall short of ensuring that it is usable by the customer and can be integrated successfully into the workflow in which it was intended. Utility speaks to whether the analytics deliverable is useful and meets the needs, implied or otherwise. Usability refers to the degree to which the product can be easily used or consumed.

The role of the analytics product manager is to facilitate the conversation between where the product development lifecycle stops to both satisfy the needs of the customer and their overall experience, while maintaining integrity with the intended value.

In this way, the perspective of the customer becomes the hierarchy of needs being satisfied (Figure 10.11). The extent to which these needs are satisfied will always be a function of value.

In Figure 10.11, note that utility determines whether the analytics product meets the need. That is, can the customer take the result and easily integrate it into their decision lifecycle. The value of the product drives additional effort in usability, the ease with which the customer's goals can be met.

The higher you go in this model, the greater the impact that automation analytics products have on the business and the totality of experience, including human factors, design, human-computer interaction (HCI), automation, as well as usability.

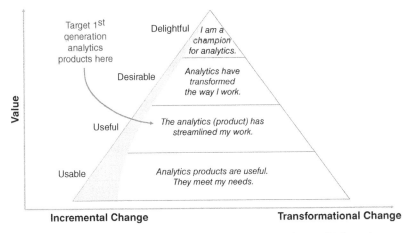

Figure 10.11 Analytics products must balance the user experience with the value.

Testing

In the Lean Startup model, an experiment is more than just a theoretical inquiry; it is also a first product.

—Eric Ries, *The Lean Startup*

Unlike physical products, the ideation and prototyping of analytics products can often be done quickly and efficiently. This, of course, is highly dependent on the tools that data scientists have at their disposal. Efficient processes demand that we have the right data structured in easily configured ways along with an analytics sandbox environment that allows for experimentation and testing.

During model development, the analytics product manager works in collaboration with the analytics team and customers to share prototypes of the product to get early feedback. At this point, ask yourself, "Does the MVP address the need effectively or is there a tradeoff we didn't anticipate?" "IT Shops" often ask for requirements and customers give answers without really understanding the implications of their decisions. It is necessary to learn how to speak together in a way that leads more quickly to shared understanding.

If you prioritize building the minimum viable product that was previously scoped, you should be able to start testing the utility of the product as quickly as possible. It is critical to strike a balance between asking for feedback too early in the process lest the customer is exposed to too much "sausage making." On the other hand, it is dangerous to seek feedback too late, as to miss the opportunity to get useful feedback on direction and validation of assumptions and on underlying business need.

TIP

Shareability in analytics is the hallmark of customer-centric, service-oriented analytics organizations.

I recommend regular customer touchpoints in order to:

- Clarify the translation of real world-ness to theories.
- Convey findings including bright spots and wrong paths.
- Validate the thinking behind analytics approaches and methods.

Launch

One of the dangers of the minimal viable solution approach to developing an analytics product is that early releases could erode confidence, or worse, that the customer believes a prototype to be fully production capable. Examples abound of customers attempting to use a proof-of-concept as the finished product.

It is in the launch phase where you finalize the selection of prototypes and results validation to the development of a final solution. Consider the initial steps of launch as a dress rehearsal. The prior steps exposed the underlying issues and risks of the solution, and based on the work that was done during problem framing, the analytics team should have a very clear idea of what the product will and won't do for the organization. That is, the opportunity was explicitly outlined, including what was in and out of scope at the outset.

In the launch phase, the project moves from a product that satisfies those needs to a production capability. The conversation around change management will be found in the next chapter, but this is where actioning analytics becomes critical for leadership to understand and champion. This involves not only technology and data, but also the human element.

It is vital to be clear about the problem the solution was intended to solve, as well as the characteristics of the underlying data required. Claims about generalizability and adoption in other domains should be made only after testing in those specific conditions.

Assessment

The only way to win is to learn faster than anyone else.
—Eric Ries, *The Lean Startup*

Sometimes we fail. The product manager is responsible for making sure that the team learns from their failures and successes. An accurate assessment of the team's accomplishments and benefits realization is critical in a learning organization.

This phase of the product development lifecycle includes assessing how the process went, how the team performed, and how the product performs, and also gauging the customer's reaction to our efforts. Measures of success defined earlier should be collected and analyzed.

Both qualitative and quantitative measures of success should be inventoried. You should know, for example, whether the results achieved your objectives and whether the solution is working as intended, as demonstrated in early prototypes. All of these lessons feed the next cycle—whether in a new iteration of this product or a completely different product.

These lessons learned and metrics inform the next iteration of the analytics product lifecycle.

Retirement

While excluded from most lifecycle models, proactive planning for the retirement of analytics products is an essential responsibility of any good product manager. At some point, the results will be old and analytics models will decay.

Ask yourselves these questions:

- What is the strategy for analytics product calibration and tuning?
- What metrics will we use to determine when a model is decaying?

- How will we know when the product needs to be replaced?

- Should we plan for future effort around retuning and improving the model?

Like physical products, analytics products have an expected lifespan. It is better to plan for that during the development lifecycle rather than letting it decay on its own. Analytics models, in particular, can have a relatively short lifespan as business conditions, data, and analytics methods change rapidly.

Product Portfolio Management

In "Theory Construction as Disciplined Imagination" Karl Weick (1989) suggests that we can improve our success by engaging in what he calls "disciplined imagination." This is a great description of what we do in analytics **product portfolio management.**

Discipline refers to the conscious, purposeful action on the part of the product manager. Imagination implies a diversity of thought and intellectual curiosity. This balance is critical in analytics product management.

> Analytics portfolio management is the art and science of making decisions about analytics product selection and prioritization, matching opportunities to strategic objectives, applying capabilities to create value, and balancing discipline against imagination.

The focus on the portfolio of opportunities and the resources used to address them requires a mindset shift from project thinking where there is a defined beginning, middle, and end, to continuous improvement. That is not to say that agile methods for managing work don't have their place. In fact, it is necessary to consider management's needs for forecasted costs and a comprehensive understanding of resources and capacity; but I believe that product management's primary focus is in linking capabilities to value creation.

Portfolio management is a way to bridge the gap between strategy and implementation.

—Project Management Institute (PMI, 2017)

Product management techniques are used to flesh out the details of the product in order to better understand the impact and effort expected for each. Portfolio management also looks at the backlog and roadmap, with the goal of setting priorities based on a variety of inputs. The process involves deciding what should be built and when, based on what will bring the most value to the user and the product. Additionally, running experiments and tracking effectiveness can be used to continually test and improve products and understand what's truly of value to the customer.

Product Roadmap

Like physical products often found in technology sectors, we must maintain a balance between short-term activities designed to delight customers today with longer-term goals. We must find the time for the evolution of an analytics capability focused on the maturation of people, processes, technology, or data designed to meet the needs of the organization. It is in the analytics product roadmap where we outline which problems are to be tackled, by when, and for what good. The capabilities needed are captured as assumptions or constraints, but the shift in focus to the business challenge helps maintain focus and priority on the customer rather than internal capabilities.

Toolkit @
www.analyticslifecycletoolkit.com

To find an example of this journey.

Analytics teams are hives of intense activity. Management is required, not just of individual projects, but also of whole project portfolios that may have interdependent components competing for resources. Competent resource management tasks for analytics teams include:

- Judicious decision making surrounding the sequencing and time commitment for components of an analytics project
- Making trade-off decisions to right-size effort based on project need

▪ Setting reasonable milestones that satisfy customers without exhausting the analytics team

▪ Implementing agile management methods so that project and products may evolve as new data about their impact and use becomes available

▪ Ensuring that team members understand the impact of a product in terms of its usage within the leadership hierarchy of an organization

The focus of the analytics product roadmap is to balance ongoing needs, and a detailed look is taken at the backlog and the analytical aspirations of the organization. The process involves deciding what should be built and when, based on what will bring the most value to the user and the product.

The linkages between the analytics product roadmap and the analytics capability roadmap are important. In the latter, integration with IT systems and processes become important and often include:

▪ Governance and management systems

▪ Data maturation strategies

▪ Quality management processes

▪ Tools and technology adoption

▪ Security, privacy, and cyber-defenses for data

▪ Key competencies for staff

Resource Management

Traditional resource management is often construed as the activities used to support forecasts or resource reports along with maintaining spreadsheets that track the allocation of personnel.

Instead of focusing energy on traditional resource management, analytics product management must broker a balance between

▪ Current and aspirational capabilities

▪ Current and aspirational competencies

▪ Team leadership and talent development

Here, the entire product strategy and vision is taken into account, and focus is put on the initiatives that line up with the big vision of the product. An analytics product roadmap is a communication tool that helps communicate where you are, where you are heading, and how you expect to get there.

Some of the tools that can be used to capture the gap between the current state and future state include:

- *Enterprise skills matrix*—A living document that captures the critical skills needed and an accurate representation of where divisions, departments, teams, and individuals are.

- *Analytics capabilities roadmap*—The roadmap is tied directly to the analytics portfolio of problems discussed earlier, the analytics capability roadmap helps to create alignment between the products that need satisfying and the analytics capabilities required.

- *Enterprise information management strategy*—This was discussed in Chapter 4 in the context of data strategy. This context refers to the organization's current readiness and intentions for information management. Elements of this roadmap should include data governance, data management, data quality, metadata management, and master data management.

- Data and analytics technology inventory—This captures the current and evolving tools and technologies used across the enterprise. The roadmap provides guidance but not governance over the recommended use cases for various tools and their current rates of adoption and accessibility.

Quality Processes

Quality processes refers to the ongoing assurance that all analytics data products meet the requirements and/or specifications. The analytics product manager is responsible for ensuring that analytics products are developed using best practices for quality assurance. Further, they should manage the maintenance and durability of analytics products and their overall lifespan of usefulness.

The elements of quality processes include:

- Translating product and process quality into actionable plans
- Developing quality assurance and quality control procedures
- Implementing quality improvement strategies
- Championing the use of risk-based approaches for testing, validation, and product verification (see below for discussion)
- Documenting all analytics product processes and product provenance

One of the activities that product management needs to establish is the definition and measures of quality for analytics products. In analytics, we often focus on discussions of data quality, but in this context, we are talking about the quality of analytics products—that is, the deliverables from our analytics efforts and the processes that produce them.

 ANALYTICS QUALITY

The overall assessment of a data product to serve its purpose in a given context.

These attributes can guide the discussion of product quality:

- Accuracy
- Comparability
- Completeness
- Consistency
- Relevance
- Reliability
- Timeliness
- Validity

Within an organization, acceptable product quality is crucial to operational workflows and business processes and to the reliability of analytics use across the enterprise. Product quality is affected by the way we ingest and transform data, how we think and develop hypotheses and the processes we use to design, develop, and deploy analytics models. Analytics product quality assurance is the process of verifying the reliability and effectiveness of our analytics results.

As with software, analytics product quality can affect usability as well as interpretation and the application of analytics to solve real-world problems.

Poor analytics product quality can impact nearly every aspect of how decisions are made across that organization, including:

- How much your analytics projects cost and how effective they are
- How accurately you can make business decisions
- How accurately you understand your organization
- How quickly you can turn analytics opportunities into business benefit

This section outlines four practices for quality management in analytics:

1. Utilize a risk-based approach to quality management.
2. Align quality measures with performance goals.
3. Engage stakeholders early and often.
4. Capture and use knowledge.

Utilizing a Risk-Based Approach to Quality Management

While the concept of risk-based approaches to validation was addressed previously, it is worth repeating here. We need to right-size the effort for managing quality with the expected benefit to the organization. Many organizations have bloated procedures they call quality processes. In my experience, we need to be smart about how we translate a requirement into a business benefit. Software development organizations may have both quality control and quality assurance processes which are intended to deliver a defect free result. But in analytics, since we rarely have a perfect model, we should prioritize our quality processes around risks including:

- What is the risk of failure?
- What is the impact of that failure?
- What is the trade-off of not taking the risk?

A risk-based approach evaluates the risks to guide the best practice areas for analytics including problem framing, sensemaking, model development, testing and evaluation, interpretation, and operationalization.

Aligning Quality Measures with Performance Goals

Donabedian proposed a conceptual model for evaluating the quality of health care (Donabedian, 1988). While it has been applied to health services and specifically to quality of care, the structure-process-outcome paradigm has relevance as a model for measuring analytics quality (Figure 10.12).

Adapted to analytics, **structure** describes the context in which analytics are conceived and delivered. The context in which analytics are delivered includes the data, systems, technology, and platforms. **Process** refers to the methodologies, frameworks, and approaches that are used throughout the delivery of insights. Finally, **outcomes** are the effects of analytics on the business.

Looking at each as aligned toward the singular purpose of supporting fact-based decisioning, the measures that are used can help create the much-needed alignment between the technology and temperament; between data and decisions; between analysis and action.

Metrics can then be applied to measuring the right thing in analytics and recognizing their place. For example, we can apply the importance of requirements traceability to testing to quality outcomes.

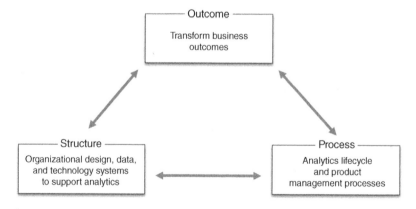

Figure 10.12 Structure-process-outcome model for analytics quality

If it often useful to consider the **structure-process-outcomes** as a system when considering the appropriateness of **quality measures** for analytics (Figure 10.13).

Another important step is to fine-tune performance measures for both teams and individuals to include quality measures. Creating alignment between incentives and outcomes is an essential part of **talent management**. People generally behave based on their incentives. By making quality part of their goals, desirable behavior is reinforced.

Engaging Stakeholders Early and Often

As you will see in the next section, stakeholder engagement is one of the key processes in analytics product management. It also serves as a foundational element in ensuring analytics quality. Engaging with stakeholders throughout the process helps to ensure that we understand the business, their challenges, how they make decisions, and how analytics models are to be used.

Quality is often defined as the degree to which something meets or exceeds the expectations of its consumers. Needs, whether stated or implied, serve as the cornerstone of every analytics product. That is, we capture the business problem as a set of requirements and frame it according to our understanding. We make sense of the data and construct theories based on perceptions of cause and effect. In each of these activities, engaging with stakeholders helps ensure that we understand better and can apply knowledge and methods with greater confidence and accuracy.

Capturing and Using Knowledge

It is said that the only constant in life is change. This holds true for analytics products as well. As with most facets of business, there is always going to be change. No one can predict every aspect from the beginning, as challenges and unforeseen tasks will appear. Adapting quickly to these changes helps keep a project on track. Documenting the changes will serve as a learning process for future projects. Additionally, other components of the Analytics Lifecycle should be captured and shared so that all of the proverbial "knowledge eggs" aren't in a single basket. Successful analytics organizations that capture

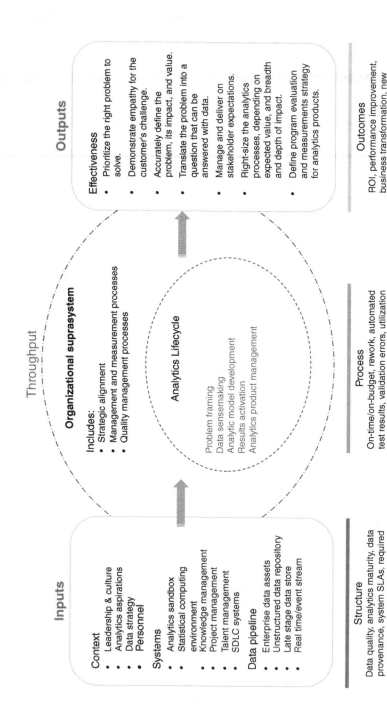

Inputs

Context
- Leadership & culture
- Analytics aspirations
- Data strategy
- Personnel

Systems
- Analytics sandbox
- Statistical computing environment
- Knowledge management
- Project management
- Talent management
- SDLC systems

Data pipeline
- Enterprise data assets
- Unstructured data repository
- Late stage data store
- Real time/event stream

Structure

Data quality, analytics maturity, data provenance, system SLAs, required capabilities, competency measures

Throughput

Organizational suprasystem

Includes:
- Strategic alignment
- Management and measurement processes
- Quality management processes

Analytics Lifecycle

Problem framing
Data sensemaking
Analytic model development
Results activation
Analytics product management

Process

On-time/on-budget, rework, automated test results, validation errors, utilization of systems (e.g., knowledge management)

Outputs

Effectiveness
- Prioritize the right problem to solve.
- Demonstrate empathy for the customer's challenge.
- Accurately define the problem, its impact, and value.
- Translate the problem into a question that can be answered with data.
- Manage and deliver on stakeholder expectations.
- Right-size the analytics processes, depending on expected value, and breadth and depth of impact.
- Define program evaluation and measurements strategy for analytics products.

Outcomes

ROI, performance improvement, business transformation, new opportunities

Figure 10.13 Example measures for quality using structure-process-output model

and continuously learn consistently do these things better than their counterparts:

- Track and document changes and impacts.
- Share knowledge and skills across teams to increase knowledge wealth and reduce knowledge and skills deficits when a team member leaves.
- Document the creation of how the knowledge is gained so it is easier for new team members.

Stakeholder Engagement and Feedback

Throughout the Analytics Lifecycle, customer feedback plays a key role in validating and improving on proposed features and products. Customer collaboration offers direct insight and suggestions that can help you understand how you are doing at solving the problems you're already trying to address, and discovering new problems you weren't aware of.

The components of stakeholder engagement include:

- Understanding and empathy
- Bidirectional communication
- Leading change

Understanding and Empathy

In Six Sigma, during the Define phase of DMAIC, tools such as the Kano Model (Revelle, 2004), critical to quality (CTQ) and house of quality (Stroud), and value stream or process maps (Stroud) are used to understand customer needs and requirements. Empathy is the first phase of the design thinking process, where the techniques we employ are all designed to get into the minds of users. Techniques in design thinking to understand the customer include:

- Persona definitions
- Empathy pap
- User journeys
- Context maps

- Interviews
- Problem statement

In analytics, similar techniques can be used to gain clarity on who your stakeholders are, what they want, what they need, what they expect, and where their current attitudes are in relation to the problems and potential solutions.

Similarly, in change management, stakeholder analysis methods are used to identify individuals and groups of people impacted by or holding influence over a change, their target change state (e.g., awareness, understanding, buy-in, commitment); and finally, managing their journey to the desired end-point via involvement and innovative two-way communications.

The objective of this process is to learn about others, the end users, and the problem to be solved.

As Idris Mootee, the CEO of Idea Couture, suggests,

Design thinking is human centric. It was always focused on the customer or end user's needs, including unarticulated, unmet, and unknown needs.
—Design Thinking for Strategic Innovation (Mootee, 2013)

Through the process of engaging in collaboration, we are able to create connections and relationships that have often been elusive in other realms including software development and business intelligence.

Bidirectional Communication

The quality of communications is a significant factor in the success or failure of analytics. When communications are mishandled or absent, analytics impact is seldom realized. Done well, communications can foster a sea change in both the quality and depth of relationships. Furthermore, integrative communication can facilitate adoption and the successful impact of analytics across organizational boundaries.

As you will see in Chapter 11, engagement goes beyond traditional "one-way" communication to truly engaging the "hearts and minds" of stakeholders.

Communication can take on a number of forms, but done well, it fosters understanding, facilitates acceptance and ownership, positively impacts morale, and increases the accuracy of the business processes and the impact of analytics. Communication done right helps to reinforce the linkage between the organization's vision and analytics activities.

Leading Change

Finally, stakeholder engagement is a way to support successful change strategies. As emphasized throughout this book, analytics done well should lead to change—in process, behavior, and impact.

More on leading change will be addressed in Chapter 11.

Capability and Talent Development

The final domain of responsibility found within the analytics product management best practice area is that of capability and talent development.

As outlined in Chapter 3, organizational capabilities are the things we need to be good at in order to be successful. Analytics capabilities are ever-evolving, and we may never truly arrive. The extent to which we can become a learning organization—one that continuously learns and adapts to the current and prospective realities in which it operates—depends on its ability to learn and grow.

Building Capabilities

Developing new capabilities depends on the current and potential competencies of the workforce. Capabilities can be built in two ways:

1. By addressing gaps in skills, knowledge, abilities, and dispositions of our workforce.
2. By reinforcing human behavior through a systematic focus on the capabilities needed to meet business objectives.

Capability development is highly linked with talent development strategies. The first focuses on the gap that exists between what is needed and current competencies, while the latter centers on performance management and improvement.

The linkage between capability development and talent development strategies is especially critical in analytics, as it is a continually changing landscape. We will never be able to hire new talent fast enough with the right skills, so it is essential to create a learning strategy, measure competencies, design learning programs, and create a supportive learning culture.

See Chapter 11 for further discussion of the importance of developing analytics competencies.

Moving from Training to Talent Development

When most people think of training, they think of an off-site location with a computer for every two people, or a cold hotel conference facility with 200 other people, with a speaker or instructor telling them what they need to know. Modern organizations are beginning to think differently about developing people; that is, a shift is occurring from training to workforce management, and specifically in the area of talent development.

The solution is not educational seminars, technical training workshops, or lectures. If organizations seriously want to get better at analytical capabilities, they must invest in selecting the right people, organize the teams for an effective, efficient, and customer-focused Analytics Lifecycle, and integrate agile project methods with talent development and performance management.

This linkage helps inform our capabilities, what business processes need to be supported, and how we organize to deliver on our analytical capabilities. From there it is critical to understand what we are good at and where we need growth. That's where the knowledge and skills assessment comes into play. Equipped with a strong understanding of the opportunities, we can staff project teams, help individuals on their own personal roadmap, and build institutional knowledge through formal and informal knowledge management strategies.

An example of how to support the alignment of organizational project needs with talent development is shown in Figure 10.14. Given that you understand your organizational priorities around data and analytics, and where all of your people are with regard to their

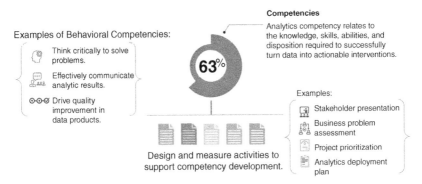

Figure 10.14 Align talent development to analytics aspirations.

competencies, you can integrate professional development plans using this framework.

As you consider the amount of time it takes to onboard new employees and bring them up to speed on the organization, its vocabulary and culture, and its technology and processes, you need to think differently about how to develop and nurture talent. In order to develop data fluency and develop talent, you will need to move to a model where learning is a continuous process and not the chilly conference room with the notebook of slides that will gather dust in a cubicle after the session is over.

CHAPTER SUMMARY

As outlined in this chapter, analytics product management is a multi-disciplinary best practice area that encompasses a wide-ranging set of activities. While the role of product manager is not widely seen in analytics today, it is certainly prominent in successful organizations that understand the importance of managing analytics products with both discipline and imagination.

The key factors of successful product managers lie in their ability to manage the integration between people, processes, data, technology, and culture. Specifically, I see the role of analytics product management as balancing the delivery of analytics products with the value created, opportunities realized, or waste or problems diverted. A critical component of this is in the development of relationships and building organizational capability.

Toolkit Summary

Best Practice Area:	Analytics Product Management	
Purpose:	*What is the intent of this best practice area?* The purpose of analytics product management is to continually improve how analytics products are developed and the value derived from them.	
Key Competencies:	*Knowledge, skills, abilities, and disposition*	
What do we need to be good at?	▪ Quality processes (including testing) ▪ Design thinking ▪ Product thinking ▪ Requirements management ▪ Service delivery ▪ Portfolio management ▪ Team processes	▪ Talent development and management ▪ Product development ▪ Process improvement ▪ Innovation ▪ Stakeholder engagement
Inputs	**Processes**	**Outputs**
▪ Analytics aspirations ▪ Analytics strategy ▪ Mature data pipeline ▪ Executive champion ▪ Learning organization	▪ Value management ▪ Analytics Lifecycle execution ▪ Quality processes ▪ Stakeholder engagement and feedback ▪ Capability and talent development	▪ Improved processes ▪ Effective analytics programs ▪ Mature and reliable analytics products ▪ Enterprise skills matrix

	What should we know as a result of this best practice?
Key Questions:	▪ Which analytics projects should we tackle? ▪ What is our analytics maturity current state? ▪ What are the critical opportunities for improved value? ▪ What areas are we most/least proficient? ▪ How do we measure and promote value with analytics? ▪ How does analytics support the organization's purpose?

REFERENCES

Accenture. (2013). Analytics in action: Breakthroughs and barriers on the journey to ROI. Retrieved from www.accenture.com/us-en/~/media/Accenture/Conversion-Assets/DotCom/Documents/Global/PDF/Technology_6/Accenture-Analytics-In-Action-Survey.pdf.

Bay, J. (n.d.) How to become a video game product manager. *Game Industry Career Guide*. Retrieved from www.gameindustrycareerguide.com/how-to-become-a-video-game-product-manager/.

Bersin, J. (2013). Big data in human resources: A world of haves and have-nots *Forbes*. Retrieved from www.forbes.com/sites/joshbersin/2013/10/07/big-data-in-human-resources-a-world-of-haves-and-have-nots.

Blasse, N. (2015). Why Product Thinking is the next big thing in UX Design. *Medium*. Retrieved from https://medium.com/@jaf_designer/why-product-thinking-is-the-next-big-thing-in-ux-design-ee7de959f3fe.

Cagan, M. (2017). *INSPIRED: How to create tech products customers love* (2nd ed.). Hoboken, NJ: John Wiley & Sons.

Consulting, A. (2016). The study of product team performance. Retrieved from www.actuationconsulting.com/study-product-team-performance/.

Donabedian, A. (1988). The quality of care: How can it be assessed? *JAMA, 260*(12), 1743–1748.

Few, S. (2015). Data sensemaking requires time and attention. Retrieved from www.perceptualedge.com/blog/?p=2052.

Howard, J., Loukides, M., & Zwemer, M. (2012). *Designing great data products.* Sebastopol, CA: O'Reilly Media.

Kotler, P., John W. Hartman Center for Sales Advertising & Marketing History, & Armstrong, G. (1991). *Principles of marketing* (5th ed.). Englewood Cliffs, NJ: Prentice Hall.

Kumar, M., Townsend, J., & Vorhies, D. (2014). Enhancing consumers' affection for a brand using product design. *The Journal of Product Innovation Management.* Retrieved from onlinelibrary.wiley.com/doi/10.1111/jpim.12245/abstract.

Magestro, D. (2016). Aligning analytics strategy to business strategy. *Analytics Experience 2016.* Retrieved from www.sas.com/content/dam/SAS/en_us/doc/event/analytics-experience-2016/aligning-analytics-strategy-business-strategy.pdf.

Moggridge, B. (2007). *Designing interactions.* Cambridge, MA: MIT Press.

Mootee, I. (2013). *Design thinking for strategic innovation: What they can't teach you at business or design school.* Hoboken, NJ: John Wiley & Sons.

Nash, A. (2012). Be a great product leader. *LinkedIn.* Retrieved from www.linkedin.com/pulse/20121002124931–8876-be-a-great-product-leader/.

Nelson, S., & Metaxatos, P. (2016). The Internet of Things needs design, not just technology. *Harvard Business Review.* Retrieved from hbr.org/2016/04/the-internet-of-things-needs-design-not-just-technology.

Norman, D. A. (2002). *The design of everyday things* (1st Basic paperback. ed.). New York: Basic Books.

PMI. (2017). Portfolio management. Retrieved from www.pmi.org/learning/featured-topics/portfolio.

Research, N. (2012). ROI of business analytics increases significantly as solution matures (Press release). Retrieved from nucleusresearch.com/press/roi-of-business-analytics-increases-significantly-as-solution-matures/.

Revelle, J. (2004). KANO model tutorial. Retrieved from asq.org/learn-about-quality/qfd-quality-function-deployment/overview/kano-model.html.

Ries, E. (2011). *The lean startup: How today's entrepreneurs use continuous innovation to create radically successful businesses* (1st ed.). New York: Crown Business.

Roed, J. B. (n.d.) *Design driven innovation through minimum viable products.* myendnoteweb.com. Retrieved from www.ntnu.no/documents/10401/1264433962/JohanArtikkel.pdf/8fb097c8-ed08–471c-8d19–8dd66593a074.

Selling the value of analytics. (2017). Retrieved from www.analyticshour.io/2017/04/25/061-selling-value-analytics-sayf-sharif/.

Stroud, J. D. Defining CTQ outputs: A key step in the design process. *Six Sigma.* Retrieved from www.isixsigma.com/methodology/voc-customer-focus/defining-ctq-outputs-key-step-design-process/.

Stroud, J. D. More value: Value stream or detailed process mapping? Retrieved from www.isixsigma.com/tools-templates/process-mapping/more-value -value-stream-or-detailed-process-mapping/.

Theus, A. (2016). Product management tips from "A Faster Horse." Retrieved from www.productplan.com/product-management-tips/.

Weick, K. (1989). Theory construction as disciplined imagination. *Academy of Management Review, 14*(4), 516–531. Retrieved from amr.aom.org/ content/14/4/516.short.

PART **III**

Sustaining Analytics Success

CHAPTER 11

Actioning
Analytics

If you want to make enemies, try to change something.

—Woodrow Wilson

THE POWER OF ANALYTICS

As suggested at the beginning of this book, *analytics* is resilient, in large part because of its ability to impact the way we work, the decisions we make, and the outcomes we achieve. Analytics is a strategy that supports effective interventions and opportunity capture and, as such, analytics strategy is inextricably linked to action—turning data-driven insights into momentum for change.

There are literally thousands of examples of how analytics have changed organizations. Here are a few:

- In pro sports, analytics are being used to increase concession and merchandising sales, optimize ticket sales, identify top talent, and predict player performance.

- In human resources, analytics are being used to understand and predict employee retention and optimize "pay for performance" opportunities; artificial intelligence is a tool to identify potential talent before someone even applies for a job.

- Health care has seen a tremendous rise in the use of analytics for predicting readmissions, optimizing care, and managing entire populations.

- Even in nontraditional fronts, organizations are seeing the value of analytics to identify high-risk shelters in disasters and to help social safety net organizations identify children at risk for neglect and abuse.

In each of these cases, the focus and problem domain are unique, but the thing that ties them all together is the resultant change. Understanding and using results from analytics is central to the idea of actionable analytics. Throughout this chapter, when we refer to change, we mean any impact to individuals because of analytics results (analytics actors) or a change in the way that analytics are generated (analytics producers).

A Case Study in Analytics and Change Management

There are many reasons why analytics projects fail, but failing to plan for how the changes will affect how people do their work has to be at the top of the list. Take a recent example of a real-world scenario in a large hospital system where a predictive model was deployed to help clinicians prioritize patient cases. (I've made a few changes to avoid the possibility of identifying or embarrassing anyone.) Key points:

- The hospital's infection rates were significantly higher than other hospitals based on their size and capabilities.

- The finance and operations teams identified this as having a significant financial impact on the organization, as hospital-acquired infections required treatment that was not reimbursed by the payers.

- The goal of the model was to identify "at risk" patients for a specific hospital acquired infection.

- A physician champion was selected to work with the analytics team to develop a predictive model.

In the context of a **change management** strategy, this had all the trappings of a great "change" project:

1. There was a shared sense of urgency (and purpose).
2. The team had developed a "guiding coalition" that included a highly respected and influential physician.
3. The model was developed with regular checkpoints along the way and included feedback regarding the importance of several clinical indicators.
4. The model was developed using solid testing and validation principles.

The sad news is that while the predictions were outstanding, the model ran automatically, with little impact to the infection rates. The reason this initiative failed was multifaceted, but the project faced two primary challenges:

- Competing priorities: this was one of literally a hundred things that the physician champion had to do on a given day.

(Continued)

(Continued)

■ No clear purpose: there was a disconnect between what the model produced and how the clinical care teams operated; that is, there was no clear linkage between the model output and the action that was required to effect change.

All too often, smart people do great work that ends up not living up to its potential, or sometimes a few heroes put the project on their backs and force it through, despite the lack of a great change management strategy. This is a dangerous de-motivator to staff and causes organizations to lose some of their best, most capable people.

Leading Change

The proper leadership of any change initiative is critical. Lacking leadership, it begs the question of whether the change is worth doing. Effective change management assures that the people, processes, and technologies are in optimal working condition. All too often, the focus is on the technology without regard to the potential impact to people and process—or worse, there is an assumption that people are smart enough to figure it all out.

The management of change, or *change management,* is more than just "training" or a communications plan; rather, it is a systematic approach that helps facilitate the transition of organizations and people from a current to a future state. In the case study example just described, the desired future state was one in which hospital-acquired infection rates would be significantly lower than the current state—a reasonable and measurable outcome.

It is unfortunate that the phrase "change management" has such a negative connotation for some people, since there are great examples of organizations leading transformation. For a success story on change leadership in action, look at Google's Project Oxygen. Google moved from a company "built by engineers for engineers" (one in which the role of management was not valued) to one in which it measured the value of management using data. In fact, it committed to leading organizational change. Google wanted "to be hypothesis-driven and help solve company problems and questions with data."

> **Learn More**
>
> Google's Project Oxygen, hbr.org/video/2761856636001/how-google-proved-management -matters.

If we truly believe that analytics can have a transformational impact on organizations, the "transformation" must be managed—or, as John Kotter would advocate, "lead" the change.

A systematic change management approach will facilitate the transition from a current to a future state. We can define organizational change as a creation of a mindset that helps individuals transition between technology and processes in the context of organizational culture. Change is realized only when people do their jobs differently and make their own transition to a future optimized state. Change management by force does not work. One successful approach is the Giving Voice to Change method that builds:

- *Awareness*—Helping people prepare for change
- *Knowledge*—Understanding the rationale and impact
- *Contribution*—Giving adopters a voice in the foreseen change
- *Adoption*—Helping staff develop skills using new tools
- *Commitment*—Integrating new skills into workflows

Change management will be discussed in greater detail later in this chapter with an outline of six change management best practice areas for analytics.

EFFICIENT AND EFFECTIVE ANALYTICS PROGRAMS

Everyone's talking about it, no one really knows how to do it—everyone thinks everyone else is doing it, so we all say we're doing it.

Deb Gage, president and CEO of Medecision during a panel
at the Becker's Hospital Review 5th Annual CEO + CFO Roundtable

Chapter 1 included a summary of the power and "why" of analytics, transforming organizations through programs that support the discovery process, to create value through organizational change to produce improved outcomes. So why don't all organizations simply do more with analytics?

To answer this, we must first talk about what's involved in analytics, and second, we must confront the challenges. A conversation about the difference between **effectiveness** and **efficiency** will help frame the potential areas for opportunity.

Effective (adj.)

Adequate to accomplish a purpose; producing the intended or expected result.

Efficient (adj.)

Performing or functioning in the best possible manner with the least waste of time and effort.

Analytics leaders typically seek to increase and improve the efficiency of data and analytics operations, including data flow and management, business analysis, discovery, results interpretation, presentation, and operationalization. As is true with most organizations, we are faced with limited resources and would prefer to maximize the use of each of these resources—regardless of the type, be it money, technology, time, human capital, and/or quality.

However, by pursuing efficiency at all costs, some companies are missing a valuable chance to step back and look at their overall effectiveness from a big-picture perspective. They should ask themselves, "Are we being effective in our data management efforts—are we creating data that is accessible, usable, trustworthy? Are we being effective at storytelling—turning data facts into insights that resonate with our stakeholders? Are we being effective at selecting projects—those that have the potential for greatest impact—and are we seeing

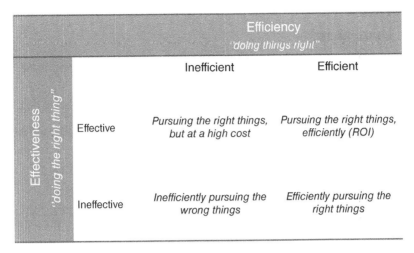

Figure 11.1   2 × 2 Effectiveness and efficiency matrix

these changes all the way through to how clinicians and front-line business users will use them to effect change?"

Analytics leaders strive to find an optimal balance between effectiveness and efficiency that ties directly back to value. One way to illustrate the difference between efficiency versus effectiveness is with a 2 × 2 matrix (Figure 11.1).

The goal for most analytics organizations is to achieve the top right of this matrix—going after the right goals and being efficient, by making full use of its analytics resources (people, processes, technology, and data), by not wasting time, and by maximizing the alignment of and collaboration between employees. While most organizations have the best of intentions in that they know what they want to achieve, the silos often make true efficiency and effectiveness elusive.

It is not usually difficult to focus on efficiency, as it is relatively easy to measure (cost, time, effort) and is perceived to be more "controllable." A great case study on the potential pitfalls of the easy path can be found in a classic *Harvard Business Review* case study describing the death-spiral of Bridgeton Industries, an automobile manufacturer. The story of Bridgeton relates to the fact that it focused on trimming the fat (efficiency) and in doing so, lost sight of the bigger, more strategic picture of purpose and value creation.

Learn More:

Keeping your industry out of the Bridgeton death spiral: precisionlender.com/blog/general/keeping-bank-bridgeton-death-spiral/.

Understanding the Analytics Lifecycle

It is a capital mistake to theorize before one has data.

Sherlock Holmes in *A Study in Scarlett* by Arthur Conan Doyle

As a matter of practical explanation, consider the differences between effectiveness and efficiency in the Analytics Lifecycle. Chapter 10 described analytics product management as an overarching set of activities that help manage and support the analytics teams and their deliverables.

Figure 11.2 depicts the various stages and activities in the pursuit of creating analytics products.

For each data product created, we all go through the various stages of analysis, exploration, analysis, interpretation, and operationalization. Note that this may seem linear, but it is often necessary to go back and revisit some activities to refine, clarify, and elaborate. Not all projects are created equally, in that some may not require all the activities outlined here. For example, for business questions that demand low fidelity, you may find that a rough-order-of-magnitude answer may be sufficient. Similarly, where the key stakeholders have high data literacy, the effort toward explanation and story framing may be less critical. In operationalizing data products, you may find that some projects never make it that far (nothing interesting here to see), or that the change requires effort beyond the value that it creates, or that it is impractical to realize the true benefit.

The difference between effectiveness and efficiency for analytics teams can be summed up succinctly: being effective is about doing the right things to create value and improve outcomes, while being efficient is about achieving maximal productivity with minimal waste or expense.

Table 11.1 highlights some common examples of effectiveness versus efficiency in the Analytics Lifecycle.

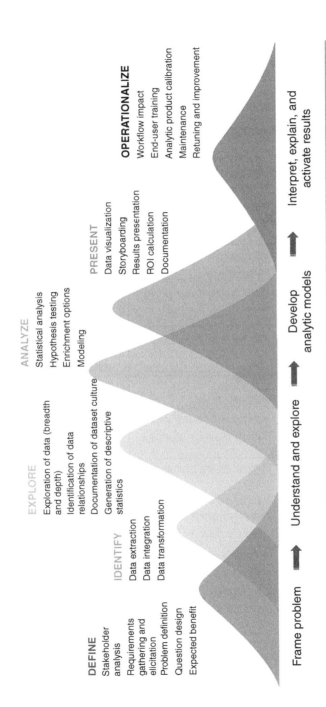

DEFINE
Stakeholder analysis
Requirements gathering and elicitation
Problem definition
Question design
Expected benefit

IDENTIFY
Data extraction
Data integration
Data transformation

EXPLORE
Exploration of data (breadth and depth)
Identification of data relationships
Documentation of dataset culture
Generation of descriptive statistics

ANALYZE
Statistical analysis
Hypothesis testing
Enrichment options
Modeling

PRESENT
Data visualization
Storyboarding
Results presentation
ROI calculation
Documentation

OPERATIONALIZE
Workflow impact
End-user training
Analytic product calibration
Maintenance
Retuning and improvement

Frame problem → Understand and explore → Develop analytic models → Interpret, explain, and activate results

Analytics Product Lifecycle Management

Figure 11.2 The Analytics Lifecycle

Table 11.1 Differences between effectiveness and efficiency in analytics

	Stage	Effectiveness	Efficiency
❶	**Problem Framing**	▪ Prioritize the right problem to solve. ▪ Demonstrate empathy for the customer's challenge. ▪ Accurately define the problem, its impact, and value. ▪ Translate the problem into a question that can be answered with data. ▪ Manage and deliver on stakeholder expectations.	▪ Expend the right level of effort for the problem. ▪ Collect and manage requirements competently (for clarity and reuse). ▪ Economically utilize stakeholder time and knowledge. ▪ Manage the project.
❷	**Data Sensemaking**	▪ Translate the problem into the appropriate data sources. ▪ Accurately assemble the data. ▪ Assess the value of the integrated data. ▪ Formulate testable hypotheses about the relationships found.	▪ Capably access and acquire the data. ▪ Proficiently integrate the data. ▪ Utilize the most appropriate tools and technology (eliminate waste, avoid redundancy/duplication/ rework).
❸	**Analytics Model Development**	▪ Identify opportunities for enrichment. ▪ Test hypotheses for their validity. ▪ Eliminate spurious relationships.	▪ Competently utilize statistical and visualization software. ▪ Create summarized information/insights.
❹	**Results Activation**	▪ Create stories that resonate and influence. ▪ Select the most appropriate mediums for communication. ▪ Master storytelling for influence. ▪ Lead change management. ▪ Assess generalizability. ▪ Imbed into workflow. ▪ Assess product durability and opportunities for improvement.	▪ Create storyboards and visualizations. ▪ Document findings and other knowledge for reuse. ▪ Validate analytics models, calibrate/retune, maintain, and retire.
❺	**Analytics Product Management**	▪ Right-size the analytics processes depending on expected value, and breadth and depth of impact. ▪ Define program evaluation and measurements strategy for analytics products.	▪ Manage enterprise portfolio. ▪ Efficiently manage resources. ▪ Capture knowledge and opportunities for reuse.

Perspectives on Effective Analytics

Never confuse motion with action.

Benjamin Franklin, American politician/inventor

Table 11.1 outlined some examples of the difference between effectiveness and efficiency in analytics. However, there may be wildly different opinions about what constitutes efficient and effective analytics programs, depending on the perspective.

It is not uncommon to hear multiple, competing perspectives from both internal and external stakeholders. Analytics leaders and analysts might have a one-sided view of the Analytics Lifecycle and view analytics process efficiency and effectiveness in different time frames and in different ways. This often differs from the "decision lifecycle" that other stakeholders utilize when attempting to capitalize on the analytics products. In short, each stakeholder asks different questions about the importance of analytics processes and their impacts (see Table 11.2).

Table 11.2 Stakeholder perspectives on analytics effectiveness and efficiency

Role	Question	Time Horizon	Incentives/Outcomes
Analytics Leaders	Are analytics having an impact, creating value?	Quarterly, annually, 3 to 5 years	Quality, benefits, costs
Analysts	How can I get better—learn, grow, become more proficient?	Days, weeks, months	Time spent on interesting, relevant, actionable, purposeful work
Front-Line Data Champions	What can I use to impact outcomes?	Minutes, hours, days	Integrated, actionable view of data
Executive Leadership	How can we transform our organization?	Mid-term, long-term	Long-term implications for operations, financial, and clinical domains Driving innovation, learning, and creating new opportunities
Patients/ Customers	What does this "risk score" mean to me?	Today, tomorrow	Data that makes sense/ resonates, drives behavior change, and is actionable
Analytics Customers	How can I get better visibility into what's going on?	Weeks, months, quarterly	Data that is accessible, accurate, at the right level of detail, and in a form that I can use

Confusing the needs (aka incentives) of these stakeholders often results in misunderstanding their priorities and misplacing your efforts.

Different perspectives can be useful in both service design and in understanding how people consume data products. One of the tools that can help create both analytics products and processes is **design thinking**.

Challenges to Effectiveness and Efficiency in Analytics

The comforting conviction that the world makes sense rests on a secure foundation: our almost unlimited ability to ignore our ignorance.

Daniel Kahneman, psychologist, author and Nobel
Memorial Prize in Economic Sciences

In the field of analytics, we face several potential challenges that range from implementing change to ensuring that we have the right skills and competencies to deliver on the organizational capabilities. These barriers can be found in the areas of leadership, the human element, and in data and technology. See Figure 11.3 on the common challenges in analytics.

Toolkit

From the companion website, access the interactive MindMap outlining barriers to analytics adoption.

While Figure 11.3 doesn't capture all the potential challenges with analytics, it certainly represents the most pressing of those challenges that impact our ability to be both effective and efficient in the delivery of analytics products to organizations.

At a higher level, this can be seen in the struggles that every analytics leader faces:

- Strategy versus execution
- Culture versus politics
- People versus process
- Data versus technology

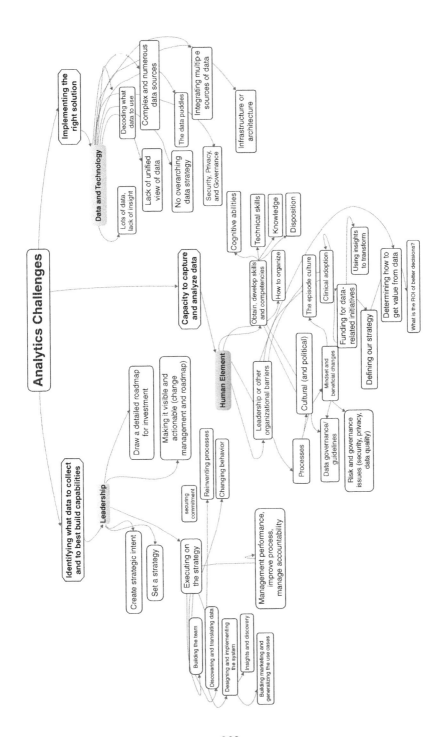

Figure 11.3 Common challenges in analytics

WHY OPERATIONALIZATION OF ANALYTICS FAILS

Once we know something, we find it hard to imagine what it was like not to know it.

Chip & Dan Heath, *Made to Stick, Switch*

As if the list of challenges above was not overwhelming enough, it is important to note that transformative change is hard. Even if you have the right strategy, the right data, the right people, and the right technology, it is still possible to fail. Here are some of the reasons why we can fail in our efforts to operationalize analytics:

- *We produce data, not insights*—Organizations are overwhelmed with data, as evidenced by massive numbers of reports and dashboards that continue to proliferate; they aim to democratize the data, pushing data to the edges of the organizations where they can be vetted, enriched, and utilized.

- *Insights are untimely*—The "time to decision" is often in minutes and hours, yet analytics insights arrive well outside the decision-making window.

- *Decisioning process is not understood*—The Analytics Lifecycle must be in sync with the decision lifecycle. When we fail to empathize with how people use the data to support decisions and problem solving, we set ourselves up for failure.

- *Technology is too general*—When technology solutions (data warehouses, dashboards, reports, etc.) are implemented, we often fail to consider how they can best support organizational decisions.

- *Trusted partners*—Producers and consumers of analytics often do not have a strong relationship that allows the analyst to understand or anticipate the true needs.

- *Data fluency*—There exists in most organizations a gap in basic data and analytics literacy. Data literacy must be evangelized and championed throughout the organization.

- *There is no silver bullet*—In general, we fail to collect deep, nonquantitative, insights about people and processes that could help position analytics insights into the proper context.

▪ *Thinking small*—While big-bang approaches are ill-advised, we cannot continue to report on the past. Our mandate is to apply analytics where we can influence change—including transforming the business and the delivery of product or services.

▪ *Poor stewardship*—We fail to inspire confidence when we provide inaccurate, incomplete data that cannot be replicated; we must ensure quality in every data product we develop.

▪ *Culture of "Haves and Have-Nots"*—When we fail to push analytics to the edges of the organizations, we fail; we need to create voracious consumers of analytics—those who solicit data, ask questions, push for insights, and take actions. We also must model the use of analytics and support our data champions.

▪ *Modest predictive accuracy*—Analytics models are only as good as they help us influence change; analytics results that perform no better than intuition (Spidey-sense) or produce predictions that are not impactful contribute to the negative narrative about ineffective analytics.

▪ *Unplanned or unintended consequences*—When we fail to understand how models are used in the context of the business and the systems of interconnectedness, we are susceptible to analytics being used for the wrong things.

What's Required for Successful Analytics Change

An idea not coupled with action will never get any bigger than the brain cell it occupied.

Arnold Glasow, American businessman

While some industries are still in their "analytics infancy" phase, others have developed mature, robust analytics capabilities. On the backs of heroes, we can see the potential benefits of analytics through leading organizations, and these use cases continue to drive our future aspirations. But how do we effect change? How do we "action" analytics in our organizations?

The opportunities can be seen in the challenges we face. It's up to us to apply what we know about behavior change, motivation, problem solving, design thinking, and so on to effect change where we can influence.

While organizations differ in the specifics, it comes down to these core elements:

1. Develop strategic intent and clarify analytics aspirations—organizational capabilities.

2. Define the data strategy—outlining what data to collect and how to govern it.

3. Build capacity to capture and analyze data—including nurturing and developing analytics talent.

4. Implement the right solutions—people, processes, and technology.

5. Apply analytics to the right problems.

6. Create a culture of innovation that reacts timely to insights.

Note that many of these elements rely heavily on leadership, people, processes. and data. Technology is an enabler and should never be confused with being "the" solution.

CHANGE MANAGEMENT

Up to this point this discussion has presented change as an ethereal concept, something that causes angst for most people. As previously discussed, change can be born out of a struggle.

> *Change does not roll in on the wheels of inevitability, but comes through continuous struggle.*
>
> —Martin Luther King Jr.

Or, change can be part of the natural evolution that we call progress.

> *To improve is to change; to be perfect is to change often.*
>
> —Winston Churchill

As noted earlier in this chapter, change management is more than just "training" or communications—it is a systematic approach that helps to facilitate the transition of organizations and people from a current to a future state.

When we talk about organizations changing, it is really about the creation of a mindset that helps individuals make a personal transition in the context of technology and processes wrapped inside an organizational culture. It is often said that a future state is only achieved when people do their jobs differently and make their own transition from their current state to their future state. Change management is not about forcing change but rather helping people prepare for the change (awareness), understanding the rationale and impact (knowledge), helping them with the tools that allow for skills development (adoption) and skills integration (commitment).

The process to manage change should depend on the impact of the change and should be scaled accordingly (see "Choosing the Right Approach"). While a number of change management methodologies are available, both commercially and otherwise, I believe that the eight-step process that John Kotter characterized in the seminal work *Leading Change* (Kotter, 1996) stands the test of time.

For my work in analytics, I utilize six best practice areas outlined in Table 11.3.

Not all projects will require every one of the processes contained within these six best practice areas. The processes should be right-sized according to the breadth, depth, impact, and criticality of the change.

Choosing the Right Approach

As noted, the level of change management effort often depends on the context of the change. Figure 11.4 outlines each of these **dimensions of change** with representative questions that help quantify the impact to the organization. The answers will serve as the basis for the impact assessment and will drive the level of governance and effort required to support the change.

Change can be measured by a structured evaluation:

- *Breadth* applies to a large number of user groups and roles.
- *Depth* involves moderate changes to the way people will work.

Table 11.3 Change management best practice areas for analytics

Change management best practice areas	What this means in practice
1. Create a shared change purpose.	▪ Create an aspirational future state. ▪ Establish clarity around why you intend to achieve this. ▪ Identify the people who will be impacted.
2. Establish a visible and engaged leadership coalition.	▪ Conduct stakeholder analysis. ▪ Collaborate to define the impact of the change. ▪ Engage change champions at the extremes (tipping point leadership).
3. Facilitate stalwart engagement and communication.	▪ Implement a robust communications strategy. ▪ Build awareness, knowledge, contribution, adoption, commitment.
4. Support strong individual performance.	▪ Conduct knowledge and skill assessment. ▪ Deploy effective training and knowledge management strategies.
5. Build a supportive organization and culture.	▪ Build a change network. ▪ Align business processes. ▪ Manage change progress. ▪ Address change readiness.
6. Create a measurement strategy.	▪ Design change governance. ▪ Track progress and issues/report status. ▪ Measure progress (bright spots, laggards).

- ▪ *Impact* has moderate impact to processes and tools and to organization and culture.

- ▪ *Criticality* is driven by an internal need to change, impacts core functions, and ties directly to a corporate strategy.

In organizations, the impact and change strategy can be determined by examining these factors. For departments with a limited number of users, the impact could be minimal and the change management strategy should be scaled accordingly. However, keep in mind that the number of users is only one dimension to evaluate. The criticality of the proposed changes and the impact to business processes must also be considered, along with the depth of the change.

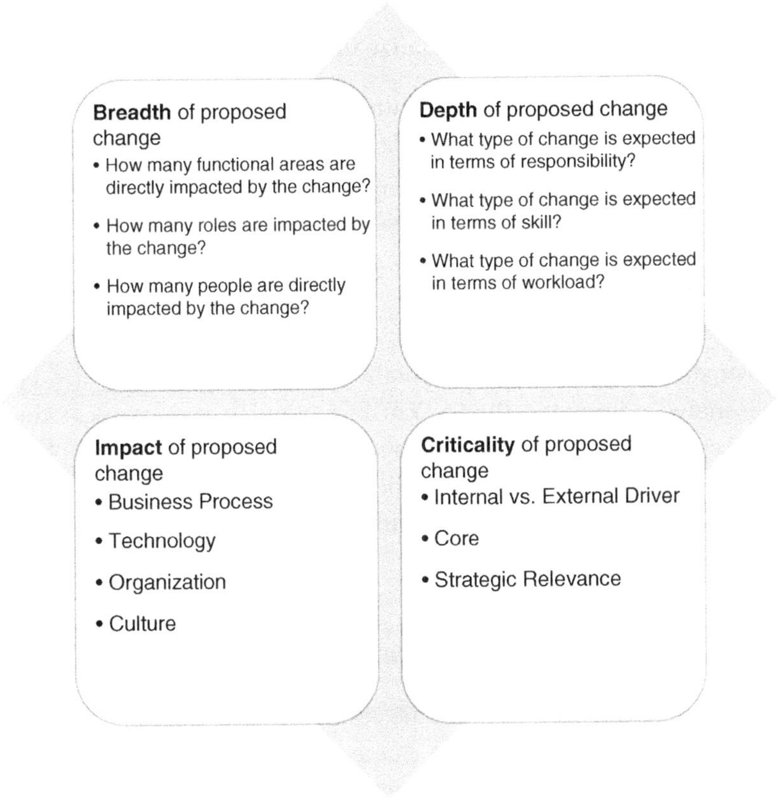

Breadth of proposed change
- How many functional areas are directly impacted by the change?
- How many roles are impacted by the change?
- How many people are directly impacted by the change?

Depth of proposed change
- What type of change is expected in terms of responsibility?
- What type of change is expected in terms of skill?
- What type of change is expected in terms of workload?

Impact of proposed change
- Business Process
- Technology
- Organization
- Culture

Criticality of proposed change
- Internal vs. External Driver
- Core
- Strategic Relevance

Figure 11.4   Dimensions of change

When assessing different types of change in organizations, they can be scored and fit into one of three types of change:

- *Transformational* affects a large number of people across the organization where the change is critical and fundamentally affects how people do their everyday job.
- *Transitional* is not as widespread as a transformational change but does affect how people perform their jobs and retooling of processes is required.
- *Transactional* is limited to a single department with a small number of users.

For example, a transformational change in the context of an analytics platform would be characterized by:

- The breadth of its impact—number of departments/organizations and number and types of roles that are affected
- The depth of change—changes to responsibilities, skills, and workload
- The impact to culture and organization
- The criticality of the change

Organizations can fundamentally transform how they use data and analytics knowing that a transformation in how work is done requires attention to change management. After all, when people are asked to use different tools to do their jobs, they need to be supported and have the necessary skills, training, and leadership support to make that transition.

Why Change Management Matters

Change management improves the effectiveness of planning, mobilizing, and ultimately executing a change program. Specifically, change management helps an organization to:

- Achieve unity of purpose around the need for change and what the future organization should look like, and create a sense of urgency or aspirational vision.
- Establish clear decision-making authority and governance, and outline how change will be managed.
- Understand the impact of the change, positive and negative, on different stakeholder groups.
- Develop a purposeful and defensible change management strategy and plan.
- Develop and support the change leaders best placed to successfully deliver the program.
- Conduct a stakeholder analysis, build a **change network**, and create change with specific communications that move people along the **commitment curve**.

- Identify competency strengths that can be used to support change, align performance and talent management processes with the direction of change, and develop training strategies to enable transitional or operational change.

- Reconfigure the organizational structure in line with the changed processes and coordinate the transition from old to new.

- Define the organization's core values, cultural characteristics, and reflect these in a specific behavior change plan.

- Develop program-specific change metrics and track the value chain linking change management interventions with business benefits.

- Establish business readiness criteria and checklists, determine when the organization is ready, and facilitate a smooth transition from old to new.

Emotional Responses to Change

A new implementation of a data or analytics technology platform often involves tools, technologies, or techniques that may be new to the organization. As with any upgrade in technology, there is a user learning curve, and changes in business processes—all of which affect productivity, efficiency, and morale. The implications and ramifications of introducing new software may not be critical in all organizations or industries. However, in a highly regulated, fast-paced, or competitive environment, change can be devastating.

At the heart of a change management plan are the activities required to address the change impacts that have been identified. These activities should move stakeholders along the commitment curve, facilitate adoption of the change solution, and achieve anticipated business benefits. The change commitment curve shown in Figure 11.5 illustrates the emotional stages of awareness, understanding, adoption, and commitment that stakeholders experience during the course of a change program requiring the adoption of new ways of working.

There are many variations in how users react, but most models depict the four stages of emotional response to change shown in Figure 11.5.

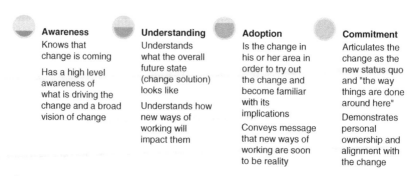

Awareness
Knows that change is coming

Has a high level awareness of what is driving the change and a broad vision of change

Understanding
Understands what the overall future state (change solution) looks like

Understands how new ways of working will impact them

Adoption
Is the change in his or her area in order to try out the change and become familiar with its implications

Conveys message that new ways of working are soon to be reality

Commitment
Articulates the change as the new status quo and "the way things are done around here"

Demonstrates personal ownership and alignment with the change

Figure 11.5 Emotional reactions to change

Stakeholders progress along the four stages depending on their starting point (current state) and desired point (future state). Different stakeholders will, of course, start at different points along the curve and mature at different rates. One factor that often drives this is "technical curiosity" that can help accelerate adoption. We know, for example, that the velocity for change will be fundamentally different for those who have been early adopters of new technology, as well as those who have been privy to the conversations regarding the change and involved in process redesign.

The change commitment curve in Figure 11.6 demonstrates how the four emotional responses to change mature to the point of full

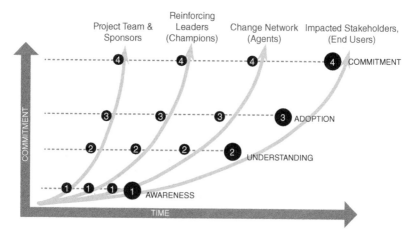

Figure 11.6 Change commitment curve

commitment, and how each stakeholder group will move along the commitment curve at the rate most appropriate and critical for that group.

Consider the potential pressures and anxieties for users learning a new software program who:

- Work in a time-sensitive environment and are not afforded the luxury of being slow or inefficient
- Must produce quality work, and
- Must be able to respond to internal or external questions and concerns in a timely manner.

Further, a number of other issues may plague the organization. Consider these examples:

- A history of inadequate communication has brewed frustration among users.
- A stigma is associated with certain software components like "open source" versus commercial vendors (much like the fight between the iPhone and Android).
- Employee on-boarding practices are fragmented and inconsistent.

If this process is done poorly, people will fail to move up the commitment curve and instead spiral downward.

Taken together, the risk of doing nothing or managing change poorly can be devastating to a project. We began this section by discussing how to measure the impact of the change. And the stage has now been set for considering why the change is important and how to create that sense of urgency.

Examples of Change Management for Analytics

In the context of modernizing data or analytics technologies, I know from my own experience that change can have a profound effect on whether organizations realize the expected return on investment. Any change in technology or process can have a great impact on those who use, manage, or administer those systems. One of the common threads is that organizations often don't recognize the potential impact of the change, so it is often seen as scary and complex. For example, if users go from using Microsoft Excel to a forecasting system, managers will often think that the change is minor, as in going from one system to another, and users should be able to make the switch easily; or they believe that a tool demonstration will suffice as change management.

Table 11.4 provides some examples of changes and their potential impact.

BEST PRACTICES FOR LEADING CHANGE

As previously discussed, my approach for managing analytics change programs includes six key best practice areas. This chapter highlights four of the areas that illustrate the importance of change management and its relevancy in analytics projects.

Create a Shared Change Purpose

Like John Kotter's philosophy on change, I believe that one of the most important steps in a project is to create a clear vision and strategy around why the change is important and what that means to stakeholders across the organization. A change management strategy should be compelling and consistent, with a vision of the future business environment and the implications for the future state of the organization.

In analytics—whether technology impacts those who develop the models or business processes change as a result of analytics model deployment—this can be documented in a way that defines the mission, vision, and strategy for the change. One example from a project that my team supported required incorporating a company's vision for a common analytics operating platform. However, the company's current state had it utilizing literally hundreds of individual PCs and servers with varying products spread across three continents. Its business objectives included standardization of processes to improve global sharing of resources and improved economies of scale.

By creating a shared sense of purpose, the company provided clarity of thinking and defined measurable targets for the change. In addition, it offered an opportunity to collaborate with employees across the

Table 11.4 Examples of analytics impacting change

Audience	Type of Change	Potential Impact
Data analyst	Adopting a new technology for data exploration and analysis	▪ File system changes: navigation, right click options, invocation parameters ▪ Operating system changes ▪ Nuances of the tool: current working directory, graphics, default options, interface navigation, query/filter data, managing projects, code management, log reviews ▪ Programming interfaces: Web to client ▪ Versioning: automatic versus third-party tool ▪ Monitoring and scheduling jobs ▪ Remote/distributed access: VDI, Desktop, Citrix
Technical data developer	Utilizing a new system for data management: data integration, data quality, master data management, data governance	▪ Understand and appreciate metadata ▪ Movement from programs to process flows and pipelines ▪ Alignment of roles and responsibilities ▪ Transparency in data ownership ▪ Data governance processes ▪ Deeper integration with data system owners ▪ Business users new to the process
Driver for logistics company	Adoption of on-truck telematics and advanced algorithms	▪ Route optimization ▪ Determination of when to turn off engine: idle times ▪ Predictive maintenance for truck downtime
Call center personnel	Systems which improve quality and customer	▪ Optimize the customer experience ▪ Reduce network error rates: telco ▪ Recommend offers for call center personnel to reduce customer churn
Call center management	Utilizing AI to proactively provide narrative feedback on call center personnel	▪ Changes to performance evaluation process ▪ Individual coaching and mentoring of staff
Insurance investigators	Using big data and data visualization to detect and prevent fraud	▪ Automatically ingesting structured and unstructured data from claims and handwritten adjuster notes ▪ Prioritizing claims for investigation ▪ Help train machine learning algorithms

organization so that the vision and strategies of the future state of the organization were shared, making it possible for measures for success to be agreed upon and visible.

The stance adopted by leadership could have been "this is what we are going to do." However, by creating a shared vision they also created a shared sense of urgency that everyone understood. That is the value of a clear, articulated vision—it creates a clear line of sight from what we are doing to why we are doing it—reinforcing the linkages for everyone involved.

In my work, I see many reasons for change, including the need to:

- Address current operational challenges.
- Reduce costs associated with a growing user base and data volumes.
- Take advantage of commodity hardware, i.e., minimize unused capacity on servers and optimize computing power.
- Improve processes.
- Reduce risks.

Regardless of the reason, it is incumbent upon us in the analytics world to overtly champion the "why" of the change and make sure that the vision is clear, understandable, and compelling. Often times this requires explicitly drawing the map that links the business strategy and the technology decisions. When documenting the change strategy, describe the reasons for changing, what you want to achieve, and how you will get there so that people can unite around a clear understanding of the change drivers and the change vision.

Similarly, when compiling a concrete business case, describe both the financial and nonfinancial benefits of the change effort and describe the overall approach to managing the impact of change. This is especially important to engender support from various stakeholders so they don't feel like this will be another one of those changes that will leave them bruised and battered.

Establish a Visible and Engaged Leadership Coalition

Successful change leaders create a shared vision for the change, gain commitment on the change goals, and lead people through transformational change. This best practice area is about helping organizations overcome potential change challenges through leadership.

I don't recommend a "boil the ocean" strategy, but rather something akin to **tipping-point leadership** (TPL). This theory suggests that conventional wisdom is incorrect in that traditional thinking around organizational change rests on transforming the mass—so change efforts are focused on moving the mass, requiring steep resources and a long time frame. Instead, TPL posits that "in order to change the mass, it focuses on transforming the extremes: the people, acts, and activities that exercise a disproportionate influence on performance." In other words, the leaders make the difference.

By transforming the extremes, tipping point leaders are able to quickly change the core and at a lower cost to execute their new strategy. Combined with this approach to change management, strategy execution overcomes four hurdles that stand in the way of change: cognitive, motivational, resources, and political. That's the part of the message that must be communicated, and that must be included in the change methodology that democratizes analytics, creates coalitions and pilot success, without trying to boil the ocean (Figure 11.7).

Change leadership is the profound ability of those who direct, plan, and guide the organization through changes in order to accomplish its goals. The change leadership process is about developing leaders

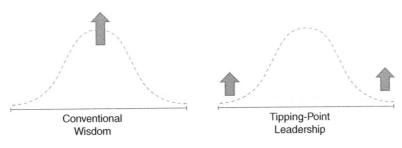

Conventional
Wisdom

Traditional thinking around organizational change rests on transforming the mass—so change efforts are focused on moving the mass, requiring steep resources and a long time frame.

Tipping-Point
Leadership

In order to change the mass, focus on transforming the extremes: the people, acts, and activities that exercise a disproportionate influence on performance.

Figure 11.7 Agility in change can occur by focusing on those with the most influence (positive and negative).

within the organization to effectively drive the change at various levels in the organization. It helps leaders understand their roles and responsibilities and serve as role models for the desired behaviors in the workforce.

Enable Engagement and Communication

Stakeholder Analysis

One of the deliverables that will be maintained throughout the lifecycle of a change program is a **stakeholder analysis** map, which documents the full list of stakeholders who may be impacted or influenced by, or will hold influence over, the change program. It does this by segmenting stakeholders, evaluating their current versus desired levels of commitment, and charting the distance between the two. This serves as a guide to managing the success of the change strategy throughout the lifecycle of the change.

Toolkit @
www.analyticslifecycletoolkit.com

Download a stakeholder map template from the companion website.

Build a Change Network

In addition to the stakeholder analysis, a critical process in this best practice area is the development of a change network. In analytics environments this is especially important, as there are natural or de facto leaders who hold referential authority in the organization. That is, the experts everyone knows and trusts, especially when they have problems.

A change network is a structure of motivated and effective sponsors and agents throughout the organization who can translate the central need for change into a broader willingness and ability to change. The change network rests on the fundamental idea that organizational members are typically less passive pawns unable to affect change and more individual actors capable of intervening in ways that can either support or undermine the change program.

Building a change network involves identifying and recruiting the best available talent—employees who are also respected and seen as representative of users, capable of discovering and addressing change network training requirements, coordinating an ongoing plan of activities, and evaluating and fine-tuning the performance of the change network throughout the change program.

Members of the change network can be deployed in a variety of ways, including serving as steering committee members, power users, influencers, surrogate trainers, role models, and opinion leaders.

Further, you might charge the change network with:

- Assisting with communications activities, such as writing blogs, knowledge-base articles, how-to documents, and/or short videos
- Providing special training
- Engaging in the design of business processes to ensure that requirements are mapped back to the project plan and/or future features list
- Participating in process redesign activities, including the exploration of process areas that feed or are fed by the core technologies that may otherwise be overlooked

Given the potential pivotal and critical role of the change network, it is important to introduce network members early in the process, give them visibility with key activities, and listen to the perspective and suggestions they bring back "from the field."

Stakeholder Communications

Communication is a central part of change management, and while it has almost become something of a cliché, identifying and "managing" the commitment of key project stakeholders through effective communication are critical components to the success of any project.

These processes aim to ensure that the right message is delivered by the right people at the right time, using the most appropriate method. There will be opportunities for individuals to derail a project, but perhaps some or many of those individuals could be converted into champions if we only knew about them. Smart stakeholder engagement and communication activities make clear what is happening, what is expected, and how to get involved, and can even remove some of the unavoidable obstacles to change.

Earlier, we saw what happens when stakeholders are actively disengaged, and the risk that it poses to a change initiative. In this best practice area, the key activities include a detailed stakeholder analysis with a heat map, which indicates how the different organizations (departments) may be impacted, as well as their current change readiness.

Finally, enabling engagement and communication addresses the "communications" part of the process. Quality of communications can be a significant factor in the outcome of a change initiative. Done poorly, it can mean that the need for change is never even fully recognized; done well, it can produce a collective transformation in organizational capability.

Stakeholder communication involves engaging and communicating with stakeholders in a way that facilitates movement along the change commitment curve. Engagement goes beyond traditional communication methods, which tend to focus on transmitting messages from leaders to end users on a one-way basis, to actually winning the "hearts and minds" of stakeholders through interventions that truly engage them.

A strong communications plan is designed to foster understanding, facilitate acceptance and ownership of the change within the organization, positively sustain morale, increase the accuracy of the transmitted information, support the implementation, and reinforce the organization's vision. Further, it will help ensure that desired outcomes are achieved.

When implementing a communications plan, project leaders must be strategic and err on the side of overcommunicating. They must address stakeholders at all levels of the organization and use all possible channels to enable the communications plan.

Users need to be assured that leadership has listened to and considered their needs. They also need to understand—and believe—that the decisions made by IT were strategic and made in a thoughtful way.

Project leaders and supporting stakeholders must attempt to make each communication as individual as possible so that each person within the organization understands the following:

- How his/her work processes will be different
- How to be successful in his/her role
- What training is available
- How he/she is being measured

With a strategic rollout of a new modernized platform and additional software, including strong change management, communications, and training plans, the IT and business support sides of the organization can align and operate more efficiently and effectively. This will ultimately demonstrate that the shared sense of urgency and the shared sense of importance are real.

Depending on the phase of the project, the communications plan should be detailed down to the level of where individual users make the transition from Awareness → Understanding → Adoption → Commitment. As you might expect, the communication goals will be different, depending on where individuals are on their own journey. The stakeholder analysis map shown above can be a useful tool to do this. Table 11.5 illustrates the changes in messaging based on where users are in their individual change curve.

Support Strong Individual Performance

Successful change allows individual employees to adopt and own new ways of working in order to enable organizational change. Training may be needed to promote the use of new products or the adoption of appropriate behaviors. Performance management processes often need to be revisited and adjusted to clarify and document expectations of the staff. The challenge is to ensure that the proper incentives, skills, and processes are in place to enable people to perform appropriately and effectively in the future state organization.

This is done by focusing on two of the processes:

1. *Knowledge and skills assessment*—Assess whether the users impacted by the change have the requisite knowledge and skills to change their ways of working in line with the business

Table 11.5 Examples of communications goals by change curve

Awareness → Understanding	Understanding → Adoption	Adoption → Commitment
▪ Communicate vision and importance of project/ problem being solved. ▪ Describe the project and anticipated changes. ▪ Share the timeline for the project. ▪ Describe impact. ▪ Explain individual roles and expectations. ▪ Build strong communication, support, and trust.	▪ Celebrate the new environment/model. ▪ Gain input and feedback from all stakeholders. ▪ Measure effectiveness and communicate results. ▪ Revise messaging as needed. ▪ Support users during the adoption phase so that they begin to demonstrate new capabilities and behaviors. ▪ Gain approval.	▪ Gain input and feedback from all stakeholders. ▪ Measure effectiveness and communicate results. ▪ Revise messaging as needed. ▪ Ensure that users have embraced change and are proficient in their work processes. ▪ Coach and support others as they adopt and adapt.

change objectives. The assessment documents the employee knowledge and skills with a view to understanding the gap between current and future capabilities.

2. *Training and knowledge management*—Ensure that all employees impacted by the change have the requisite knowledge, skills, and abilities required to deliver the change. Significant change may require training to support both the behavioral as well as the product elements of the change. This includes the right learning curriculum along with the right tools for on-the-job performance support and updated processes.

The tools used in this process include a performance management map, training and knowledge needs analysis, and a methodology for evaluation. The benefits seen when properly executing these best practices include:

▪ Clear alignment of employee objectives with strategic direction of change

▪ Support for people who need to develop knowledge, skill, and competency in their new roles

- Allocation of the right resources with the right skills assigned to roles critical to drive change
- Faster time to competency—employees more quickly able to perform in new jobs, use new systems, etc.
- Realization of benefits made from human capital investments
- Improved on-boarding/transition time

Toolkit @
www.analyticslifecycletoolkit.com

Access the performance management map template from the companion website.

TROUBLESHOOTING CHANGE

Regardless of which of the many change management gurus you follow, such as John Kotter (1996) or Heath and Heath (2010), change is hard. Following a prescribed set of steps is necessary but not sufficient for leading change. The importance of spending the time and energy in developing a change strategy, documenting the drivers of change, and following good methodology cannot be underestimated.

That said, there will likely be initiatives that just struggle. This section will explore just a few real-world challenges you may encounter.

The change management literature is replete with horror stories of why change failed. These failures cut across mergers and acquisitions, IT, industry transformation, and business model innovations. There are always excuses as to why the time, energy, and money cannot be spent on these efforts. Potential barriers to success include the following:

- **Team members having competing priorities based on their job functions**
    - Leading change requires a commitment to doing it well.
    - If resources cannot be freed up to do important work, it won't be perceived of as being important.

- **Not involving the right people (either intentionally or through oversight)**

  - Honest and broad-reaching stakeholder analysis is critical to ensuring that the impact is understood by all.

  - Technology change is not merely a technology project; be wary if you hear of a project where someone says that this is simply a technology refresh.

- **Multiple major change projects concurrently taxing the organization and involving/affecting many members of this project**

  - Change management requires experienced leadership.

  - Transformational change requires commitment.

  - If you don't have seasoned change management experts inside the company, find help outside from those who fit your culture and approach.

- **A legacy of less-than-desirable technology rollouts**

  - Leadership won't solve everything, but a strong, visible leadership coalition will go a long way to ensure that your change management initiative is different from what may have been done before.

- **Lack of an effective communication strategy**

  - Fix it. This is where experts in communication, psychology, and behavior change are essential.

- **An implicit culture that change is good as long as it doesn't get in the way of people doing their day jobs**

  - This is akin to saying that this is important, but get back to work. This strategy will fail. While the project may get to a completed state, there is little doubt that the quality bar will not have been met. It doesn't take a monumental effort to do change management right, just a commitment.

- **Lack of a clear, unified, and shared sense of why the change is being made**

  - The project should be put on hold until everyone has a clear line of sight as to why it is important and what their role is in ensuring its success.

CHAPTER SUMMARY

Actioning analytics is perhaps one of the biggest challenges we face in accelerating the value of our work. As I have outlined, understanding the barriers that get in our way and thinking about designing for change are critical to ensuring that our analytics matter. Leading change is part of our role as analytics leaders—to support and influence change that helps facilitate the transition of organizations and people from a current to a future state. This necessarily includes best practices, processes, tools, and techniques to help deal with the people, process, and organizational aspects of change.

While there is no simple solution or off-the-shelf answer, change management does not have to be expensive. It should be right-sized in accordance with the breadth, depth, criticality, and impact to the organization.

Change management is a systematic approach that helps facilitate the transition of organizations and people from a current to a future state. As a management methodology, this includes best practices, process, tools, and techniques to help deal with the people and organizational side of change.

Change management incorporates the methods that can be utilized to help individuals make successful personal transitions resulting in the adoption and commitment to the change, thus yielding the business benefits of change.

In this chapter I discussed the definition of change management and why it is an important component for any organization that seeks to transform itself. Modernizing data strategies and developing an analytics mindset supported by technology changes are important areas where change management should be considered as essential to success.

REFERENCES

Heath, C., & Heath, D. (2010). *Switch: How to change things when change is hard* (1st ed.). New York: Broadway Books.

Kotter, J. P. (1996). *Leading change.* Boston: Harvard Business School Press.

CHAPTER 12

Core Competencies for Analytics Teams

Analytics competency relates to the knowledge, skills, abilities and disposition required to successfully turn data into actionable interventions.

Greg Nelson, Founder and CEO, ThotWave

INTRODUCTION

One of the single biggest challenges in building an analytics team is defining the blend of skills that will suit the team mission and the enterprise culture. To understand how to develop staff to achieve future **capabilities**, I strongly recommend the use of a competency model that maps analytics functions, skills, and competencies to specific organizational roles.

Developed through a process of workplace analysis and expert knowledge, the model includes nine domains of **knowledge, skills, and behaviors** that need to be demonstrated within the analytics team. It is noteworthy that many of the **competencies** that are critical for analytics have several nonstatistical and nontechnical features. The reason for this is because the model seeks to address the entire analytics lifecycle, not just analytics model development.

Analytics Competencies Defined

Analytics competency relates to the knowledge, skills, abilities, and disposition required to successfully turn data into actionable interventions.

The "data scientist" is sometimes seen as the warrior—the lone Spartan—who carves his way through data to conquer his would-be foes. As an experienced consultant, I think about this differently. The data champion is a participant in a robust analytics process that helps deliver an analytics capability for the organization. As you can sense from the variety of processes and best practices outlined in this book, my view of the analytics lifecycle is broad and requires skills that go well beyond the capabilities of a single warrior.

In fact, the wide range of necessary competencies includes the technical skills, but puts them to work to solve real-world problems. For example, the behavioral view can include:

- Data wrangling
- Data storytelling
- Framing questions
- Dynamic problem solving
- Communication and results explanation
- Project prioritization
- Navigating the business context
- Data journalism
- Method selection
- Data imputation
- Outlier detection and handling
- Presenting data results
- Determining what's important in data

I choose to differentiate *competencies* from *skills* in the following way: competencies include the totality of a person's ability to masterfully execute their role. They include the right **mindset** and the right skillset, supported by skills in the toolsets that enable people to successfully perform their work.

Competencies refer to a person's ability to do something successfully or efficiently.

Whereas, skills are specific, learned activities are necessary but not sufficient to perform a role.

Skills support a person's ability to do something well.

Developing Analytics Competencies

So how do we find, grow, and nurture analytics talent? It's clear from well-known resources such as McKinsey's Report on Big Data analytics that there is a talent gap across all industries (Manyika et al., 2011).

A number of my customers report disparities between their ability to meet the priorities of their business and the capabilities of the consultants, vendors, and innovators who serve them.

In particular, I've seen a significant shift in the core competencies that organizations are looking for in analytics. There is movement away from the traditional mindset of "skills" building, where tools and technology knowledge took center stage. This is being supplanted by the new "data mindset"—where organizations are looking for people with more comprehensive, modern competencies that include design thinking, innovation, analytics product management, storytelling, understanding of IT policy, and business and operational workflows, along with a mindset toward the ethical use of data (Figure 12.1).

Similarly, there has been a significant shift in the way that talent is nurtured. Instead of chasing the high-priced data scientist, organizations are investing in modern approaches to **talent development**, adopting novel strategies.

Past and Future Workforce Competencies Needed

As discussed in the last chapter, we need to rethink our strategy for nurturing analytic talent. It doesn't have to be a one-time educational seminar, technical training workshop, or lecture. If we seriously want to get better at analytics capabilities within our organization, we must

SHIFT FROM TOOLSET TO MINDSET

Old World:

New World:

Traditional Skills

Modern Competencies

SAS	SQL
JMP	ETL
STATA	Java
MATLAB	XML
Business analysis	.Net
Reporting	
Warehousing	

Design thinking	Question design	SAS	Hadoop
Innovation	Data profiling	JMP	Spark
Product mgmt	Influence	Tableau	R
Storytelling	Team mgmt	Qlik	Python
Health policy	Quality	D3	Lua
Ethics	Tool selection		Machine learning
Workflows	Knowledge mgmt		
Security/Privacy			

Figure 12.1 The point at which there is a shift from toolset to mindset

invest in selecting the right people, organizing our teams for an effective and efficient analytics lifecycle that is customer focused and integrate agile project methods with talent development and performance management.

This linkage helps inform our capabilities, what business processes need to be supported and how we organize to deliver on our analytics capabilities. From there it is critical to understand what we are good at and where we need growth. That's where the knowledge and skills assessment comes into play. Equipped with a strong understanding of the opportunities, we can staff project teams, help individuals on their own personal roadmap, and build institutional knowledge through formal and informal knowledge management strategies.

An example of how we can support the alignment of organizational project needs with talent development is shown in Figure 12.2. Given that we understand what our organizational priorities are around data and analytics and we understand where all of our people are with regard to their competencies link to organizational competency model landing page, we can integrate professional development plans using this framework.

Analytics Career Lattice

My position is that existing staff should be incentivized to learn new skills and broaden their capabilities as to benefit both personal and organizational development. *Traditional career paths have not awarded this individual agility.* I follow the approach of other industries in eschewing the career ladder in favor of the **career lattice**, which is a diagonal framework that relates lateral experiences, skill acquisition, and peer networking to show employees how to move to a variety of positions. Figure 12.2 is a career lattice for the standardized job families described in Chapter 2. In applying this model, leadership should consider how their job families interrelate into a career lattice in making hiring, talent retention, and professional development decisions. This model is intended as a starting place to reformulate organizational design.

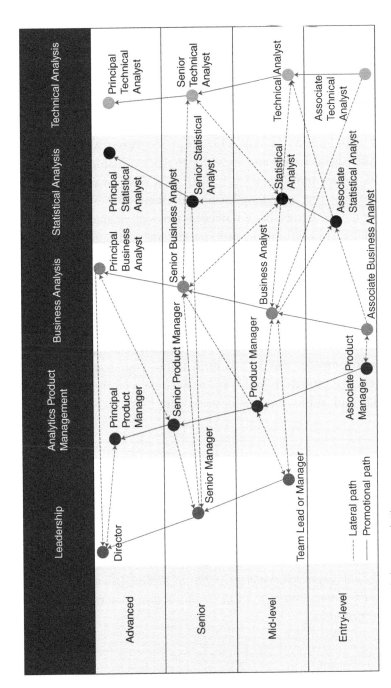

Figure 12.2 Analytics career lattice

ANALYTICS COMPETENCIES DETAILED

As was mentioned in Chapter 3, analytics is a team sport, and we cannot rely on the fictitious unicorns. There is no single soul that I have met who has mastered all of the competencies required for the breadth and depth of the analytics lifecycle. With that said, there are individuals who are very good at solving problems.

In this section, I outline a competency model that I developed in concert with Monica Horvath, PhD, from ThotWave. As you consider the knowledge domains and the competencies contained within each domain, realize that I view each of us as a work in progress. I am, and always will be, a life-long learner. In Chapter 3, I talked about the four key competencies that are needed across all of analytics (analytical thinking, critical thinking, problem solving, and systems thinking). Here, I add one more: curiosity. In my experience, I can teach people the nuances of things like question design or data exploration, but I think curiosity is a prerequisite to any successful growth.

While technologies, approaches, and methods will continue to change, I encourage you to not think of the nine competency domains and 42 competency areas below as an overwhelming list of things to master. Consider this as a way to frame your learning for your own personal growth. If you want to become a business analyst, for example, look at the competency areas with those skills highlighted.

Toolkit

To access learning resources by knowledge domain, please see the companion website.

Competency Domain: Business

There is a growing recognition across industries that analysts with a solid command of the business workflow are those who, in turn, most effectively support their business units.

The analytics professional with business domain expertise makes the following unique contributions:

- Developing relevant data and analytics products that suit the needs of business, financial, and operational customers
- Translating unstructured business problems into a solution discovery framework with statistical underpinnings
- Improving existing services that rely on data
- Participating strategically and tactically in decisions that impact the organization
- Analyzing organizational data to understand how to optimize experiences of both the internal customers and external

The model represents the business domain as the sum of four competencies: operational workflows, IT policy, organizational and team roles, and organizational structure.

Operational Workflows

The analytics professional is intimately familiar with some portion of the greater organizational data, and as a result, should be able to recognize when practices change or oddities seep into data repositories. Accomplishing this requires a sufficient understanding of business workflow. In accepting this charge, analysts are supporting the integrity of operational workflows that support the business.

The operational workflows competency contains the following capabilities to incorporate business-specific factors on analytics:

- Describing the personas and workflow for supported products or service lines
- Speaking the terminology and vernacular of the business
- Describing the role of analytics regarding both strategic goals and specific tactics that serve business unit

IT Policy

Many organizations are highly regulated with incentives and pressures supplied by local, state, federal, and international entities. These varied pressures drive significant activity in how workflows and analytics solutions are chosen, rationalized, and deployed. As a result, the analytics professional should understand how evolving policies may impact those workflows and eventually alter the interpretation of data. The IT policy competency contains the following capabilities to integrate internal and external influences on analytics:

- Describing how IT policy impacts the organization's data ecosystem

- Making decisions surrounding the feasibility of projects by understanding the web of financial incentives that pressure customers, employees, suppliers, and other stakeholders

- Planning for the implied changes to existing data products given new policies that impact business workflows

Organizational and Team Roles

The analytics professional role is highly consultative in nature and has a place in every business unit. As a result, they are responsible for understanding the breadth of business roles so that they can build effective relationships. The analytics professional should never rely on guesses or assumptions when faced with workflow questions. The organizational and team roles competency contains the following capabilities for relationship building:

- Collaborating with other workers and understanding their unique perspective on data given the business unit they support

- Building a circle of influence in an organization by identifying and networking with data consumers

- Identifying subject matter experts to consult when information about a process or business function is needed

Organizational Structure

The organizational charts for many large organizations are exceedingly complex. Navigation of the myriad corporate entities, departments, and affiliated groups within an environment allows one to develop a holistic picture of the user base for data. The organizational structure competency contains the following capabilities for stakeholder identification:

- Navigating the leadership structure across the enterprise and identifying the executives and other upper-level management responsible for business decisions
- Collaborating with staff representing a diversity of business needs and perspectives to tackle complicated problems
- Working through issues of data product actionability that can arise in delicate scenarios when business units seem to have conflicting missions and purpose

Competency Domain: Analytical Thinking

The analytical thinker is one who has a strong sense of the business and thinks through business problems to identify what questions can be asked using data.

We can ask many questions about the data, but are they the right questions to ask? The analytical thinker has the ability to ask the right questions and use the results to solve the problems in creative ways.

The analytics professional with analytical thinking expertise makes the following unique contributions:

- Applying the data to a project goal to evaluate a hypothesis
- Performing statistical analysis to find correlations and dependence
- Reviewing the results to determine the impact on the project
- Advocating the value of analytics to improve the business
- Communicating insights and results

The model represents the analytical thinking domain as the sum of five competencies: question design, statistical and analytics methods, results interpretation, operationalization of insights, and evangelism.

Question Design

Each analytics project begins with a fundamental question. This question must be designed to identify the business problem we are addressing as well as the actionability of results. The question design competency contains the following capabilities to ask the right questions:

- Determining the needed questions before working with the data
- Employing a structured methodology to design the question
- Using a study design that fits the incoming data

Statistical and Analytics Methods

Statistical methods, such as creating measures, identifying correlations, calculating p-values, and other techniques help address hypotheses about business data. The statistical and analytics methods competency contains the following capabilities to perform valid and effective analyses:

- Using many different statistical methods against a variety of data
- Deriving and applying risk scores and adjustments
- Identifying and characterizing statistical variation

Results Interpretation

Once the analysis is complete, the results need to be interpreted to identify what impact they have on the business problem. This requires deep thinking and a clear and logical approach to separate assumptions from reality. The results interpretation competency contains the following capabilities to accurately evaluate findings:

- Identifying patterns in data and the source of variation
- Distinguishing whether the outcome represents a "one off" or is representative of the whole population
- Understanding correlation does not always mean causation

Operationalization of Insights

Managing analytics insights as part of a repeatable workflow reduces repetitive effort and provides a factory-like setting for analytics to "take off." The operationalization of insights competency contains the following capabilities to streamline the process of generating and employing analytics products:

- Measuring return on investment for analytics products
- Choosing an analytics product that is robust enough to handle the problems
- Creating a plan for how the organization can implement the product rollout for full adoption

Evangelism

Many great and expensive analytics products have languished on the shelf because no one was there to champion their adoption. Without a team driving the adoption of a product, as well as continuing to innovate the business process, the business problems don't get solved and the ROI diminishes significantly. The evangelism competency contains the following capabilities to promote the continued application of data analytics and analytics products:

- Conveying the value of analytics and the benefit it provides to the organization as a whole
- Informing how the results can be used in other areas of the business as well as where they are not applicable
- Communicating results in ways non-analytics employees can understand

Competency Domain: Data Management

Data management focuses on data extraction, transformation, evaluation of its suitability for use, and governance.

Having well-defined, governed, high-quality data is the foundation of the entire analytics structure. Furthermore, you need a plan for data governance and for ensuring a repeatable process.

The analytics professional with data management expertise makes the following unique contributions:

- Providing quality data for quality decisions
- Extracting data from a variety of data sources
- Governing data for documentation and security
- Joining data from the different data sources

The model represents the data management domain as the sum of four competencies: data wrangling, data quality, data governance, and data modeling.

Data Wrangling

Data can come in many forms, from many sources. Reading and formatting the data correctly for analytics is a key first step. The data wrangling competency contains the following capabilities to obtain and prepare data for analysis:

- Extracting large volumes of data
- Transforming data that can be used to answer business questions
- Cleaning dirty data

Data Quality

The quality of business decisions formed from data is directly dependent upon data quality. The data quality competency contains the following capabilities to analyze and preserve data integrity and validity:

- Profiling and characterizing data
- Developing a reproducible approach to process data
- Evaluating data suitability/quality to answer a business question considering its quality

Data Governance

Appropriate use of the data, as well as documenting data structure, meaning, and provenance, is key to proper data governance. Developing a process for these tasks helps articulate why the data is used.

The data governance competency contains the following capabilities to develop and document the process for data management:

- Describing where the data originated
- Describing the relationship between governance and quality
- Modeling how to document and improve data standards and definitions

Data Modeling

Working with disparate data means the data must be joined together. Data modeling focuses on how the different data sources relate to each other, which fields are important, and how to create a reusable model to tie the pieces together. The data modeling competency contains the following capabilities to model and analyze the structure of the data:

- Understanding different data model constructs
- Creating entity relationship diagram models that fit the pieces together
- Implementing the diagram models in a database construct

Competency Domain: Data Exploration

Data exploration entails a variety of activities to examine distinct data sets and adjudicate their suitability for different business questions and further interrogation.

Clearly defining the data is only half of the battle to answer a business question. The decisions made in exploring, interpreting, and explaining data speak to the true art of analysis.

Data exploration expertise allows individuals to make the following unique contributions:

- Quantifying the breadth and depth of a given data set and considering its suitability for an analytics purpose
- Identifying previously unrealized connection points between data
- Assessing the fidelity of the data capture process to create information that describes business workflow

The model represents the data exploration domain as the sum of three competencies: profiling and characterization, data relationships and connections, and underlying business workflows.

Profiling and Characterization

Knowing what you have in a data set is the first step toward developing novel insights. Data profiling involves performing a variety of activities to describe the aggregate trends, features, and "personality" of a data set. The profiling and characterization competency contains the following capabilities to learn about the nature of the data:

- Using a structured, repeatable process to explore and summarize the personality of a data set in terms of measures of central tendency, variation, and data types
- Identifying extreme values, outliers, quality issues, and missing data values
- Deploying a variety of charts or graphs to describe the data visually

Data Relationships and Connections

Those with strong data exploration skills can uncover connections and interactions between data that may not have been previously appreciated. They will use a variety of narrative and visual formats to explain this interrelatedness to organizational leaders. The data relationships and connections competency contains the following capabilities to identify and model the interconnectedness of the data:

- Creating a data dictionary to describe linkages between different data sets that are joined together
- Doing extensive subset analysis to see how data values may co-vary
- Leveraging master data files to enhance connection options for data

Underlying Business Workflows

While the business competency domain emphasized the operational workflows competency, good data exploration relies on being able to envision how the data in front of an analyst connects to the application that created it. Increasingly, enterprise systems such as electronic health records, inventory management, human resources, financial, and operational systems are used in nearly all aspects of running the business. The underlying business workflows competency contains the following capabilities to model and analyze business processes and data flow:

- Creating and interpreting workflow processes so the path of a data element can be mapped throughout a workflow system
- Providing deep expertise in the workflow nuance of one or more business roles
- Identifying how data feeds and values may change when the underlying workflow is either altered or not followed

Competency Domain: Data Visualization

Telling a story through graphical representations of the data is a compelling way to engage the audience and communicate meaningful information.

Being able to effectively communicate insights that guide recipients toward a conclusion or encourage them to ask deeper business questions that involve them in the overall process.

Data visualization expertise allows the analytics professional to make the following unique contributions:

- Employing a variety of visualization software packages
- Creating meaningful graphics and observing design factors and ideologies
- Communicating stories from data and explaining outcomes clearly

The model represents the data visualization domain as the sum of four competencies: storytelling, visualization techniques, actionability, and visual design principles.

Storytelling

Every story should have a beginning, a middle, and an end. Creating a story from data, depicting it in a visual way, and guiding the audience to draw a logical conclusion takes time, talent, and a variety of skills.

The storytelling competency contains the following capabilities to develop effective stories:

- Creating pictures of the data analysis that the viewer can easily understand

- Crafting storyboards to take the audience from beginning to end through a sequence of events

- Applying best practices from the industry to create compelling visuals

Visualization Techniques

The creation of great visualizations requires an eye for design as well as technical fluency with visualization software. This can be accomplished by programming, point-and-click tools, or a combination of both. The data visualization competency contains the following capabilities to facilitate the presentation of data and information:

- Choosing the appropriate software package or packages

- Embracing new tools and techniques when they become available

- Creating the visualizations in a variety of ways using the appropriate tools

Actionability

What use is putting all the work into analyzing data if the findings are not communicated to those who can act on them? Designing questions and formulating hypothesis is only as good as the ability to make change based on the answers from the data. The actionability competency contains the capabilities to use data to effect change:

- Verifying the results can be implemented

- Leading the effort to implement the solution to the defined business problems

- Helping others explore the tools and empowering them to be self-sufficient in answering some of their own questions (e.g., self-service tools)

Visual Design Principles

Creating graphs is easy. Creating meaningful graphs that adhere to design principles is more difficult. A graph needs to be created to convey information that is accurate and does not mislead the reader to jump to an inappropriate conclusion. The visual design principles competency contains the capabilities to generate effective data graphics:

- Applying design elements of line, shape, color, and other optical components
- Applying design principles of alignment, space, balance, and other area elements
- Ensuring the graph is easily readable (and interpretable) by the intended audience

Competency Domain: Technology Literacy

Technology is constantly evolving. An analytics professional must have a working knowledge of a multitude of software packages and tools to be able to find the one best suited to do the job that is at hand for making the best decisions.

There is no "one size fits all" solution when it comes to technology. The only constant is the fact that technology changes. The analytics professional must keep up on the changes in the software industry to implement the best tool.

Technology literacy expertise allows the analytics professional to make the following unique contributions:

- Analyzing the correct tool or software package to solve the business problem
- Ensuring governmental privacy and security regulations are adhered
- Exploring technology alternatives

The model represents the technology literacy domain as the sum of five competencies: tool selection and use, security and privacy, tool agility and fluency, systems thinking, and enterprise systems architecture.

Tool Selection and Use

With the wide variety of software, each with its own benefits and drawbacks, it is important to have a solid understanding as to what each software package brings to the table. The tool selection and use competency contains the following capabilities to promote effective decision making about software and technology:

- Evaluating tools for application with the business problem
- Knowing how a tool fits into the existing organization infrastructure, or recommending infrastructure changes
- Knowing the architecture supported and various programming languages

Security and Privacy

Privacy is a key concern for most businesses. State, regional, federal, and international regulations all require some measure of ensuring customer privacy. It is imperative that organizations have employees responsible to ensure this privacy by planning for, and securing the data. The security and privacy competency contains the following capabilities to protect data and information assets:

- Maintaining a secure environment that is private as well as incorporates ethical pathos
- Using internal protocols and protected information standards to protect the data processes
- Sharing security and privacy regulations with other team members as necessary

Tool Agility and Fluency

The need to keep up with ever-evolving software keeps an organization relevant and on the forefront. The tool agility and fluency competency contains the following capabilities to prevent an organization from languishing with obsolete tools and software:

- Staying active in learning the latest tools and technology
- Investigating the interoperability between tools and systems
- Switching between and integrating different tools as needed

Systems Thinking

Many times, employees are so focused on their work, they don't see the bigger picture. Systems thinking engages the thought process of stepping outside day-to-day life to illuminate the whole context in which the analytics effort sits. By gaining a better understanding of the entire system, we can make better choices about the impact and value of individual work tasks. The systems thinking competency contains the following capabilities to maintain an awareness of the linkages and interdependencies within systems:

- Understanding the entire system and applying that knowledge to the data and analytics
- Being open to doing tasks in new ways
- Formulating a 360-degree approach focusing on how the analytics will benefit all business stakeholders

Enterprise Systems Architecture

Since enterprise data assets such as large operational systems or data systems (i.e., warehouses and data lakes) are host to most enterprise analytics data, it is vital to understand the architecture and commonalities of the products. Determining a reliable workflow model will result in a better series of analytics products. The enterprise systems architecture competency contains the following capabilities to model and understand data systems:

- Designing a workflow that focuses on the impact that warehoused data has on business processes
- Understanding enterprise data assets at a deep level—not only what they are collectively but also what each individual field means
- Using IT to learn about the people and processes behind the data

Competency Domain: Strategic Thinking

Strategic thinking requires applying innovation and systems thinking to support fact-based decision making. Experience, judgment, professionalism, and ethics all play a role in leading toward a strategic solution that provides answers to important business problems using analytics.

Strategic thinking expertise allows the analytics professional to make the following unique contributions:

- Identifying various approaches to problem solving
- Evaluating solutions for implementation
- Executing strategy in line with the organization and the industry
- Critically evaluating large volumes of information
- Employing ethical criteria in the decision-making process

The model represents the strategic thinking domain as the sum of four competencies: innovation and design thinking, strategic alignment, data-driven decision making, and professionalism and ethics.

Innovation and Design Thinking

Generating a wide variety of approaches to problem solving results in new and innovative ideas and solutions. The innovation and design thinking competency contains the following capabilities to promote adaptive and inventive problem-solving approaches:

- Being creative with thinking of novel solutions
- Embracing ambiguity during the process
- Realizing that not all ideas are viable but can be used as springboards for additional ideas

Strategic Alignment

Given that the industry is constantly changing, it is essential to develop a strong personal strategy to avoid becoming obsolete. Strategic alignment competence ensures employees keep abreast of the constant changes and align and change as needed. The strategic alignment competency contains the following capabilities to ensure appropriate responses to change:

- Creating a personal strategy to stay informed on the latest events and advancements in analytics in your industry

- Communicating newfound knowledge via presentations and publications
- Engaging with others through social media and community channels

Data-Driven Decision Making

The data-driven decision making competency ensures that individuals can make sense of large volumes of data and turn the data into meaningful information to make informed business decisions. Using analytical capabilities, employees can perform in-depth analysis on data. The data-driven decision making competency contains the following capabilities to use data effectively:

- Interpreting data and measuring it
- Ensuring consistency of business data processes
- Understanding the impact of data variability

Professionalism and Ethics

Regardless of industry, data is rife with confidential information. Misuse of this information can cause serious ethical and professional concerns. It is imperative that all members of an organization recognize how confidential information can easily be misused, even with the best intentions. The professionalism and ethics competency contains the following capabilities to promote responsible stewardship of data and information:

- Demonstrating respect, integrity, and compassion
- Committing to ethical principles related to data, business practices, and analytics use
- Committing to excellence and professionalism in all regards

Competency Domain: Leadership

Leadership can, and should, happen at all levels in an organization. Cultivating an environment where individuals are encouraged to grow and mentor moves an organization forward and results in a strong, motivated workforce.

As one of the most important domains, the analytics professional with leadership expertise makes the following unique contributions that include:

- Encouraging a nurturing environment
- Recognizing opportunities for collaboration
- Identifying expectations
- Responding to changes
- Mediating conflicts
- Establishing credibility

The model represents the leadership domain as the sum of seven competencies: change leadership, coaching and development, collaborative leadership, conflict management, influence, team leadership, and finance.

Change Leadership

Cultivating an environment that adapts easily to change is a difficult process. Many people are resistant to change. Ensuring that you have an environment that recognizes change management philosophies and obtaining buy-in from all levels of an organization is crucial to adopting better processes. The change leadership competency contains the following capabilities to help the team effectively adapt to change:

- Developing and implementing change management processes and procedures
- Mentoring employees on changes and expectations
- Analyzing the impact that change will have on people, processes, and systems

Coaching and Development

The vast majority of employees want to grow and learn. There is no "one size fits all" approach for growing in one's field. Employees need a tailored plan to understand what their current skill sets are and where they want to go. The coaching and development competency contains the following capabilities to empower the team:

- Mentoring employees
- Developing an actionable, tailored learning plan for staff
- Providing resources to help the employees achieve their goals

Collaborative Leadership

Nature abhors a vacuum, and so do progressive organizations. Collaboration between individuals within a department and across departments inspires new ideas and innovations. Creating collaborative leadership fosters both individual and organizational growth. The collaborative leadership competency contains the following capabilities to promote effective teamwork:

- Brainstorming with others on how to solve business problems
- Seeking input from, and actively listening to, others
- Willingness to adapt to someone else's views that are contrary to your initial stance

Conflict Management

If everyone always agreed, the world would be a mighty dull place. Conflict management is a good tool to help resolve those differences in the workplace. The leadership domain recognizes that conflict exists and contains the following capabilities to help manage and mitigate conflict:

- Using a variety of styles to resolve conflict
- Identifying early intervention opportunities
- Using solution-driven approaches

Influence

Some people have influence because they are in a position of power. Others have influence because they are natural leaders. Those with proven leadership skills exert greater influence because people have established a trusting relationship. The influence competency contains the following capabilities to help build trusting relationships:

- Encouraging people to work together to problem-solve
- Providing valuable feedback at critical times
- Listening to others and sharing credit when due

Team Leadership

Leading a team is a tremendous responsibility, but it is also enormously rewarding as you help employees grow in their career. Making sure employee goals are aligned with company goals results in a focused and productive team. The team leadership competency contains the following capabilities to encourage and support the team:

- Providing timely feedback and setting expectations
- Recognizing outstanding performance
- Identifying strengths and weaknesses

Finance

Getting a good return on investment is a motto that has survived the business jargon test of time for a reason. Every organization should be consistently aware of the impact each project or decision has on the business. Instilling strong financial capabilities in each employee is crucial to trusting them with decisions. The finance competency contains the following capabilities to conduct the projects in a financially responsible manner:

- Describing the ROI for analytics projects
- Documenting resources and budgets
- Prioritizing projects

Competency Domain: Analytics Product Management

Analytics product management contains the competencies needed to monitor the fidelity, health, and wealth of the analytics product lifecycle.

The analytics professional with analytics product management expertise makes the following unique contributions:

- Enforcing process that governs the **disposition** of deliverables
- Applying established project management methodologies
- Managing scope, cost, and schedules as deputized by analytics leadership
- Identifying linkages and dependencies between data products, business policies, and real-world workflow

The model represents the analytics product management domain as the sum of six competencies: quality processes, portfolio resource management, business impact assessment, product maintenance and durability, requirements management, and knowledge management.

Quality Processes

Quality processes need a strong champion to ensure all team personas use data in the proper manner and do due diligence in considering the impact of different analysis decisions. Without documented, robust processes, team performance and overall effectiveness is as risk. The quality process competency contains the following capabilities to promote quality in the process and products:

- Effectively executing improvement methodologies both for data quality as well as team processes
- Ensuring that proper testing and evaluation takes place before analytics products are released to customers
- Astutely considering quantitative and qualitative costs when making decisions regarding project prioritization

Portfolio Resource Management

Analytics teams are hives of intense activity. Management is required not just for individual projects but also for entire project portfolios that might have interdependent components that compete for resources. The portfolio resource management competency for analytics teams contains the following capabilities to manage project resources and assets:

- Judicious decision making surrounding the sequencing and time commitment for components of an analytics project
- Implementing agile management methods so that project and products may evolve as new data about their impact and use becomes available
- Ensuring that team members understand the impact of a product in terms of its usage within the leadership hierarchy of the organization

Business Impact Assessment

In some form, business impact assessment responsibilities are shared by all members of an analytics team if there is true alignment between projects and organizational strategic goals. The business impact assessment competency contains the following capabilities to interrelate analytics process to business outcomes:

- Proactively identifying unintended consequences as well as business benefits
- Discussing and negotiating around any data difficulties with project stakeholders
- Implementing quality monitoring processes so business gains from use of an analytics product don't degrade over time

Product Maintenance and Durability

Implementing a software solution requires a learning curve by all who use it. Identifying technology solutions that will last longer than the latest fashion will maximize the learning investment and leverage the technology investment. It is imperative that the invested technology remains operational and that hotfixes and other maintenance is applied regularly to ensure continued growth and operations. The product maintenance and durability competency contains the following capabilities to obtain optimal returns on technology investments:

- Managing software integrations and processes
- Performing analytics product maintenance on a timely basis
- Integrating and managing additional new technologies as needed

Requirements Management

Building project plans requires a significant level of effort in identifying the subject matter experts (SMEs), coordination of those involved, documentation of requirements, and task analysis. If you have a destination (i.e., a business problem to solve), you need a detailed map of how to get there. The requirements management competency contains the following capabilities to transform business needs into project requirements:

- Involving SMEs to support the project
- Documenting requirements for all team members so that they can be used for reference
- Creating a work plan that identifies the tasks, and the dependencies, to manage the project and determine the effort involved

Knowledge Management

Every analytics project will require some deviation from initial assumptions as the effort unfolds. Documenting these changes will serve as a learning process for future projects as well as ensure there is record of analytics decisions made to arrive at a product. The knowledge management competency contains the following capabilities for brokering critical and essential project knowledge:

- Tracking and documenting project changes
- Sharing knowledge and skills across teams to increase knowledge wealth and reduce risk when team composition changes
- Documenting the creation of how the knowledge is gained so it is easier for new team members

IDEALIZED COMPETENCIES FOR ANALYTICS JOB FAMILIES BY KNOWLEDGE DOMAIN

Business Domain

The accomplished analytics professional is a subject matter expert in the business and operational aspects of the business. In order to facilitate change from the analysis and visualization of data, the professional must understand the relationships between the various actors in the business (patients, customers, suppliers) and their roles dynamics; how they interact with employees, departments, divisions; and the business (including operations, data flows, etc.).

Legend: ● Developing ● Proficient ● Strength ● Mentor

Competency	Competency Statement	Analytics Product Management	Business Analysis	Technical Analysis	Statistical Analysis	Leadership
Operational Workflows	Create and maintain operational workflows to manage patient care and the revenue cycle.	Strength	Strength	Developing	Strength	Strength
IT Policy	Explain the overall value chain of the organization and how workflows are impacted by policies within processes and systems.	Strength	Strength	Developing	Strength	Strength
Organizational and Team Roles	Build effective relationships between all stakeholders.	Strength	Strength	Developing	Strength	Strength
Organizational Structure	Successfully navigate the myriad organization structures to deliver analytics services across business settings.	Strength	Strength	Developing	Strength	Strength

Analytical Thinking

The analytics professional is an analytical thinker who asks the right questions to guide the statistical methods that explore data patterns. They apply the interpretation of these results to solve problems in new ways.

● Developing   ◉ Proficient   ◎ Strength   ◎ Mentor

Compe-tency	Competency Statement	Analytics Product Manage-ment	Business Analysis	Technical Analysis	Statistical Analysis	Leader-ship
Question Design	Reflect on a project goal and available data to determine an evaluation framework capable of evaluating a hypothesis.	Proficient	Strength	Proficient	Strength	Proficient
Statistical and Analytics Methods	Implement statistical routines that quantify measures of correlation and dependence among data.		Developing		Strength	
Results Interpreta-tion	Interpret the results of data analysis to determine impact on the organization.	Developing	Strength	Developing	Strength	Developing
Operation-alization of Insights	Incorporate a set of analytics insights into business workflow such that a continual, positive benefit is seen and the learning organization paradigm is realized.	Strength	Strength	Developing	Strength	Mentor
Evan-gelism	Champion the value of analytics products as well as an analytics team in improving and innovating business processes.	Strength	Strength	Proficient	Mentor	Mentor

Data Management

The analytics professional is able to manage data to ensure its availability, usability, integrity, and security.

Legend: ● Developing ● Proficient ● Strength ● Mentor

Competency	Competency Statement	Analytics Product Management	Business Analysis	Technical Analysis	Statistical Analysis	Leadership
Data Wrangling	Extract, transform, and curate raw data into a format that is suitable for further analysis or visualization.	Developing	Proficient	Strength	Strength	Developing
Data Quality	Champion processes and procedures to ensure data integrity and quality.		Proficient	Strength	Strength	
Data Governance	Support and co-develop processes that document and preserve the provenance, meaning, structure, and appropriate use of data.	Developing	Strength	Strength	Strength	Strength
Data Modeling	Create the appropriate processes and framework to identify, capture, evaluate, retrieve, structure, and share enterprise information.			Strength		

Data Exploration

The analytics professional is an innovative data explorer who develops structured processes to describe aggregate trends and relationships between sources of data.

● Developing ● Proficient ◉ Strength ◉ Mentor

Competency	Competency Statement	Analytics Product Management	Business Analysis	Technical Analysis	Statistical Analysis	Leadership
Profiling and Characterization	Develop and execute a structured process to describe the aggregate trends, features, and culture of a data set.		●	●	◉	●
Data Relationships and Connections	Identify and describe the interrelatedness of data created in execution of the business processes.	●	●	◉	◉	●
Underlying Business Workflows	Translates data into a clear description of the workflow processes that generated it.	◉	●	●	◉	◉

Data Visualization

The analytics professional is a storyteller who creates graphical representations of data using a wide variety of techniques and technologies. The analytics professional communicates insights to drive business decisions and enable fact-based change.

● Developing ● Proficient ◉ Strength ◉ Mentor

Competency	Competency Statement	Analytics Product Management	Business Analysis	Technical Analysis	Statistical Analysis	Leadership
Storytelling	Communicate a series of events to provide an audience with the context and insight that drives them toward either desired conclusions or the development of important business questions.	●	◉	●	◉	●

(continued)

Compe-tency	Competency Statement	Analytics Product Manage-ment	Business Analysis	Technical Analysis	Statistical Analysis	Leader-ship
Visualization Techniques	Learn and deploy a variety of program-matic and menu-driven visualization tools.		Developing	Strength	Mentor	
Actionability	Communicate find-ings effectively, in plain language, to make them useful to nonanalytics stakeholders.	Proficient	Strength	Proficient	Proficient	Proficient
Visual Design Principles	Create graphics and visual representa-tions that adhere to design elements and principles for professional quality.		Proficient	Proficient	Proficient	Developing

Technology Literacy

The analytics professional is a technologist who is literate in multiple platforms, software, and tools that can be deployed to build the frameworks and infrastructures required to support fact-based decision making.

● Developing ◉ Proficient ◎ Strength ○ Mentor

Compe-tency	Competency Statement	Analytics Product Manage-ment	Business Analysis	Technical Analysis	Statistical Analysis	Leader-ship
Tool Selection and Use	Select and use a wide variety of tools that are fit for use to analyze statistical data, build frameworks, and create infrastructure.			Strength	Proficient	
Security and Privacy	Evangelize, plan around, and adhere to all codified regional, state, and federal privacy and security regulations.	Developing	Proficient	Strength	Proficient	Proficient

Competency	Competency Statement	Analytics Product Management	Business Analysis	Technical Analysis	Statistical Analysis	Leadership
Tool Agility and Fluency	Use agility in adopting and working across different analytics toolsets.		Developing	Strength	Strength	Developing
Systems Thinking	Use habits, tools, and concepts that demonstrate an understanding of how sociological and technical systems are interdependent.	Strength	Strength	Strength	Strength	Strength
Enterprise Systems Architecture	Understand the architecture and commonalities of data products and how model workflow contributes to reliable system behavior.	Strength	Proficient	Strength	Proficient	Strength

Strategic Thinking

The analytics professional is a strategic thinker who excels at innovation and systems thinking to support fact-based decision making. They use their role to champion the ethical and professional application of analytics to solving important problems in business.

Legend: ● Developing ◉ Proficient ◎ Strength ⊚ Mentor

Competency	Competency Statement	Analytics Product Management	Business Analysis	Technical Analysis	Statistical Analysis	Leadership
Innovation and Design Thinking	Generate a wide variety of approaches to solving problems and evaluate for possible implementation.	Strength	Proficient	Proficient	Proficient	Strength

(continued)

Compe-tency	Competency Statement	Analytics Product Manage-ment	Business Analysis	Technical Analysis	Statistical Analysis	Leader-ship
Strategic Alignment	Develop and execute a strategy to keep current with the latest advances in the field.	●	●	●	●	●
Data-Driven Decision Making	Interpret and critically evaluate statistical information within large swaths of data and discuss it to share understanding, opinions, and concerns.	●	●	●	●	●
Profession-alism and Ethics	Consistently demonstrates the characteristics of ethics and professionalism in responding to organizational members, clients, and customers.	●	●	●	●	●

Leadership

The analytics professional is an organizational leader who facilitates the development of individual team members, navigates growth and change, and provides mentoring and coaching for a healthy work environment.

● Developing　　● Proficient　　● Strength　　● Mentor

Compe-tency	Competency Statement	Analytics Product Manage-ment	Business Analysis	Technical Analysis	Statistical Analysis	Leader-ship
Change Leader-ship	Cultivate an environment that is agile in responding to organizational and process changes.	●	●	●	●	●

Competency	Competency Statement	Analytics Product Management	Business Analysis	Technical Analysis	Statistical Analysis	Leadership
Coaching and Development	Provide personalized support and guidance to individuals for skill and behavioral growth.	●	●			●
Collaborative Leadership	Foster opportunities to collaborate between individuals and teams.	●	●	●	●	●
Conflict Management	Mediate conflicts to settle differences and find common ground between individuals and teams.	●	●	●		●
Influence	Establish credibility within the organization to gain support from key decision makers.	●	●	●	●	●
Team Leadership	Support staff to narrow the gaps between actual, expected, and aspirational performance through feedback, recognition, and clarity.	●	●	●	●	●
Finance	Support economic decisions based on business concepts including revenue, accounting, and organizational value.	●	●	●		●

Analytics Product Management

The analytics professional is a product manager who ensures that the team achieves its goals through collaboration, allocation of resources, planning, documentation, and communication.

Legend: ● Developing ◉ Proficient ◎ Strength ◉ Mentor

Competency	Competency Statement	Analytics Product Management	Business Analysis	Technical Analysis	Statistical Analysis	Leadership
Quality Processes	Maintain and monitor processes and procedures to ensure organizational performance and effectiveness.	Strength	Proficient	Developing	Strength	Mentor
Portfolio Resource Management	Forecast and logically document the sequence and time commitment for the events and tasks needed to complete the project.	Strength	Strength	Proficient	Strength	Strength
Business Impact Assessment	Manage and evaluate the impact of analytics process on the overall business outcomes.	Strength	Proficient		Developing	Strength
Product Maintenance and Durability	Implement technology solutions that will enable or augment the quality, expediency, reliability, and longevity of data and analytics products and services.	Strength		Developing	Developing	Strength
Requirements Management	Consider the requirements for expert knowledge, effort, and time allocations when building project plans.	Strength	Strength	Developing	Strength	Strength
Knowledge Management	Track and document changes to a project, process, or initiative to convey a clear picture of current status, desired outcomes, and change impact.	Strength	Strength	Strength	Strength	Strength

CHAPTER SUMMARY

The process of finding, selecting, onboarding, training, and nurturing analytics talent is a critically important part of any analytics organization. In this chapter, I outlined nine domains that are critical in order to deliver on the analytics capabilities needed in the modern enterprise. By defining the expected proficiencies of analytics talent across the knowledge domains and competencies that matter, I have given you the tools to be successful at knowing where you need to focus your energies on talent development.

REFERENCE

Manyika, J., Chui, M., Brown, B., Bughin, J., Dobbs, R., Roxburgh, C., & Hung Byers, A. (2011). Big data: The next frontier for innovation, competition, and productivity. *Digital McKinsey*. Retrieved from Digital McKinsey website: www.mckinsey.com/business-functions/digital-mckinsey/our-insights/big-data-the-next-frontier-for-innovation.

CHAPTER 13

The Future
of Analytics

... throughout the whole history of science most of the really great discoveries which had ultimately proved to be beneficial to mankind had been made by men and women who were driven not by the desire to be useful but merely the desire to satisfy their curiosity.

—Richard Feynman, Nobel Laureate

THE ANALYTICS LIFECYCLE AS A FRAMEWORK

Arguably, there are many ways to think about the topic of analytics. My purpose in writing this book has been to present ideas that will help analytics professionals solidify their own thinking about key concepts and how they can be applied.

The framework for analytics and the associated best practices offered here are based on my own trial-and-error efforts at explaining these concepts to both clients and students. In a nutshell, that framework is presented in Figure 13.1.

These important lessons for all of us are described throughout this book:

- Analytics strategy should be rooted in the overall organizational strategy.
- Our analytics aspirations should be rooted in the capabilities derived from that strategy.
- What we need to be good at—our analytics capabilities— is a direct result of our purposeful effort at defining those capabilities.
- The role of analytics leadership is to manage the alignment between people, process, technology, and data; that is, the achievement of capabilities in support of the strategy.
- The analytics lifecycle best practice areas are meant to be multi-disciplinary. There is no "analytics unicorn," but rather, a team that is disciplined, engaging, and creative.
- The analytics lifecycle depends on a robust data pipeline and should support the decision lifecycle.

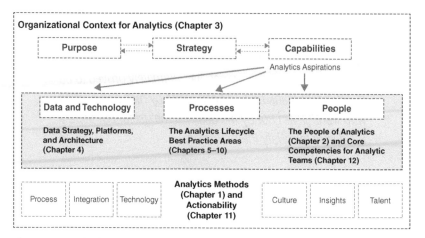

Figure 13.1 The linkage between analytics strategy and execution

- The actionability of analytics is heavily influenced by organizational leadership and culture, along with our ability to align its resources to lead change.

While there are likely very few novel ideas presented in this book, I do hope that the framing of these concepts, coupled with a unique perspective that empathy should play a critical role in the design and development of data "products," helps anchor the idea that best practices will help to move analytics from the mystical to the mainstream—where everyone can play an important role.

The future of analytics will be attenuated by our human ability to learn. We have massive amounts of information at our fingertips. I believe the future of analytics will be led by those who learn how to learn more quickly and find relationships and patterns in data that may not have been possible to discover before. Curiosity and lifelong learning is, and will always be, the hallmark of explorers.

THE ROLE OF ANALYTICS IN OUR FUTURE

One of the central themes behind design thinking is empathy. Think back to the IT of yesteryear—when data was scarce and computing resources were rationed. The schism that started as a way to prevent "users" from doing stupid things is being broken down every day. Business is the largest consumer of analytics today, and we are doing everything we can to protect data from malice and to democratize its use throughout the enterprise. No longer should database administrators, chief security officers, or report writers be seen as keeper of the keys, but rather, as curators and enablers of an information economy.

We are forever changed.

The analytical thinker is nascent and valued. That is, we are beginning to appreciate the data champion who can translate a business problem into a question that can be answered with data. We are moving from valuing only mathematics skills to the well-rounded competencies needed for success. Analytics is out of the bag and there is no going back. It is infecting everyone—empowering us to think critically and support decisions with data.

As Dr. Bertalan Mesko, PhD, the Medical Futurist, suggests, "The future is about empathy, not coding." Indeed, the future will no doubt involve artificial intelligence, self-driving cars, and ambient analytics embedded in everything from insulin pumps to icemakers. But it is those with evolving competencies "such as the futurist mindset and social skills coupled with sound digital literacy who might be more important" (Mesko, 2017).

It has been suggested that AI will replace 50 percent of all jobs in the next decade. Those who are problem-solving, empathy-driven data champions will differentiate themselves from the rest. In this final chapter of the book, I leave you with some of my own lessons learned and what we can do to ensure our continued relevance.

A Futurist Perspective

I consider myself a futurist and find passion in framing present realities in both historical and future context. Even in 1999, I wrote on the skills for the next millennium (in 1999, we were approaching the doom of gloom of Y2K) (Nelson and Barnes Nelson, 1999.) This paper highlighted what I saw as the need to move from a traditional skillset to a new mindset. While this paper was written for a SAS audience, the relevancy of the lessons remains, and include guiding sentiments such as:

1. Obtain the knowledge of different industries (and interests outside of your primary field of endeavor), as well as a greater understanding of your own business.

2. Become a one-person learning organization; that is, become adept at processing different types of data and concepts, while drawing on past learning and experiences.

3. Develop the ability to think like an "intrapreneur."

4. Demonstrate agility and flexibility in all aspects of work and personal life.

5. Learn the art of creativity, new ways of thinking, building, and problem solving.

6. Communicate ideas through verbal, nonverbal, and written modes, including visuals.

Nearly two decades after first writing those words, I have a few more lessons that I would like to share.

1. Ubiquitous Computing and Analytics

Data is the kind of ubiquitous resource that we can shape to provide new innovations and new insights, and it's all around us, and it can be mined very easily.

—David McCandless, Data journalist

We have more computing power in our mobile devices and televisions than ever before. The lines between technology, consumer and business applications, and analytics will continue to blur. Today, we argue over the differences between operations research, mathematics, computer science, and statistics. As ambient analytics finds its way into our daily lives, we won't always be able to tell when analytics are at play, and likely we won't care!

2. Big Data Will Drive Innovation

We're entering a new world in which data may be more important than software.

—Tim O'Reilly, Founder, O'Reilly Media

In the past decade, we have seen tremendous advances in technology. For example, visual analytics was introduced in large part because traditional analysis methods limited our ability to "see" all of the data.

Similarly, the speed of data introduced us to new terms like *event stream processing*. Paradigms for how we store data, from data warehouses to data lakes, and process data, such as in-database and in-memory, were in large part responses to the massive amount of data that we have at our disposal.

In the coming years, we will continue to see innovation in response to the Internet of Things (IoT) as well as novel methods for cataloging and processing nonstructured data (e.g., video, images, sound, narratives, voice). Further, we will see techniques to automate the mundane. For example, I think of all of the activities that we do in analytics and imagine a day where the manual work of model building, variable selection and transformation, and visualization will be replaced by algorithms. What we see as expert processes are already being codified into algorithms.

3. Insulated Industries and Perspectives Will Become Extinct

> *The first rule is that you've got to have multiple models—because if you just have one or two that you're using, the nature of human psychology is such that you'll torture reality so that it fits your models ... and the models have to come from multiple disciplines—because all the wisdom of the world is not to be found in one little academic department.*
>
> —Charlie Munger, one of the world's top investors and Warren Buffett's longtime business partner, *Poor Charlie's Almanack.*

No longer will we see industries remain isolated from others but, rather, they will actively seek out the lessons learned and apply techniques across organizational and industry boundaries. Even in analytics, we are seeing a shift from reliance on the "quants" to multidisciplinary problem-solving teams that value multiple perspectives, including behavioral economics, psychology, statistics, computer science, and linguistics.

Further, we will see industry more quickly apply research into practice as organizations align with universities and stand up innovation and translational research centers to more quickly apply lessons from academia into competitive advantage.

4. Purpose Will Be a Differentiator

Our ability to do great things with data will make a real difference in every aspect of our lives.

—Jennifer Pahlka, founder and executive director for Code for America

Technology will no longer be an organizational differentiator but will be seen as the greatest equalizer. Just like the Internet made access to information ubiquitous, the technologies that we use to manipulate data and create insights will be commonplace.

It will be our ability to apply inventiveness for purpose that will become our differentiator. Organizations with a heart and purpose that people can believe in will be the standard, not the exception. These organizations will support national and international "analytics tours of duty" where they apply lessons and expertise to solve humanitarian issues.

5. Competencies over Skills

Abilities should not limit access to the possibilities provided by analytics.

—Oliver Schabenberger, SAS executive vice president & chief technology officer

Finally, it is my hope and belief that analytics competencies will be valued over specific skills. In an economy where certifications and technical boot camps still dominate, we are seeing a recognition that competencies matter more than skills alone. Competencies that emphasize application to effectively perform a job such as leadership, influence, communication, empathy, and critical thinking will rise in stature. We've seen this over the past decade in analytics organizations that have added people with graphic design and data journalism skills. No longer is it sufficient to give the technical answer; rather, we must be able to communicate for both influence and change. I think continued focus on user experience (UX) will result in new, unforeseen roles such as the UX writer.

We live in a time when artificial intelligence has begun to influence our everyday lives. In organizations, machine learning and natural language processing are commonplace. Evolving innovations in security such as blockchain all help to speed the application of analytics. It is our right and responsibility in the world of analytics to get better at learning and to embrace change. Besides evolving our technical skills, we need to hone our "soft" skills in order to successfully navigate the automated world of "intelligent machines."

FINAL THOUGHTS

As anyone knows who has had to maintain their livelihood, their friendships, health, and marriage while memorializing their ideas, this book was a labor of love. During the writing of this book, my first grandson was born. It is my hope for him and for all future generations that we will learn from history, continue to balance agility with intentional planning, remain humble in what we know about the world, and use technology to aid noble, human-centered pursuits.

Throughout this book, I have attempted to make analytics real. That is, instead of preaching and theorizing, I provided actual examples as well as a rich set of tips and tools that can help leaders understand what is needed to achieve their analytic aspirations, and I offered grounded advice to practitioners on the realities of participating in the Analytics Lifecycle.

I hope I have achieved this mission.

I find myself invigorated at the prospect of analytics being able to help solve some of the most important issues of our time, as well as those my grandson will confront. The passion of purpose in analytics is an important touchstone in our collective work. Algorithms will be replaced. Techniques will be improved. Processes will evolve. Technologies will morph. Transforming organizations and outcomes is entirely possible. Analytics is having a profound impact on the world today.

Despite the perception that young people lack curiosity and problem solving, I am nevertheless optimistic. There is, and will always be, the curious, the problem solvers, the inventors, the passionate, and the empathetic. I meet them every day—these are the data champions.

REFERENCES

Mesko, B. (2017). The future is about empathy, not coding. Retrieved from http://medicalfuturist.com/future-empathy-not-coding/.

Nelson, G. S., & J. Barnes Nelson. (1999). SAS skills for the next millennium: A geek peek into the future. Proceedings of the 24th Annual Meeting of *SAS Users Group International*. Miami Beach, FL: SAS Institute.

About the Author

Greg Nelson is the founder and Chief Executive Officer of ThotWave, an expert for the International Institute for Analytics, and adjunct faculty at Duke University's Fuqua School of Business. He teaches analytics in both the School of Nursing and at the Fuqua School of Business at Duke University. Greg has authored over 200 papers and publications and is a regular speaker and keynote presenter at national and international events in both technology as well as for private companies and events.

Greg, an analytics evangelist and futurist, has brought his 20+ years of analytics advisory work to bear to this important topic – the people and process side of analytics. Through this pragmatic treatment of the analytics lifecycle, Greg speaks to both the practical and human-centeredness of analytics in a way that is accessible and useful for all data champions.

Greg earned his bachelor's degree from the University of California, Santa Cruz in Psychology, a Masters in Clinical Informatics from Duke University, and conducted Ph.D. level work in Social and Cognitive Psychology from the University of Georgia.

Having once flown to Alaska on a one-way ticket with a tent, a sleeping bag, and only $100 to his name, Greg has settled in rural North Carolina, where he lives with his wife Susan and their four-legged menagerie on a farmlet.

You can connect with Greg on twitter @gregorysnelson or on LinkedIn at www.linkedin.com/in/gregorysnelson/. You can also visit his website, analyticslifecycletookit.com, to learn more about some of the tools and techniques outlined in this book.

About the Companion Web Site

On the Analytics Lifecycle Toolkit website (http://www.analyticslife cycletoolkit.com/), you will find a variety of resources, including the tools and templates mentioned throughout this book. In addition to the checklists, templates, and other materials that you can use to reinforce the concepts covered in this book, the site also contains links to resources, references, and other information related to analytics. In addition, you will be able to sign up for e-mail updates whenever content is added or updated. You'll also find a blog where I discuss practical implications of analytics across the lifecycle.

Index

Printed and bound by CPI Group (UK) Ltd, Croydon, CR0 4YY

16/04/2025

14658510-0004